BEST DAMN
HIP HOP
WRITING
2018

Guest Editors

GARY SUAREZ
KIANA FITZGERALD
MARTIN E. CONNOR
DART ADAMS
YOH PHILLIPS

Edited by
Amir Ali Said

Series Creator & Editor
Amir Said

Superchamp
Books SB

New York

Editor, Amir Ali Said
Series Creator and Editor, Amir Said

Guest Editor, Gary Suarez
Guest Editor, Kiana Fitzgerald
Guest Editor, Martin E. Connor
Guest Editor, Dart Adams
Guest Editor, Yoh Phillips

Back Cover blurb by Yoh Phillips

DESIGNED BY AMIR SAID

Cover, Design, and Layout by Amir Said

Print History:
March 2019: First printing.

Best Damn Hip Hop Writing: 2018
/ Edited by Amir Ali Said
Series Editor Amir Said
1. Said, Amir Ali 2. Said, Amir 3. Hip Hop Music Criticism 4. Rap Music Criticism
5. Music Criticism
I. Said, Amir Ali; Said, Amir II. Title

ISBN 978-0-9997306-5-2 (Paperback)

CONTENTS

FOREWORD   ix

INTRODUCTION   1

PART 1: CRITICAL OBSERVATIONS   5

Award Shows Need Rappers More Than Rappers Need
Award Shows by Erin Ashley   6

The Gospel According to Pusha T by Josie Duffy Rice   13

What Kendrick Lamar's Pulitzer Prize in music means for
hip-hop by Donna-Claire Chesman   23

Why So Many Hip-Hop Producers Are Putting Business
Before Beats by Cherie Hu   27

Inside UK drill, the demonised rap genre representing a
marginalised generation by Yemi Abiade   32

Sorry, Drake And Nicki, But Hip-Hop Is Changing
by Gary Suarez   37

Hip-Hop's Love/Hate Relationship with Chance The
Rapper by Kathy Iandoli   41

Hip Hop Writing in 2018 by Martin E. Connor   44

Migos' Crossover Win at the AMAs Signals an Imminent
Industry Shift by John Vilanova   47

Hip-Hop Is Already an Inclusive Artform & an Exclusive
Culture. Mainstream Rap Isn't... by Dart Adams   51

Inside 6ix9ine's Outrageous Sentencing
Hearing by Rich Juzwiak   57

How do we stop black grief from
becoming a commodity? by Sharine Taylor   62

Did Kanye West's "Five-For-Five"
Album Release Strategy Hinder Teyana Taylor's *K.T.S.E.*?
by Amir Said   68

The Greatest Year in Hip-Hop
History by Christopher Pierznik 73

PART 2: PROFILES/RETROSPECTIVES/REVIEWS 94
The Perfectionist: Mac Miller is finally making the music
he's always wanted to make. by Craig Jenkins 95
Thank You, Mac Miller by Donna-Claire Chesman 105
Bad Bunny: Life in Puerto Rico for a refreshingly weird Latin
trap star by Julianne Escobedo Shepherd 109
Tu Pum Pum: The Story of Boricua Guerrero,' the Hip-
Hop & Reggaeton Album That Paved the Way for Latin
Trap by Eduardo Cepeda 120
Bhad Bhabie Isn't Going Anywhere
by Meaghan Garvey 124
"I Don't Remember the Samples I Use. Hell No."—The
Story of 'Madvillainy' by Gino Sorcinelli 137
Let's Take a Moment and Care for Saba
by Alec Stern 148
Review: 21 Savage Shows Tremendous
Growth On "I Am > I Was" by Eric Diep 163
Album Review: DAYTONA by Zach Quiñones 167
Eve & Dr. Dre, "Let Me Blow Ya Mind"
Rap Analysis by Martin E. Connor 171
'Invasion of Privacy' Is Cardi B's Victory Lap
by Lindsay Zoladz 177

PART 3: FRESH PERSPECTIVES 184
Hip Hop Writing in 2018 by Gary Suarez 185
Donald Glover's 'This Is America' Is a Nightmare We Can't
Afford to Look Away From by Tre Johnson 188
To Be Seen Is to Be Heard: Visibility Is No Longer an
Option by Yoh Phillips 191

Why Can There Only be one Dominant Woman in Rap?
by Kiana Fitzgerald 198
Nothing Lasts Forever: The rise and fall of Kanye and Drake
by Bijan Stephen 205
How Desus & Mero Redefined Hip-Hop in Late Night
by Dylan "CineMasai" Green 210
The Rise of the Rap-tor: Inside Hip-Hop's Complicated
Relationship With Hollywood by Shawn Setaro 214
Today's Fun Hip Hop is Good, but It Needs a Deeper
Message by Amir Ali Said 215
Black Skinhead: Vic Mensa and the Distortion of the
Skinhead Culture by Elijah C. Watson 226
The Real Story of South Florida Rapper XXXTentacion
by Tarpley Hitt 230
When It All Falls Down: The Twisted Nightmare
Of Kanye West and Trump by David Dennis, Jr 248
From 40 to Dilla: The Beauty of Raging Against the
Dying Light by Yoh Phillips 256

CREDITS 267
ACKNOWLEDGMENTS 271

FOREWORD

The Importance of Music Education

Music is deeply embedded into our personal and collective existence. Music adds depth and dimension to our environment, it elevates the human spirit, and it contributes in many important ways to our quality of life. Moreover, music is one of the primary ways that we learn about ourselves and others. Music is crucial to our understanding of the different traditions and beliefs that exist in the world. And, of course, music is also one of the fundamental ways that we create and communicate in and draw meaning from the world around us. This is why everyone — regardless of age, cultural heritage, or socio-economic background — benefits from a diverse music education. Thus, the purpose of music education, and by proxy music education books like the *Best Damn Hip Hop Writing* series, is not only to inform but to enrich and enlighten us all. With music education books, people increase their awareness of rich and diverse cultures, beliefs, and societies; and they learn how and why almost nothing in contemporary society is created or communicated without the influence of music.

About the *Best Damn Writing* Series

There is a lot of good writing happening today. From the explosion of talented essayists to freelance writers to independent authors to DIY poets and more, this era is rapidly producing some of the most engaging and culturally influential writing ever published. At the same time, however, much of this writing is being missed by the very readers who would likely appreciate and gain from it the most. This is not to say that a lot of the great writing of today is being overlooked, but rather that the number of literary channels — and their outdated publishing methods and often non-inclusive traditions — is insufficient to the growing body of interesting writing that's taking place right now. And this is especially the case when it comes to contemporary anthologies.

Anthologies are a great way to discover new writers and a means for further understanding the art and craft of writing. For classic Western literature, the task of assembling an anthology tends to be a foregone conclusion, at least in terms of the writers (nearly all old white men) that readers supposedly should know. But I don't believe that contemporary anthologies need to suffer from a similar ideological, non-inclusive fate.

More specifically, the inclusive kind of anthologies — that I believe better serve new voices in writing — do not exist in tall order. Anthologies, which have typically been fashioned by a narrow group of people whose tastes are tuned to an even more narrow corner of writing, are often positioned well outside of the mainstream. Because of this, I think the potential of the anthology, as a pop culture item, is largely unrecognized. That's why I've created the *Best Damn Writing* series. I want to help anthologies become a more recognizable part of pop culture, not something merely for so-called literary types. Moreover, I want to reimagine what the anthology is; how it's shaped, who it's for, and how it works.

I think book anthologies are like music playlists for readers. And just like music playlists, literary playlists benefit from the specific tastes and backgrounds of its curators. Within this context I believe that there is a premium for curated literature that stands beyond bloated listicles or selection archetypes commonly found among literary elitists. I've cultivated my taste from a broad consumption of literature, music, film, art, and pop culture. Certainly, this is not to say that my taste is superior to anyone else's, but rather it's fine tuned to the areas of culture that I've long had deep interest in and, in many cases, that I have written extensively about. Thus, I want the *Best Damn Writing* series to be an anthology series that promotes some of the finest writing in popular culture, specifically in the areas of hip hop, poetry, film, memoir, art, and technology — all of the corners of culture that occupy my deepest interest and exploration.

As to what I believe constitutes the "finest" or "best damn" writing within these areas, well, I base this not so much on my personal taste but on what I believe are the three things that anthologies should do. First, I believe an anthology should be about discovery. It should introduce writers to new audiences; and, conversely, it should introduce audiences to emerging and established writers whose work deserves further amplification. Second, I believe that an anthology should offer insight into the craft of writing. That is to say, it should offer a close-up on style and form and the different ways in which themes are developed by writers. Finally, I believe that an anthology should always offer fresh perspectives and insights. The kind that illuminates current cultural moments and shed light on important points from the past.

—Said (Amir Said),
Paris, France
January 3, 2019

Introduction

About the *Best Damn Hip Hop Writing* Series: Documenting Hip Hop Culture; and The Rise of Hip Hop Music Criticism and Hip Hop Studies

Hip hop culture has always been a central interest of mine. From my very first book, *The BeatTips Manual,* which explores the history of the art of beatmaking, to my book *The Art of Sampling,* which examines copyright law and music sampling, I've continually aimed to document hip hop culture and demonstrate why it is such a powerful cultural force around the world. Further, since I first began reading *The Source Magazine* as a teenager in the early '90s — my first introduction into hip hop music criticism — I have continued to be impressed by the level of writing being done in this corner of cultural criticism. Moreover, the academic discipline commonly known as hip hop studies, which has also produced a number of notable works over the past 30 years, has helped inspire my own writing in this field.

But today, hip hop music criticism is a pretty mixed bag. And hip hop studies often feels stuffy and dominated by scholars who seem to be outside of the hip hop community. The freedom of the internet has made it more possible than ever for individuals to publish their own ideas and observations about music. That music writers have been able to do so as an alternative to what the so-called tastemakers have to publish is particularly liberating. And to be certain, there are some really terrific (highly knowledgeable) hip hop/rap music writers. That being said, most hip hop music writers of today tend to be three types: (1) Highly subjective fans — of one artist, sound, style — who write glowing write-ups; (2) News writers whose main objective often leans more into the world of gossip and muckraking than journalis; and (3) Think-piece writers who carry the analytical skillset and writing chops that you would expect from any good journalist.

So while the quality of hip hop music criticism has risen in some places, the overall quality of hip hop/rap music criticism has become a bit of a crap shoot: A zone where overzealous subjectivity, disconnected analysis, and/or poor writing often drowns out the signal of terrific writing.

As an academic discipline and literary category, hip hop studies is fairly new. Within this space there have been some important works written by various recognized scholars. But the voices, often buried in exhaustive research and dense prose and academic speak, are often kept inside the walls of academia and are therefore not exposed to pop culture and the people (practitioners) most vested in hip hop culture. In order for hip hop studies to grow, I believe that the walls between academia and pop culture must come down. This point is key because the work of many hip hop scholars is often disconnected from the actual pulse of hip hop culture. Likewise, the writing of far too many hip hop music writers demonstrates a serious lack of awareness of the pivotal work that has been published by scholars. Thus, scholars will be better served by more inclusive peer reviews (if you will), and those who engage with hip hop culture primarily from a non-academic paradigm will certainly benefit from a more direct exchange with the work of scholars. In this context, I want the *Best Damn Hip Hop Writing* series to serve as a link between the interrelated worlds of hip hop music criticism and hip hop studies.

Lastly, whether it be hip hop music criticism or hip hop studies, the primary goals of the *Best Damn Hip Hop Writing* series is to provide a pathway to a deeper understanding to some of the critical themes in hip hop, while also offering critical observations on some of hip hop's most influential artists and developments; and to amplify the voices of writers of who have demonstrated excellence in this field of study.

About *Best Damn Hip Hop Writing: 2018*

What exists here in *Best Damn Hip Hop Writing: 2018* is an example of what quality, long-form analysis can look like. All of the pieces in this anthology, chosen by guest editors Gary Suarez, Kiana Fitzgerald, Dart Adams, Martin E. Connor, and Yoh Phillips, along with Amir Ali Said (editor) and me (series editor and creator), provide readers with a broad spectrum of hip hop culture, in the specific, as well as hip hop's impact on pop/ mainstream culture in general. From Erin Ashley's deft piece about why award shows need rappers (more than rappers need award shows) to Yemi Abiade's piece about the demonization of UK drill to Rich Juzwiak's fascinating coverage of a 6ix9ine sentence hearing to Craig Jenkin's remarkable profile of the late Mac Miller to Julianne Escobedo Shepherd's engaging profile of Latin trap star Bad Bunny to Tre Johnson's excellent examination of Donald Glover's "This Is America" to Tarpley Hitt's superb investigative reporting on the story of the late controversial rapper XXXTentacion to Donna-Claire Chesman's analysis of what Kendrick Lamar's Pulitzer Prize in music means for hip hop, *Best Damn Hip Hop Writing: 2018* highlights the cultural and political power of hip hop culture and it reminds us all of the joys, challenges, and pitfalls of humanity.

All of the writers who appear in *Best Damn Hip Hop Writing: 2018* are committed to the serious exploration of hip hop culture, and their work represents a gold standard for music journalism. The pieces in this book not only offer critical observations and fresh perspectives, they also shed light on the artistic, economic, social, and emotional impact of hip hop culture. In this regard, I hope that readers find *Best Damn Hip Hop Writing: 2018* to be not only an anthology that is informative, engaging, challenging, and inspiring but also a crucial source of reference of hip hop culture.

—Said (Amir Said),
Paris, France
February 21, 2019

Part 1
CRITICAL OBSERVATIONS

Award Shows Need Rappers More Than Rappers Need Award Shows

by Erin Ashley

On the eve of the 1998 Juno Awards, Vancouver group The Rascalz[1], who were nominated for 'Rap Recording of the Year' for their album *Cash Crop*, sat amongst their peers at the annual gala awaiting the results. Given that the ceremony was untelevised, and rap music had propelled into being one of the most popular genres in music, admittedly, the trio joked about refusing the award if they won[2], which would not only be a Juno first but also a presumed career killer. The group would win that night, and what started as a jovial conversation quickly turned into an explicit decline of the Juno Award.

In an effort to rectify their errors of not having the category televised previously, in 1999 the Junos invited The Rascalz to perform their chart-topping, and now classic Canadian anthem "Northern Touch" on the televised broadcast. The single not only became a domestic chart-topping single—a rarity for hip-hop music at the time, but it was the first rap song to be performed live during the televised portion of the prestigious award show. Moments after their performance, The Rascalz would be once again awarded 'Best Rap Recording', this time for "Northern Touch", becoming a moment that would cement itself in history as the first time the award would be handed out during the televised portion of the show.

Nevertheless, Rascalz manager Sol Guy's statement following their win in 1998 still rings true: "In view of the lack of real inclusion of Black music in the ceremony, this feels like a token gesture towards honouring the real impact of urban music in Canada. Urban music, reggae, R&B, and rap: that's all Black music and it's not represented at the Junos. We decided that until it is, we are going to take a stance." Unbeknownst to the Rascalz, the statement they made that night would foreshadow a strained relationship between the Junos and the hip-hop community for years to come.

Since 1970, the Juno Awards have been an annual ceremony that recognizes the artistic and technical achievements of Canada's music industry—however, Black music categories, as well as genres made by marginalized communities in general, are rarely, if ever, televised. Little change appeared in sight for more than a decade until 2011 when Drake, who was nominated in six separate categories that year, was asked to host the Juno Awards. He would not only be the first rapper to ever be asked to host the award show, but also the first Black host in its 41-year history. But what should've been a trophy sweep resulted in Drake snubbed in every single category for his debut *Thank Me Later.* "He had one of the biggest years ever in rap history as far as being a Canadian, they have him hosting the entire thing.... and to me, it's disrespect, what they did. Absolute disrespect," Kardinal Offishall would later tell the *Toronto Star*[3].

Since then, Drake has not attended the national award ceremony. And though he's been nominated and won several awards since, some of his biggest achievements[4] have failed to be recognized. More recently, Jazz Cartier's 2017 speech following his win for 'Rap Recording of the Year', addressed the awarding committees directly and in a since-deleted Instagram post saying, "...also @thejunoawards while you guys enjoy all the hip-hop in the world at your after parties, next year you gotta have this category filmed on television."

This year marks a turning point in hip-hop's relationship with the Juno Awards, and it probably stands to be its most volatile position to date. According to Nielsen's 2017 Canada Music Year-End Report[5], Hip-Hop/R&B was the "fastest-growing music genre of the year, with an 86% increase in audio on-demand streaming consumption over 2016." Additionally, seven of Canada's most streamed artists of the year came from the Hip-Hop/R&B genre, including Drake and The Weeknd. With those statistics, it would only make sense that the most popular genres in Canada—and North America, overall—would finally receive their due praise. Twenty years after The Rascalz first rejected their Juno Award, the conversation continues, but this time a new question is on the horizon: do our homegrown talents, who've earned accolades and praise elsewhere in the world before Canada, still need the Junos?

Three-time nominee and Juno-award winning producer and rapper Rich Kidd says, "Speaking for myself and a few others [who] I've talked to about this, the Junos only sort-of matter. They matter when we see people we know from the community that are nominated or performing [un-televised]. After that, it's an after-thought—the generations after don't put any emphasis on it because their OG's don't give a shit." Race, according to Rich Kidd also plays a role in how the Junos operate. Similar to Macklemore's success across the border, both Classified and SonReal have benefitted from being white in an vastly white music industry, allowing for a 'safer' image to be associated with a 'dangerous' genre. "Even though Class[ified], who I respect, put years of work in his craft, he's still benefiting off white privilege in a majority white country. His image relates to the average Canadian and he doesn't rap about issues that may make white people uncomfortable or critically think about shit that's going on like [what] Eminem's 'trying' to do right now," he says.

Traditionally, Black music has always functioned in coded languages[6] only understood by those involved directly. And while that coding has started to be deciphered as these genres gained mainstream popularity, it's still misunderstood by the governing committees that oversee them. While hip-hop culture becomes a fashionable marketing tool for Canadian entertainment industries, the return on investment for the community producing it, especially in Toronto, falls flat, time and time and time again. "When you can win one of what is said to be one of Canada's top honours or music prizes and it not revered by anybody as something significant, there's a real problem with the infrastructure. The silence there speaks volumes," Juno-award winning rapper Tona states. Sean Leon, one of Toronto's most promising artists who opted out of submitting this year, shares similar thoughts, "Canadian award shows are bad, period, in the sense that they're not going to change your life in the way that a Grammy would, but to apply and go through all that and to lose based off these Canadian politics is exhausting and I don't see the point of it, at all."

For Quebecois artists like rapper Wasiu, the awards seem even more out of touch, partly because Francophone releases are largely overlooked by the vastly English-speaking committees. "In Quebec, we don't care about the Junos. The francophones only care about ADISQ⁷ (Association québécoise de l'industrie du disque, which also hosts an award gala), and if the anglos in Quebec care about an award show, it's whatever the Americans are watching," he says. "Whatever happens at ADISQ can change how people view you over here in Quebec. Whatever happens at the Junos doesn't change your social status in Quebec at all."

Akin to the 1989 Grammy Boycott led by Will Smith and DJ Jazzy Jeff, whispers of a Juno boycott have lingered through the Canadian rap community for a while, but in some cases, it's already happening. This is the first year that none of the artists signed to OVO, including Drake, DVSN, Baka and Majid Jordan, submitted for Juno nominations. It's also the first year where several artists were reportedly approached to perform on the televised award show but turned it down.

"If all of the hip-hop community boycotts, I mean, what are we trying to change? If it's to get our awards televised, I don't know if it really matters. What matters is the exposure of these

artists," Rich Kidd states. "Maybe they should let Belly or Tory [Lanez] perform on Sunday because that's more helpful to me than giving me an award for a category that has no clear definition what a rap recording is." Sarah F., a corporate music professional, shares a different view. "We have to care. Backing off of the Junos alone would only send the message that they don't need to do the appropriate amount of work to be an accurate representation of all music in Canada."

There's an overwhelming sentiment that if the Juno Awards and their administrative body, the Canadian Academy of Recording Arts & Sciences, truly want to elevate their worth, their infrastructure needs to be uprooted from the top down in all departments. As it stands, the initial voting process for many Juno categories, including hip-hop and R&B, is done by approved community members who serve as initial and secondary judges. It's a voluntary position, rather than a paid one, which Sarah F. feels needs to also change "by doing the work to engage and pay the members of the community who are active in the scene and finding innovative ways to support the music." While these concerns have been echoed for years, it seems as if they're finally being heard.

In a recent statement provided by Allan Reid, President & CEO of CARAS and The Juno Awards, he says that,

" We value our relationship with all music communities that make up our dynamic industry. The rap/hip-hop/R&B community is a significant part of the Canadian music landscape, and our job at CARAS is to ensure that we are providing the right avenue to educate, develop, celebrate and honour artists in these genres, as we do for all genres," states Reid. "This year we are happy to share that the rap/hip-hop/R&B community will be represented on JUNO Weekend through performances

by Clairmont The Second at the JUNO Gala Dinner and Awards, and Daniel Caesar and Jessie Reyez on the JUNO Awards Broadcast. The Rap Album of the Year category will also be included in the 2018 JUNO Awards Broadcast, along with some exciting initiatives during JUNO week, and throughout the year, celebrating the legacy and future of Canadian hip-hop." As per Reid, not only will the 'Rap Album of the Year' be presented 2018 Juno Awards broadcast, but to celebrate "Northern Touch" once more twenty years later, the Rascalz, as well as Checkmate, Kardinal Offishall, Thrust, and Choclair will be the artists presenting it."

Though this may still feel like an afterthought for many artists, in an additional statement, CARAS and The Junos note that they are making long-term adjustments such as switching the Rap category's final voting procedure from "judge-voted to member voted" to ensure that the entire voting body is able to weigh in on the selection with the hope that it "will encourage more members of the rap/hip-hop/R&B community to become CARAS Academy Delegates and have their voices be heard."

Though the changes reveal a step in the right direction, Rich Kidd and journalist and XL Recordings A&R Samantha O'Connor sum up the hesitancy of these communities celebrating them too early. "I think it will help change the relationship of present to future rap artists from our country. I don't think it changes shit for the older generations of Canadian hip-hop/rap, who have seen their time come and go without being properly acknowledged, and [will] look at the Junos involvement with urban music now as a contrived method of reaching for relevance and ratings because rap music is the most popular and streamed genre," says Rich Kidd.

"We're used to putting in the work and only relying on

11

ourselves for the earned respect and praise for art that... has gone on to change the face of the global music scene," says O'Connor. "The Grammys still haven't completely gotten it right. The Brits are just coming around. The Junos [have] to take the first step by putting away their politics, look around and realize that it is our rap and R&B communities that birth superstars who are going to shine with or without them."

The Gospel According to Pusha T

by Josie Duffie Rice

The cover art for Pusha T's album *Daytona* is a picture of Whitney Houston's bathroom. It was taken in 2006, but it appears older and more worn than it is, perhaps because of the border of what seems to be faux water damage. The décor is distinctly '90s, an aggressive attempt to look soft. The counters are cluttered, strewn with all the ingredients required to sustain an addiction—spoons caked with powder, pipes, papers, cigarette butts.

That Houston is not in the photo is irrelevant. There is plenty we know about the occupant by instinct. The person who commands this space is not broke. They are not a new user, nor a casual one. At this point, Houston was more than a decade into a battle against crack and cocaine addiction, an addiction that she often denied. "I feel like the cover represents an organized chaos," Pusha said. "Looking at that cover, I'm sure whoever frequents that bathroom or area knew whatever they wanted to find and knew where it was."

Tina Brown, Bobby Brown's sister and Whitney's then-sister-in-law, took the photos and sold them to the National Enquirer. She also divulged deeply intimate details about Houston's addiction, family, and relationships. "Whitney won't stay off the drugs. It's every single day. It's so ugly," Brown said. The tabloids reported on it with a mix of smug derision and hollow lament. They expected no more from a drug addict. "It's hard to believe that [this] drugged, dazed woman ... was once one of the most beautiful and popular singers in the world," wrote one reporter. "But today that woman, Whitney Houston, is just another crackhead."

Pusha is a protégé of Kanye West, a disciple of the church of provocation. West produced *Daytona* and it was West who

13

insisted on paying the $85,000 licensing fee to use the picture for the cover. "This what people need to see to go along with this music," Pusha said West told him.

And the photo is provocative. It's visceral, even. Photos tend to rely on the living to turn stomachs, but this picture manages to pull it off insensate. There are no pretenses here. It's uncomfortable, like walking past a couple screaming on the sidewalk. Just by existing, you barge in uninvited. By no fault of your own, you invade.

Over the past 30 years, hip-hop has garnered a reputation as lawless, angry, and violent. Throughout the '80s and '90s, politicians, community leaders, and journalists inveighed against the music, blowing racist dog whistles and invoking well-worn theories of black defect, while steadily laying the blame for any issue plaguing poor black communities at hip-hop's feet. "Gangster rap reveals the pathology of its creators," The New York Times wrote in 1990. Other publications went further. Billboard magazine published a piece by Michelle Shocked, a white folk singer, in which she argued that hip-hop was the minstrelsy of our time, and managed to blame rap music for white racism: "The chicken-thieving, razor-toting 'coon' of the 1890s is the drug-dealing, Uzi-toting 'nigga' of today … [The mostly white] audience will eventually feel justified in all manner of acts of racism." Listening to certain mainstream rap was like entering "a nightmare world of brute criminality, unrelenting bloodshed, and African American self-loathing," wrote David Mills of *The Washington Post* in 1991.

Drug dealing has always been a major character in the persistent myth of the scourge of black criminality in rap music. Given the coverage, one could be forgiven for believing that rappers were the first artists to ever reference drugs, violence, or casual sex. But as far back as the 1930s, when Cab Calloway sung "Reefer Man," drugs and popular music have been entangled. From jazz and heroin, to marijuana and reggae, to whiskeys in country music, and the great range of substances in rock and roll, drugs and alcohol have had major influences on both art and artist. If anything, hip-hop has simply followed in this tradition.

What was legitimately new about hip-hop was something more subtle: While most pop music concerns itself with drug consumption, hip-hop spans the whole market. It's been 30 years since N.W.A's "Dopeman," a song that begins with a skit of an addict showing up to Eazy-E's door trying to sell his chain. The rapper turns him away. "To be a dope man, boy, you must qualify," Ice Cube instructed. "Don't get high off your own supply / From a key to a g it's all about money." It's a mantra Biggie would repeat 10 years later in "Ten Crack Commandments."

Hip-hop's focus on the supply end of the drug market—the drug dealer—is understandable, given the comparably meager conditions of much of black life in America, and the government's perpetuation of those conditions. The successful drug dealer manages to secure vast wealth while defying a criminal-justice system that has long brutalized black people. For N.W.A., formed in the tumult of 1980s crack-era Los Angeles, and besieged by all the material values of capitalist America, the horror of drug addiction was beside the point. The point was money in communities that had almost no access to capital. The point was the rejection of the legal system that had long rejected them. By the time Biggie came along, very little had changed. "Juicy" might well be the kind of song now played at white people's weddings, but when Biggie talked about the people that "called the police on me when I was just trying to make some money to feed my daughter," he was speaking in earnest. The dealing was seen as a way of surviving in a world that had bet they would not.

And yet, hip-hop long regarded the drug addict as a figure of scorn and comedy. This has changed somewhat as the genre has evolved. Today rappers such as Future and Young Thug speak frankly about the ways they use drugs to manage inner turmoil. But for a long time the user was incidental, a weakness to exploit.

15

"On the corner, betting Grants with the Celo champs," Nas rapped. "Laughing at baseheads trying to sell some broken amps." They are fodder for derision, the users. Addicts, if not casual users, are regarded with a pervasive contempt. "Just another crackhead."

Hip-hop, for all its creative force and ingenuity, has long subscribed to an image of addiction that corresponds with the culture it professed to reject—the image projected by fear-mongering politicians, the one that undergirds the criminal-justice system that launched the War on Drugs. The drug dealer in hip-hop is a resourceful antihero, part Robin Hood, part CEO. But the addict in hip-hop is like the addict everywhere else. Hopeless. Deserving of shame. Off to the side. Something subhuman—weaker, stranger, more destructive than the rest of us.

Pusha is a product of this tradition. He has, in his 41 years, worked largely in two professions—the rap industry and cocaine dealing. He describes first dealing[8] drugs as a junior-high kid. When he was 15, Pusha followed his brother into hip-hop; together they forged the rap duo Clipse. Like many of their contemporaries, Clipse's music was a mix of nostalgia and bravado, and cocaine was a major piece of their repertoire. Whatever money they made from rap was built on the glamorization of their former vocation. But in 2010, they parted ways—Pusha's older brother, Malice, recommitted to his Christian faith and sought more anonymity. Pusha, on the other hand, sought more of the same. He signed to Kanye West's G.O.O.D. Music that same year, where he's released four albums, including *Daytona*.

Coke and Pusha's music are inseverable. He is part of a larger cohort of rappers who came to the music industry in the wake of drug dealing, but Pusha has centered his past much more than his peers. This is what he's known for now, perhaps less because of the dealing he actually did and more because he references it persistently.

Hyperbole finds a home in all music, and rap is no exception.

Drug dealing is especially ripe for exaggeration. It is near impossible, then, to present even the basic reliable details of the years Pusha spent dealing. And yet it is not hyperbole to say that coke harnesses some sort of magnetism over Pusha's music. He is almost effortlessly clever in his self-conception—"L. Ron Hubbard of the cupboard," the "last cocaine superhero." It is the consistent thrum throughout his whole body of work, including Daytona.

Pusha is older now, with money that he didn't have before. Titles, too—in 2015 he was named president of G.O.O.D Music. He seems to have retired from the drug game. "Young enough to still sell dope, but old enough that I knows better," he said at 36, on Future's "Move That Dope." And yet his gravitation to the past is persistent, line after line heavy with bombast and nostalgia. One gets the sense that dealing, not rapping, is the dream job. Other rappers managed to escape the game. He begrudgingly aged out of it. "Who don't wanna sell dope forever?" he asks incredulously.

Like all of us, Pusha is a victim of his own cognitive dissonance. In interviews, he seems genuinely perplexed by the reputation he's earned over the years. He repeatedly downplays the extent to which coke dealing is central to his music.

"You get a lot of heat from people who say you only rap about cocaine—," one radio host asked him in 2015.

Pusha cut him off, agitated. "I don't care what they say," he said. "Listen, people can't even talk to me about that anymore. That bothers me. Cuz I feel like if you say that, then you're only listening at a surface level."

"It takes a more introspective viewpoint to sit here and talk about the science of it," he said in another interview. "I'm talking about how it's dog eat dog, the level of loyalty you have with these people, because it's a team, and when it breaks down, what happens to your life. The competitive nature of these guys in the street, that vie for the biggest prize or the hottest girl. It's all about ego."

There's something to this, surely. When Pusha is rapping about

17

cocaine he's referencing it in a musical tradition of black people creating industries in places that had none. He's talking about much more: the economics, his subversion of the law, capitalism, his youth, the thrill. And yet it narrows to the same thing each time. He's laser focused—obsessed might be an overstatement, but there's no denying his fixation. Every metaphor is this metaphor.

The delineation between user and dealer is inexact and often illusory. The myth of a distinct supply chain—where a person either cultivates or deals or possesses or uses, but never more than one—doesn't tend to map onto reality. But it's a frame that has persisted through the drug war: suppliers as kingpins, dealers as evil, and users as weak. It is this fiction that allows us to criminalize the whole chain of illicit drugs, from creation to consumption. We view these different tiers in the market as distinct because it makes it easier to ascribe wrongdoing. I understand why this is attractive to lawmakers and moralizers—we can punish the sinners. We can wipe our hands clean of them. And ultimately this brings us back to an analysis of pathology—one that allows us to blame the individual rather than grapple with the fundamental causes of addiction and the transactional market of illegal substances.

In a time when society seems to have a newfound pity for drug users, it's easy to understand our era as a post–drug war one. This is a mistake. Sympathy shifts on a dime. In many parts of the country, the opioid crisis has motivated a return to failed tactics, some even worse than before. "Using laws devised to go after drug dealers, [prosecutors] are charging friends, partners and siblings," The *New York Times* reported[9] in May. "Many are fellow users, themselves struggling with addiction." Many of these people purchased drugs and decided to share with a friend. But when that friend overdosed, the user was suddenly no longer a pitiable drug addict, but an evil murderer. In Louisiana, a heroin addict named Jarret McCasland injected[10] his girlfriend, Flavia Cardenas, also a heroin addict, with drugs. The injection killed her. In 2015, McCasland was tried for second-degree murder and convicted; he was eventually sentenced to life without parole.

The increasing trend of prosecuting users for murder is a disturbing reminder that criminal law is no place for a drug crisis. The return to a failed drug war, one that manipulates addiction into pure weakness and dealing into murder, is bound to fail. It's also a reminder that there is not as much of a difference between scorn and pity as one would hope. The perception of drug addiction is still predicated on weakness, sin, and shame—all of which deserve punishment or justify exploitation. The portrayal of addicts as pathological shapes everything from our drug policy to our coke rap.

The difference between users and dealers is, again, often fictional. But in Pusha's case, like many of his predecessors and peers, the separation is real. He boasts about—and, much less rarely, grapples with—dealing, not using. And the failure to fully comprehend the life of a drug addict is what allows him to exploit Whitney Houston for his own benefit.

There are glimpses, brief moments of more complicated self-reflection from Pusha—guilt, regret, and a fear of what karma might have in store. "I started out as a baby-faced monster / No wonder there's diaper rash on my conscience," he says on "Nose-talgia." But the moments are short-lived, and any accountability is internal. There is much more grandstanding than self-reflection. There is no person at the end of the dealing, no character at the end of the rhyme. Transaction necessitates multiple people, but Pusha is onstage alone. And because of that, he spends precious little time focused on the wrongs. As he says on "Drug Dealers Anonymous," "The money count is the only moment of silence / 'Cause hush money balances all this drugs and violence."

There's a braver approach, one that both rejects didactic anti-drug rhetoric that conflates use with addiction and addicts with hopelessness, and does not avoid the very real damage literal "pushers" facilitate, if not inflict. Countless examples are sprinkled throughout the genre—Tupac's "Dear Mama" ("Even though you was a crack fiend, Mama / You always was a black queen, Mama") or Jay-Z's "You Must Love Me" ("All you did was motivate me, don't let 'em hold you back / What I do, I turned around and I sold you crack"). In fact, it's what Kendrick Lamar manages to do on the second verse of "Nosetalgia." Lamar excavates a litany of emotions about his father's drug dealing and addiction, the possibility of prison, his promise to support his family, his aunt stealing from him to feed her habit. ("My daddy turned a quarter piece to a four and a half / Took a L, started selling soap fiends bubble bath / Broke his nails misusing his pinky to treat his nose.") It's not an ethical reprimand, but an accounting of the wins and losses, an assessment of the various ways hard drugs are lucrative and dangerous.

But by focusing on his market prowess almost exclusively, Pusha avoids the weight of his past and present exploitative behavior. He has built a career from others' drug addiction—first by selling drugs, then through two decades of constant rhymes about selling drugs. One could argue the former was more defensible.

Ultimately, he's created a persona that benefits from the same desperation that killed Houston in the end. One sees hints of that reflection in the album cover—not the money, not the exchange, not the person, but the day-to-day banality, the accoutrements of a life centered around using, and the various people that enable such a life.

Dying of addiction is a particular cruelty—it kills you and then haunts the collective memory. If you die by heart attack, or cancer, or in your sleep, it's a tragic postscript to your life story. If you die of addiction, it is your life story. It becomes the whole plotline. Whitney Houston was the greatest pop vocalist of her time, a luminescent woman, joyful, a black woman built of the church. But as an addict she became a sideshow—mocked in her long struggle, and ogled in her death. How she lived has been overawed by how she died, so much so that the scene that led to her death can now be packaged, like her music, as a commodity.

It is impossible to map the struggle of someone you don't know publicly or personally, but by all accounts, Houston spent years of her life in combat, on the frontlines of her own personal drug war. One of the world's greatest singers was treated not with empathy, but with derision. She was ridiculed in the press, betrayed by her family, exploited by her loved ones. Media used the term pathology to describe her life, too. The former editor of *Us Weekly* described Being Bobby Brown, the reality-television show featuring Whitney; her husband, Brown; and her child, Bobbi Kristina, as "a show where you probably saw more pathology than you needed to." She died in a bathtub. You know what they say: that you can't ever beat this kind of addiction. You either spend years outrunning it, or it kills you instead.

Ten years ago, my friend Lisa overdosed on heroin and died. She's not the first person I knew to die from an overdose, nor the last, nor the most surprising. But her death weighs particularly heavy on me, especially now. Lisa was theatrical, strong willed, sharp, but never self-serious. She was a storyteller, with a limitless capacity for invention. On New Year's Eve 2000, when I was 13, my parents insisted that I spend the evening before the new millennium at church. I was devastated. But the next day Lisa threw me a surprise New Year's party, inviting all our friends over to her house in the middle of the afternoon. There were party hats, I remember. We all stood in her living room, holding hands, counting down to fake midnight. I remember being stupefied by how extravagantly kind this was.

And yet, when I think about Lisa, I have to fight for these memories of life because they are all obscured by the manner of her death. It's not out of judgment or disappointment, not because her death says anything about who she was, or who she was to

21

me. It is because the tragedy of a life ended so abruptly can be all consuming. This may be understandable. But it's less than she deserves. It warps her humanity to remember her merely by the disease of addiction.

This is about more than my own memory of a friend felled by addiction, or hip-hop's exploitation of it. We are in a moment when the ethical expectations of art and artists—especially when it comes to the mistreatment of women—have exploded. Art is supposed to make us uncomfortable, expose the cracks in the foundation, and strip bare what we've deified. But it also exposes the artist. Bill Cosby kidding about Spanish Fly is not so funny anymore. Woody Allen's *Manhattan* simply doesn't play the same. The rendering of people as objects to be deployed however an artist chooses is at last coming into question.

For Pusha T, the addict is nearly always an object, a means more than a human—"A nigga got rich from what you snort through a straw," he recounts. And the portrait of Houston's addiction plays the same role, transforming a scene of personal strife into a package to be distributed out on the streets. In all the times I replay her death in my head, I have never wondered where Lisa got the drugs. I am not interested in laying blame. Similarly, it is easy to imagine circumstances in which drug dealing is not a choice, but an imperative; not a question of morality, but one of survival. But there is no imperative in making the dead collateral damage in a quest for profit. And there is something particularly brazen about profiting from the addictions that killed a person, and then pillaging their reputation for more.

Honest art is not always honorable art—which is to say, there is no honor in laying bare the failings of others when you are unwilling to interrogate your own. Honesty that asks no sacrifice lacks truth; honesty at someone else's expense lacks virtue. Profit and provocation are easy. Honorable art, hard art, is in the reckoning.

What Kendrick Lamar's Pulitzer Prize In Music Means for Hip-Hop

by Donna-Claire Chesman

Let's begin with the obvious: Kendrick Lamar and hip-hop do not need awards to be validated.

In terms of acclaim and mass discussion, hip-hop is the dominant outsider, commanding the charts and the sonic epoch we find ourselves in, while simultaneously being maligned and scapegoated by toxic institutions. That said, these awards are necessary armor, a way to take the unfair burden of proof off of the artists and temper conversations about "real" music to a simple nod at the trophy case. In many ways, this award is a utility to the artist, a means to reduce their emotional labor and let them focus on delivering prize-worthy music—business as usual.

A Pulitzer in music for Kendrick Lamar is a Pulitzer in music for hip-hop when, for so many heads, casual fans, and the mainstream at-large, Lamar's music plays as their definition of the genre. In large part due to the GRAMMYs' constant snubs[11] and the Pulitzer's distance from hip-hop culture, this award feels weightier than any Album Of The Year recognition.

Of course, the Pulitzer fills a void for fans who are gutted year to year when Lamar misses out on AOTY by a hair. More importantly, it's the legacy of the Pulitzer as a high art curator that turns this award into a blooming cultural moment. The message has been sent: hip-hop is high art. When we consider the ways in which high art and pop art have been historically racialized, this award is not only revolutionary, it is a moment of overdue reclamation.

We see the question raised, then, "Why not *To Pimp A Butterfly*?" If we are speaking strictly tactfully, awarding *TPAB*,

Lamar's most forward-thinking and consequently most timeless effort, would not have been as revolutionary as awarding *DAMN.* *DAMN.* is as of-the-moment as it is boundary breaking. An award for *DAMN.* speaks to hip-hop's command of the contemporary sphere as much as it does speak to hip-hop's stewarding music on the whole.

In a pleasant twist, classical composers don't disagree with that sentiment. A finalist for the same Pulitzer, Ted Hearne told *Slate*[12] that hip-hop's influence does reach the classical pools traditionalists are vying to keep exclusive. "Hip-hop as a genre has been important to me as a composer, but Kendrick's work in particular," Hearne said. "He is such a bold and experimental and authentic artist. He's one of the people that is creating truly new music."

With a finalist in the category praising Lamar, we have to address the source of the looming fear of progress. For every Ted Hearne, there is a ripe think piece tearing down the accomplishment as political pandering and selectively quoting Lamar's music to fit their narrative of hip-hop as a string of empty profanity.

Speaking with *The Washington Post*, composer Alex Temple, when asked if there was something "sonically threatening" about hip-hop, explained[13] away the threat with a hard truth: people let the stereotype presuppose the research.

"I've seen some pretty shocking dismissals from people who listened to Kendrick for two minutes, lacking any kind of cultural or artistic context, heard some swears and an angry tone, and concluded that his music wasn't worth listening to," Temple said. "The funny thing is, these same people would respond to a casual dismissal of their music by saying 'you need to educate yourself.' They're so secure in their elitist worldview that they don't notice the irony."

Those not trapped in an elitist bubble see Kendrick Lamar and hip-hop for all it's worth. Also speaking with *Slate*, other

Pulitzer finalist Michael Gilbertson recalls a moment where Lamar transcended both awards and music, and rose to the terribly exclusive pantheon of higher education. "I remember when I was at Yale, I heard some other grad students give a talk on some of the theological and conceptual narrative depth in his work, and I was really struck by that," he said. "It changed the way I listen to his music."

Gilbertson's reaction to this Yale lecture entirely re-frames the misunderstanding Temple brings to light. The connotation of "Yale" alone is enough to reconsider these divisions between hip-hop and higher thinking. The message has been sent, again: hip-hop is higher education. It is a transcendent art form that deserves to be recognized within and outside of the scope of music.

So, just how far can Kendrick—can hip-hop—go?

Recall 2016's institutional shake-up, when Bob Dylan won the Nobel Prize for literature, wherein his Nobel lecture was a four-thousand word thesis on the link between music and literature. Obviously not racially motivated, Dylan also faced critical backlash from a score of outlets. He also received a wellspring of support.

Former United States poet laureate, Billy Collins even argued[14] in favor of Bob Dylan as a poet, saying, "Bob Dylan is in the 2-percent club of songwriters whose lyrics are interesting on the page even without the harmonica and the guitar and his very distinctive voice. I think he does qualify as poetry."

Now, could Kendrick Lamar win a prize for his poetry? Per the committee, Dylan won the Nobel for "having created new poetic expressions within the great American song tradition," which is not too dissimilar from the language Hearne used to praise Lamar. Within this context, Kendrick Lamar is one of the most qualified poets within the American poetic tradition.

"Not once have I ever had the time to ask myself, 'Are my songs literature?'" Dylan confessed[15] in his 2016 Nobel Banquet speech. For Kendrick Lamar, the question of literary merit is not rooted in time, but space. That is, what institutional spaces can Black artists occupy before a White majority lashes out? Allowing Kendrick Lamar the space to answer with an earnest "Yes!", that will be revolutionary—not only for hip-hop, but for poetry.

Consider how poetry by Black women continues to be undercut by White critics, who see the confessional nature of the work as low-brow. For every accolade awarded to a Morgan Parker or Eve Ewing, there remain sprawling onslaughts on contemporary poetry by Black women and women of color, ostensibly because the content and form does not qualify as "true" poetics. Meaning, their work does not align with the comfort of the critic.

Would Lamar receive a similar strain of backlash? Of course, even with the privilege of being male, it's not unrealistic to imagine critics taking to their keyboards to undercut the business of giving literary awards to rappers. Even so, a message would have been sent: hip-hop is the American literary tradition. With this Pulitzer in music, that message is coming.

"This is no longer a narrow honor," Gilbertson rightly concluded. Hip-hop, art, institutions, none of these bodies should remain insular. In the age of sold-out 'Yeethoven' performances held at the Lincoln Center, there's really no stopping these inter-sections; rather, there is only acceptance and acceleration.

Hip-hop is classical, is Pulitzer worthy, is and will be Nobel worthy. The world is catching up, and all the while, hip-hop continues to run away with victories.

Why So Many Hip-Hop Producers Are Putting Business Before Beats

by Cherie Hu

"If y'all knew the amount of f–king money I give up just to make sure a song comes out, 'cause people are so f–king stingy, you would not believe it."

These are the words of Kenny Beats[16]—a producer who has worked with rappers like Rico Nasty, Key!, and Freddie Gibbs—as cemented in a fiery 15-second video that the producer uploaded to Twitter from his car recently. But if we're being realistic about the harsh demands of hip-hop's loose, rapid-fire release culture and haphazard record-keeping that comes along with it, Kenny Beats' words may as well have come from any other producer in the genre.

Going back as early as when budding rappers and entrepreneurs were selling cassette tapes and CDs from the trunks of their cars, fast money from moving physical product has taken precedence over long-term revenue from royalties that said artists might never see. Of course, the industry landscape is much different today; fans are effectively renting access to music via streaming services like Spotify and Apple Music, previously unprofitable catalog now has a longer lifespan[17], and rappers are coming out on top.

According to the latest HITS Daily Double Song Revenue[18] Chart, the top 20 rap songs are generating nearly $1.8 million in streaming revenue in a single week. Label bidding wars are heating up as a result, with record deals ranging from $1 million for Lil Xan[19] to a reported $15 million for BROCKHAMPTON[20]. But producers, who are often forced to stay behind the scenes both culturally and financially, are still paying the price—and speaking

27

up about it.

Last year, "Pull Up Wit Ah Stick" producer Lil Voe revealed that Warner Bros. Records sent him a mere work-for-hire contract for the song, and took all his publishing and wiped his official credit from the track in the process. Atlanta producer DJ Burn One then confirmed[21] that he never got paid for producing two tracks on A$AP Rocky's 2011 debut mixtape *LIVELOVEA$AP*, which the rapper is still monetizing and currently performing for global audiences on tour.

"You can blame the business and say it's dirty—which it is—or you can put one foot forward at a time, hire a lawyer to look over your contracts, arm yourself with knowledge, and help others in your arena," says Burn One, who is currently forming a nonprofit organization called Fast Forward United to educate and empower producers with business resources. "I think it starts with baby steps."

On the corporate level, inaccuracy around ownership leaves billions of dollars on the table. Spotify has faced two copyright infringement lawsuits[22] over the past three years, adding up to $1.75 billion, for allegedly failing to secure the necessary licenses for certain songs. An estimated $2.5 billion[23] is currently sitting in pools of "black box"[24] royalties, some of which are collected when streaming platforms are unable to identify who owns a song.

While who exactly is "responsible" for this problem remains an open debate, one indisputable fact is that artists and producers aren't capturing as much ownership information during the creative process as they used to. Even the phrase "at the source" itself has diluted in meaning, as collaborators are increasingly recording verses in hotels or bedrooms while on tour on opposite hemispheres of the world, rather than together in the same studio.

"Producers need to take initiative in the studio from the beginning and say, 'I think what I've added has X value to this project,'" says Deborah Mannis-Gardner, owner and president of DMG

Clearances, which has handled global music rights clearances for clients like DJ Khaled and Eminem. "The problem is that once you have six to eight writers or producers on a track, everyone has their own opinion on what percentage everyone gets. I don't think people are being intentionally combative, but it's hard to get that many people on the same page."

In addition, remote work norms often put indie artists at a disadvantage in contract negotiations. "If you're an indie producer working with a major label and not everyone's in the same room to sign a split sheet, you don't have a lot of leverage," adds DJ and artist manager Adam Golden, who manages emerging producer Yung Skrrt. "Labels will get the sound they want, regardless of whether the original producer is willing to cooperate with them."

As a result, securing the proper credits for songs is often retroactive, even at the major-label level. Lawyer sources say that many major rap albums, including Drake's Scorpion and Migos' Culture II, are still securing the proper clearances weeks or even months after release.

The credits problem is also arguably a chicken-or-egg dilemma with respect to producers' business models. Industry sources say that producers today can command four- to six-figure upfront checks per track. At those rates, producing even just three songs a month can already lead to substantial annual income, to the point where said producers might not necessarily be prioritizing proper credits or metadata.

That said, "if you're getting an advance, you should also be getting a contract with details about how many points, mechanical royalties and other basics you're getting on the backend off the song," says Burn One. "If someone tells me they have an advance but no royalties, that's telling me they didn't get the proper deal in place."

Given the amount of money at stake, building a solution for these enduring issues around credits is potentially big business—

and a growing number of music-tech companies are jumping on the opportunity. In April 2018, Spotify acquired Loudr, a startup using machine learning to streamline licensing and royalty payments. Later in August 2018, City National Bank, which has several high-profile clients in Hollywood, acquired Exactuals, which similarly trains algorithms to match ownership data across disparate sources to ensure the proper rights owners are paid.

Both Spotify and YouTube have also added sections for songwriter and producer credits to their platforms. The one big catch: because they're still ingesting these credits primarily from labels, much of the output is still incomplete or erroneous[25] for now—a classic case of "garbage in, garbage out."

There is also a burgeoning, if not overcrowded, startup ecosystem around credits: at-the-source solutions like Auddly and Sound Credit, publicly-searchable databases like Jaxsta, and even a handful of blockchain-based initiatives like JAAK and DotBC. While each of these startups is tackling a different, necessary piece of the gargantuan credits puzzle, there's a lot of politics involved in positioning a new startup to labels as an authoritative data source—and a given major label cannot realistically work with all of these startups at once.

Amidst this complex tech landscape, many producers are realizing that the solution they can control most directly is simply elevating the value of their own brand. A-listers like DJ Khaled and Benny Blanco are no longer relying solely on advances or residual royalties for income, but are also tapping into other revenue streams such as merchandise, brand endorsements, and even touring, altering public perception of producers in the process. The underlying argument is that producers are no longer just "secret weapons"[26] for artists, but are also creative leaders and backbones for hip-hop culture that deserve the proper value and recognition.

"A lot of us think putting business first taints the energy of the music, but now I think business is what allows the music to flow," says Burn One. "You just need to protect your interests, learn your rights and negotiate what you're worth. The moment you take your eye off the ball, someone else will take the ball from you."

Inside UK Drill, the Demonised Rap Genre Representing A Marginalised Generation

by Yemi Abiade

London feels like a war zone. In 2018 alone, the Metropolitan Police has reported 50 knife and gun-related deaths in the UK capital, with an ominous rise – the highest in a decade – in the past two weeks.[27]

What seems like indiscriminate, inexplicable crime[28] is having its root causes dissected and, in a state of moral panic and unfolding debate, mainstream media is clumsily pointing to one direction: the current soundtrack of the UK's streets, drill.

A form of trap-style rap taken from Chicago and pioneers such as Chief Keef in the early 2010s, then exported into south London some years later and popularized by 67, K-Trap, 150 and others, drill has enveloped UK music's underground with its rampant, energetic and domineering sounds, reflecting the harshness of these rappers' respective neighbourhoods.

Until recently, mainstream media have actively ignored it, but are now jumping on the bandwagon of blame, not hesitating to pinpoint blame on the music and its disciples for perpetuating violence. Some even go the extra mile and flat out demonise everything about it – to ludicrous levels and with a failure to grasp slang in their criticisms – and are left exposed as the proverbial relics and proprietors of white privilege that they are.

Let's be clear, drill music is no picnic. In it, rappers detail vivid accounts of cooking up drugs, facing up to their rivals (or opps) and harming those who dare to disrespect them. Yes, lines referring to cleaning kitchenware after doing away with a person exist, and their presentation (visuals of young black men in all-black tracksuits, faces covered in balaclavas, spewing street slang and throwing up frequent gunfingers) can be ominous from the outside looking in.

While street politics, social media antics and the inevitable violence they produce are issues rife within this music, drill is the new sound of the disenfranchised as they make sense of a neglectful nation. Scratching beneath the surface of their explosive and territorial bravado further, you discover that these drillers are really crying out for help, speaking to a mental anguish that has engulfed them but fails to be addressed.

This is a reality far removed from the idyllic British society the media likes to perpetuate when they fail to even report most murders in the capital. Their fantasy is just that, and violence on our streets embodies this notion. What mainstream media and the government continuously fail to grasp is that these tales, accounts and personas rife within drill music are simply reflections of their localities.

These are communities that are constantly being let down by cuts to local services, such as youth clubs and school services that would take would-be gangsters and murderers off the streets, channelling their energies into positivity.

Just last week the home secretary, Amber Rudd, denied that cuts to police services have anything to do with the recent spate of violence, ignoring a leaked report that spoke to the contrary, another tale of politicians and authority figures skirting responsibility.

Rather than looking inwards, admitting the failure of a generation and putting systems in place to begin rectifying the damage, higher forces continue to show little care, and the result is bloodshed. To implicate a musical genre for such violence – something that has existed generations before UK drill became a factor – is, frankly, unfounded. These problems would exist without drill, so why is it now the fashionable thing to heap blame upon?

Prominent MC Abra Cadabra eloquently expresses this best, telling the *The Guardian*[29] last week: "Targeting musicians is a distraction. The cuts that affect schools, youth clubs, social housing and benefits are making life harder for the average person living on or below the poverty line in this city.

"There are people doing mad tings, not because they want, but because the situation has forced them to."

His sentiments were echoed by prominent DJ Bembah, speaking to BBC Radio 4 last Monday: "[Drill] is just real-life content, you talk about things that happen from day to day. Music can affect your emotions, but it can't affect what you do outside. It can't make you go outside and stab someone."

And, despite the best efforts of POC writers such as Ciaran Thapar – a journalistic authority on the genre and a youth worker in Brixton, drill's ground zero – to communicate these issues on a national scale and link them to its rise, their efforts are either ignored or coopted (without credit) by an establishment quick to jump on the hot topic of the day.

"I think it is remarkable that paying attention to this rich, complex type of modern subculture has required a context of blame," he says, "rather than a willingness to appreciate drill as something worth studying for the sake of better engaging with young people. Or, a willingness to criticise powerful forces in society that have created an environment that is ripe for this music being made violence and disenfranchisement being realised."

Clearly, it is a greater case of music being shaped by its surroundings than teenager and young adult rappers being spurred by drill's various anthems.

Thapar continues: "If a given teenage boy cannot disassociate from the content of a type of music, to the extent that it is making him want to kill someone, then surely that's the failure of us as a society to allow education and parenting and community relations to get that bad? It's not music's responsibility."

British media's moral frenzy of late simply presents the detachment between them and these communities, but instead of trying to close the gap and deal with what causes these issues, they widen it further by demonising an entire subculture.

This is nothing new; grime's rise in the early 2000s coincided with Operation Trident, a state-wide police initiative to tackle gang violence. There, the new sound was also victimised – sensing a pattern here? That drill is merely another chapter in this blame game is indicative of a society in which its representatives have been placed on the periphery by a nation that ought to protect them from the dangers of street life.

The collective attitude of the mainstream therefore brings up the old (or maybe not) adage that black communities remain aliens – punching bags for when the going gets tough – and that black boys are forever the problem of British society.

"That's what it feels like," says *Complex* senior editor and *Trench* editor-in-chief Joseph "JP" Patterson. "Especially when you've got papers like the *Daily Mail* consistently attacking successful black men in Britain. It's almost like, no matter which route you take, it's never good enough for these people."

An endless cycle of interrogation may put these forces at ease, but ignoring these problems breed contempt, giving birth to more violence. Regardless of London's murder rate, drill will continue to offer a voice to those without one because, for many of them, it's all they have to survive.

"As long as our country is being delivered austerity," Thapar says, "and people in London are happy to watch gentrification completely isolate long-forgotten communities of young people, the music is going nowhere, because it will connect with people who are believing and resonating with its message."

Mainstream media, the government and public services have the tools to transform some of these communities for the better, but it requires a real change in mentality that, based on the current chain of events, is not achievable in the near future.

Sorry, Drake and Nicki,
But Hip-Hop Is Changing

by Gary Suarez

Trend watching is a core component of success in the music business. From keeping up with the latest SoundCloud up-and-comers to mining local scenes for burgeoning talent, the industry depends on such active monitoring and engagement in order to thrive. Today's star can easily be tomorrow's has-been, struggling to reach new heights or even find a place for themselves as tastes shift and fans migrate in pursuit of something fresh.

In hip-hop, now the largest genre grouping by consumption thanks in no small part to the streaming revolution, the challenges increase and compound regularly. A viral hit could signal the onset of a promising career, as seems the case for Lil Pump, or a false start with little room to recover, as Stitches no doubt knows in the years since "Brick In Yo Face." Even artists that achieve tremendous prosperity in short order may find themselves very much out of vogue without warning, as evidenced by the almost inexplicable fall of once vibrant rap romantic, Fetty Wap. With an abundance of new music dropping each week, few second chances are granted and, as O.T. Genasis can attest after "Coco" and "Cut It," third ones can prove maddeningly slippery.

While established hitmakers overwhelmingly occupy our ears, as patrons we often take a passive approach to hearing new music, letting the platforms we listen on and social media influencers we listen to drive our consumption. Getting a placement on one of Spotify's branded playlists or a shout out from a prominent Instagrammer can have a significant impact on a single's lifespan and an artist's prospects. With discovery a less individual practice than the Internet age posited, hip-hop remains a game to be gamed by those with the power and savvy to do so, making it vital for insiders to stay on top of what's happening.

Still, amid all the fads and frauds coming at us almost daily, hip-hop is a living thing, one that grows, adapts, and, ultimately, changes to suit its times. Through the genre's 45-year history, seismic shifts have disrupted the status quo time and time again, with heavy hitters nudged or shoved aside for the next defining wave. And while day-to-day it may not be apparent, we are once again in the midst of such a transference.

The summer of 2018 rages on, and so too does the veritable donnybrook of rappers dropping new albums to beat the heat. Already in the mix are full-lengths by known quantities Drake, Future, Nicki Minaj, Kanye West, and the unexpected tag team of Beyonce and JAY-Z as the imaginatively named duo The Carters. Travis Scott stunned his haters with the massive first week performance of *Astroworld*, which officially went RIAA gold in that opening frame, while tabloid target Mac Miller returned with a soul searching outing for his fans in *Swimming*. Imminent entries from Young Thug and the aforementioned Lil Pump promise to shake things up, with plenty of blazing hot weeks ahead for other contenders to join in.

While it seems premature to suggest Canada's biggest export will fall off anytime soon, especially with the strong performance of his latest double album *Scorpion*, reactions to that record were mixed. So too, it appears, is the case with *Queen*, a rap-centric release that even has some of the Minajerie's faithful Barbz questioning their stan status. Even the comparatively shorter *Beast Mode 2*, the existence of which delighted fans of the Zaytoven-helmed first installment, failed to produce a single close to the Atlanta rapper's Metro Boomin hits. And the less said about *Ye*, that hastily assembled rap miniature, the better.

"Our longstanding faves are putting out underwhelming albums now because that's generally what happens."

This, assuredly, is the natural order: the inevitable slide of big names from the last decade or so into the legacy artist category. Whether we like it or not, our longstanding faves are putting out underwhelming albums now because that's generally what happens. We witnessed it 11 years ago when Kanye's *Graduation* bested 50 Cent's *Curtis*, the initial sales disparity signaling the demise of G-Unit's days of dominance, which in turn had its ascendance at the expense of the once formidable Roc-A-Fella. There was a time when Cold Chillin' was the name in hip-hop, summarily replaced by gangsta and hardcore rap on both coasts courtesy of N.W.A., then Wu-Tang, then 2Pac and Biggie and so on.

The possibility of Drake or Nicki or Kanye ever putting out great and groundbreaking albums again remains open. Survivors of the 1990s and early 2000s, JAY-Z and Nas dropped their summertime projects to much fuss and little else, the former obviously benefitting from the superstar standing of his wife. And seeing how well younger acts like Travis Scott are doing, it's safe to say we've transitioned away from the aging powerhouses controlling the musical conversation.

Indeed, hip-hop is driven by the youth, and in just the last two years we've seen a rising generation of listeners with a corresponding collection of new artists generally ranging in age from teens to mid-20s. One example, Lil Uzi Vert took the momentum from 2016's breakthrough "Money Longer" and ended up making even bigger waves with 2017's "XO Tour Life" and Migos' "Bad And Boujee." His erstwhile collaborator Playboi Carti appears to be on the same path, leveraging "Magnolia" into this past May's debut album *Die Lit*. Barely legal, Lil Pump captivated audiences with the repetitive "Gucci Gang" and continues with his *Harverd*

Dropout tracks.

Thanks to support from these young audiences, Cardi B and Post Malone went from presumed one hit wonders to international festival headliners. And the pool of prospects keeps expanding, with new entrants like Juice Wrld and Lil Baby making it onto Billboard's Hot 100 this year. Latinx artists like Bad Bunny and Ozuna are challenging the norms, with Spanish language hip-hop approaches making for major chart hits too. Admittedly, some of the figures coming up do so with considerable legal baggage and troubling behavioral characteristics, yet their music nonetheless connects with young consumers.

Looking at the landscape, we're clearly in the middle of another generational shift in hip-hop. Today's tweens and teens are removed from 31-year-old Drake by as much as two decades, and the idea that he will direct this segment's tastes seems questionable given the way things have always gone. The kids will always be right, determining for themselves what's cool and what isn't.

Conversely, the choice now for maturing listeners who've grown accustomed to being on top is to decide whether or not to keep overlooking the new and young talents in hip-hop in favor of aging ones. In truth, we're probably about two years away from an undeniable turnover. Those who opt to stick primarily to what they know stand to officially become the new oldheads. Choose wisely.

Hip-Hop's Love/Hate Relationship with Chance The Rapper

by Kathy Iandoli

I'm really not an expert on Chance The Rapper at all. The only thing I know is that if Apple Music admitted to behaving like a record label, then Chance would be their flagship artist. That's about it. That and he's pretty fucking talented. 2013's *Acid Rap* was one of those projects geared to shape-shift the next five years of hip-hop had mumble rap not taken over like, "Just kidding!" However, it did solidify Chance as a force; the "indie rapper" tag not withstanding.

When he dropped his mixtape *Coloring Book* in 2016, it quickly became an "album" in the Grammy world, as he took home three awards that following year, including Best Rap Album. Funnily enough, other rappers like Drake would challenge the Grammys for their stiff categories, though *Coloring Book* would somehow bypass that categorization glitch and fit perfectly into that fantasy ambiguity. Performances on The Ellen DeGeneres Show, Harvard talks, hanging out with Obama, and doing a Kit Kat commercial all propelled the Chicago native to the next level. And of course, every new level comes with a whole new set of haters.

So here we are, five years following *Acid Rap*, and Chance drops off four new songs this week ("I Might Need Security," "Work Out," "Wala Cam," and "65th & Ingleside"). These all drop in the midst of a self-concocted new album rumor that he's since squashed, yet he's "def been in the stu tho." Apparently the elusive project was supposed to arrive timed with the Special Olympics on July 21. (If that still happens before this column posts, then whoops! I don't write in real-time.) Anyway, the four songs he did offer up were in the signature style of the man we now casually

41

call "Chano." Chance has kind of made his music this podium of bars where each line is a carefully constructed quotable. As soon as these tracks dropped, we got the Twitter storm of: "When Chance said [insert line from song], I felt that."

The one song of the four that's been getting the most social media burn is "I Might Need Security." The cover art is an abstract embodiment of the Arthur meme, the song and title are inspired by Jamie Foxx's "I Might Need Security" standup bit, Chance admits to buying the Chicagoist on the song, and he gets political as fuck, but then also says things like, "Still in my bag like the fries at the bottom." So yeah, it's a nice cross-section of the internets, nostalgia, current topics, and internet-quality #bars.

However, half of the web hates everything Chance-related.

Scanning both Twitter and Facebook, it's really a mixed bag of superlatives used to describe Chance the Rapper and his music. Tweets like, "I will listen to anything Chance drops" are chased with tweets like, "I will never listen to anything Chance drops." This is due largely to his flimsy social media politics back in the Spring, where he expressed that not all Black people have to be democrats but then turned around and slammed Donald Trump arguably for effect). This was all during Kanye West's weird MAGA spasms. And while Chance was one of the major players on Kanye's 2016 *The Life of Pablo*, we also learned earlier this month that he too is joining the full-Kanye-produced project bandwagon and working with his Chicagoan elder on an effort as well. This did nothing to Nas in the way of criticism, but it may do everything to Chance since he has a whole cannon full of naysayers ready to blast off.

The critiques delve deeper into his catalog beyond the 'Ye stigma. Some feel that *Acid Rap* was his last quality project. Others feel like his lyrical content has drastically shifted ever since the fame trickled in. The retorts from fans are more regional, on these new releases in particular. Apparently, if you're not from Chicago then you can't appreciate "Wala Cam" (I like the song and I've only been to Chicago once, so…I guess). But there's no denying that Chance is a philanthropist, especially for the Windy City, so that loyalty runs deep.

The problem with this whole debate is not in the now-polarizing opinions of Chance, but with the temporary pedestals that artists are placed upon whenever they do something against the grain. That will only result in disappointment. Every time.

We saw that many moons ago with Lupe Fiasco, when he "Kick Pushed" his way into our hearts and everyone deemed him the messiah. Shit, rewind back a little earlier to 20 years ago next month when Lauryn Hill dropped *The Miseducation of Lauryn Hill*; Lauryn forecasts it herself on the album: "They hail you, then they nail you. No matter who you are."

You have every right to love an artist, just as much as you have every right to dislike them. You don't have a right to determine their fate in music based upon one isolated project, song, tweet, comment, Instagram post, charitable offering, engagement, etc. — mainly because it's futile. And the reason why is because nothing is fixed. There is nothing so monumentally grandiose that an artist can do that will forever keep them in the public's favor. This also plays in reverse, unfortunately, as there's nothing ever too heinous that an artist can do that will stop their continued success with their loyal core. We can look to another Chicago native R. Kelly for further proof of that. But for the record, Chance has neither done something so amazing to keep him permanently lifted nor something so awful to stage a protest. He's just out here flourishing, with some evident mistakes sprinkled in.

So devour these new Chance the Rapper songs or hit unsubscribe. It really doesn't matter. For better or worse. *Kanye shrug.*

Hip Hop Writing in 2018
by Martin E. Connor

Hip hop writing has never been more important than it is in 2018. With more artists to go through than ever before, hip hop writers today have a duty—not a job. They do not separate the "must-hears" from the "pretty goods", and the "could-be" artists from the "never-gonna" ones. Their judgments are no longer of the black-or-white nature: "5-stars!" "Two thumbs down!"

This shift from critical judgment to subjective positioning is the result of several forces that have changed not only music writing, but the entire music industry itself. These include the huge amount of content; the immediacy of social media; the rise of podcasts and vlogs; and the blending of musical genres.

Take that first point: the huge amount of music that gets made today. This makes critics less like judges, and more like musical guides who must lead us through a tangled pop jungle that's bound to have something for everyone. For example, here's a (partial) list of rappers who have charted on Billboard within the past year: Drake, Future, Kanye, Eminem, Uzi Vert, Migos, Post Malone, DJ Khaled, J. Cole, Rae Sremmurd, Big Sean, Childish Gambino, Logic, Nicki Minaj, Cardi B, XXXTentacion, Lil Pump, Kendrick Lamar, Chance, 2Chainz, Lil Wayne...and yet, it's hard to imagine rap today with just one of those names.

So writers today position new artists and albums within the larger sweep of history, or encourage us to relive our favorite musical moments from the past, rather than grade it and judge it. Throughout this process, they keep up a healthy respect for their readers' own specific tastes and choices. The most popular critics do not take sides in G.O.A.T. debates, so much as they bring alive the experience of listening to a specific person's G.O.A.T. album or artist. This conversational aspect of today's hip hop writing is one of its defining features. In this setting, the listener here is not an uneducated amateur: they are a hip hop expert in their own right, one who needs a bit of help fleshing out their own beliefs.

Social media's blurring of that line—the one between the professional and the personal—is one reason that such writing has become more subjective. The nerdiness of Fantano, the emotion of Yoh, the energy of Quint—any differences in their reviews is proof of a different way of relating to music as a whole, and not necessarily an artistic disagreement. Having just as many rap critics to choose from as they do rappers, article readers (and video viewers, and podcast listeners) choose writers whose approach to music is similar to their own (whether playful, curious, serious, historical, etc.) Just like the larger number of artists, this leads to a larger number of writers, who now can work together collaboratively to tackle difficult topics. Data scientists team up with critics at innovative outlets like the *New York Times*, *The Pudding*, and *Central Sauce*, in order to create articles that are not only revealing, but also shareable.

That reference to videos and podcasts is telling, since so much of "hip hop writing" is now "hip hop talking," or "hip hop acting." The dominant formats of the podcast and the vlog have done much to drive and accelerate these changes to hip hop writing. Their influence ranges from the increase in subjectivity, to the increase in content, to the elevation of social media to being many journalists' main (and only) platform.

Lastly, rap is now so popular that "hip hop writing" is basically "music writing." Migos won Favorite Pop/Rock Duo at the 2018 American Music Awards; Kanye West submitted his Kid Cudi collaboration "Freeee (Ghost Town, Pt.2)," from their Kids See Ghosts album, for "Best Rock Song" and "Best Rock Performance" at the 2019 Grammys. This means that rap is no longer a genre, but the grand unifying force of pop music. When a genre's dominance becomes this thorough, accusations of selling-out, or of whitewashing, become not only toothless, but meaningless. Rather than watering down rap, it encourages the genre to present itself as the intersection at which other genres, like EDM, neo-soul, R&B, dance hall, and jazz can all meet to exchange ideas. The most incisive rap writers will know many genres besides rap, if they are to help their readers the most.

If writers have a responsibility to their readers, than those readers have a responsibility to their favorite artists. They must continue to present the genre to listeners at its best, in order to make sure that rap does not forget its roots or its pioneers. In the age of 140 characters and hot takes, this may seem like a tall task; but the same genre that went from Bronx to Brixton to Brazil is surely up for it.

Migos' Crossover Win at the AMAs Signals an Imminent Industry Shift

by John Vilanova

One thing guaranteed to get people's attention around awards shows is when a film, song, or artist is nominated in an unexpected category. *Get Out*, Jordan Peele's surrealist horror thriller, was nominated for the 2018 Golden Globe for Best Musical or Comedy (despite the director's wry suggestion that it was, in fact, a "documentary" on systemic racism), which infuriated many. Beyoncé's submission of *Lemonade*'s "Daddy Lessons" for consideration for Best Country Song at the 2017 Grammys incited spirited debate and was ultimately rejected, despite support from many in the country-music community.[30] And after the British folk/prog-rock group Jethro Tull won the 1989 Grammy Award for Best Hard Rock/Metal Performance Vocal, beating out Metallica, which seemed destined to receive the award, the announcement was booed loudly by the Shrine Auditorium audience (including artists themselves). The upset spawned major criticism and the development of special screening committees to ensure songs stayed in their proverbial lane for years to come.

So when Migos, the Atlanta-based rap trio whose influence on the culture has ranged from helping to popularize the dab to introducing the triplet flow[31] to mainstream audiences, won its first American Music Award on Tuesday in the category of Favorite Pop/Rock Duo or Group, one could have expected cries of "foul" from the corners of the internet and from the commentariat where these things tend to originate. There were a few tweets criticizing the decision, but generally the announcement was met with bemusement akin to Lil Uzi Vert's shoulder shrug in his guest appearance in the video for "Bad and Boujee," the group's breakthrough single. "We did not know we was winning this at all," admitted the Migos lead, Quavo, who accepted the award with his groupmate Offset. No one else did either, but the award certainly didn't generate the usual amount of outrage in the wee hours of the evening.

This might be due to awards-show fatigue, caused by the fact that every decision is covered with the breathlessness of a papal conclave, in which we're waiting for the fumata bianca to emit from Kanye West's ears. It may be due to the AMAs' model, where fan voting via Facebook and Twitter delegitimizes the idea that the show is anything more than a popularity contest. But it could be due to something else: a shift in music-consumption mechanisms that is blurring the once-sacred lines of genre division in favor of a more fluid ecosystem. Migos is a pop/rock group now. So what?

As a means of connecting discrete cultural texts and finding their sameness, genre is a sacred cow of sorting mechanisms. It traces its roots as far back as classical Greece, where Plato's Republic contains an argument from Socrates that it might not be possible for the same person to write or act in both comedy and tragedy, the twin genres of the day. Genre also served as a means of codifying high/low binaries, where symphonic and classical music were "art" made for the bourgeois (or "boujee") while popular music was a lower, more debased form fit for mass consumption. The Grammys, for instance, started as a way of asserting the musical significance and excellence of acts like Frank Sinatra and Henry Mancini above the menace of pop and rock music like Elvis Presley.

But it's always been slippery: Is Adele pop, soul, R&B, or some combination thereof? Why was Beyoncé's 2017 country Grammy submission denied and her rock nomination for the Jack White collaboration "Don't Hurt Yourself" affirmed?[32] How is it that the Carpenters, Bon Jovi, Ace of Base, Hootie & the Blowfish, Spice Girls, 'NSync, Outkast, One Direction, and now Migos could all win the same pop/rock award? Maybe the AMAs really are just a popularity contest. Or maybe instead they're an index of the shifting signifier of pop/rock and Migos really does have its finger on the Culture after all.

In terms of consumption, genre long functioned in a quotidian sense as a cataloging structure for retail stores of yore: If you liked Migos, you were likely to find the group's jewel cases sorted neatly between Method Man and Mos Def. Genre effectively functioned as free advertising; it assumed that if fans liked one musical group, they'd be likely to want to hear more things similar to it. But with the decline of the record store and the rise of streaming and digital platforms (which were responsible for 75 percent of total U.S. music-sales revenue in 2017),[33] these rigid boundaries are falling away.

Apple Music, one of the industry's three major streaming services alongside Spotify and Jay-Z's Tidal, boasts the availability of more than 40 million songs at any given time, many of which are thoughtfully sorted for listeners into curated playlists based around moods or spaces rather than strict genre convention. "Songs to Sing in the Car" on Spotify, for instance, has previously filed Lauryn Hill's hip-hop standard "Doo Wop (That Thing)" between the classic rocker Tom Petty's "American Girl" and Ryan Adams's meditative "Come Pick Me Up." Other playlists on the service capture the soundscape of "Your Favorite Coffeehouse" or curate a hodgepodge of "Today's Top Hits." Genre still exists, but it no longer divides culture, cleaves fandoms, or crystallizes identity[34] in ways it once did. The listening public now consumes music omnivorously and ravenously at the digital buffet.

There's reason to be concerned about this, for sure—trading the grungy hand of the record-store employee for the invisible hand of the algorithm or the curator[35] runs the risk of exacerbating systemic industry issues, such as the extreme biases revealed in Liz Pelly's recent reporting[36] on Spotify playlists' gender imbalances.

But genre itself has always been an imperfect means of categorization: organized by a variety of shared conventions, including lyrical themes, geography, song structure, and cultural context. And a stubborn insistence—on the part of awards shows and music fans alike—to use genres has created questionable and inorganic distinctions (particularly with categories like the Grammys' Urban Contemporary, which is an obvious stand-in for "music composed by black artists"). These walls are incompatible with the current culture, and breaking them down—with their racist, sexist, and ageist legacies—is the right thing to do.

Migos' victory is thus illustrative of both contemporary fan tastes and an industry structure that's changing, in which acknowledging a group that just tied the Beatles' record[37] with 14 simultaneously charting Billboard songs feels more important and necessary than debating into what box it fits. Pop is contextual, and in 2018, Migos is a pop group. That might be a good thing after all.

Hip-Hop Is Already an Inclusive Artform & an Exclusive Culture. Mainstream Rap Isn't...

by Dart Adams

Last week, Yoh wrote an op-ed[38] which quoted a line from a piece I was commissioned to write[39] for NPR commemorating the 40th anniversary of the inception of hip-hop culture, as well as a tweet from Freddie Foxxx stating the need for hip-hop to once again be exclusive.

Yoh, 26, added the disclosure that he never experienced any of the previous eras when hip-hop culture and rap weren't already mainstream fixtures and emphasized that his perspective was shaped by growing up in a post-Telecom Act/post-rap apartheid world where two separate and unequal rap industries co-existed simultaneously.

Since Yoh never saw the events unfold in real time, nor did he witness the fallout over a full calendar year afterward, he's only known the rap scene as a thriving environment. Like many younger hip-hop fans who are currently under the age of 40, Yoh made the understandable mistake of conflating rap, the rap industry and all of its corporate byproducts as being included under the umbrella of "hip-hop."

They aren't.

When Freddie Foxxx was talking about making hip-hop exclusive again, I understood exactly where he was coming from. Hip-hop culture and rap possess a unique space in the continuum

51

of American Black music due to several odd factors. First, early Black music forms such as gospel, blues, jazz, doo-wop, soul/R&B and rock & roll relied on someone with white skin privilege in order to get financed, recorded, distributed and/or get radio airplay. This was due to racism, economics and a lack of access. In turn, this led to a cycle of exploitation and inequality, which stemmed from a lack of ownership. Not only were these Black artists often stripped of their own creations and intellectual property but that meant they couldn't receive any royalties or future compensation for their own innovations or pioneering. It did, however, make the children of label owners that signed these acts to recording deals rich, since they owned the rights to their back catalogs. Cue the theme song to *The Neverending Story...*

In the case of rap music, there were several Black-owned record labels that sought to benefit from the Bronx's burgeoning hip-hop culture by recording the first big rap hit. Both Sylvia Robinson of Sugar Hill Records and Bobby Robinson of Enjoy Records saw the potential of rap music early on, but rather than sign up an elite hip-hop crew, they scouted and gathered information on all the leading crews—and the scene as a whole—to better determine how to gain an advantage. They soon realized that the DJ—not the emcees—was the focal point of the hip-hop crew and sought to exploit that appeal.

The emcees would audition for the DJ in order to be in the crew and oftentimes, after being paid, emcees were encouraged to kick down some of the money to help maintain the sound system and purchase better equipment. Both Sugar Hill and Enjoy sought out emcees and offered them, at one time, approximately 25 to 50 shows worth of pay to sign. They were then told they didn't need to split the pot with the DJ. Also, they'd record over a live band so the DJ (the very backbone of hip-hop culture) wasn't necessary. From its inception back in 1979 to today, the rap music industry has NEVER been "pure."

While early hip-hop crews and rap artists were being exploited, taken advantage of and suppressed by Black-owned labels like Sugar Hill, Enjoy and Winley, to make matters worse, rap wasn't even regarded as "real" music by the Black music community at large. Black radio programmers mostly abhorred rap. At best, they tolerated it. Even crucial Black music advocates and gatekeepers like Frankie Crocker and Don Cornelius were resistant. Major labels eventually began to record rap acts—Tommy Boy, Profile, Jive/Zomba—but they were few and far between.

In time, Def Jam would set forth the blueprint for the fortification of a rap label, thanks in large part to label co-founder Russell Simmons who also owned Rush Artist Management, which oversaw the careers of rap's biggest draws at the time. This is the kind of early ownership that no other form or subgenre of Black music had previously enjoyed.

Critically, it helped that rap was also directly attached to hip-hop culture. There's a passage in Yoh's article where he writes, "The hip-hop I know has saved the lives of all creeds and brought joy to every color. Exclusive art doesn't change, help, or save lives." The hip-hop culture I know of has done the very same—from the very beginning it changed, helped and saved lives, including my own—but only when it was a subculture far away from the prying eyes of the mainstream, Madison Avenue or Hollywood.

Hip-hop was always inclusive from the outset. Everyone brought influences from their ethnic backgrounds, countries of origin, neighborhoods and their own individuality into their chosen means of self-expression within hip-hop. Although there were few early on, white kids were among the legendary graf writers, b-boys and eventually even emcees and DJs alongside their Black and Latino peers.

White folks such as Henry Chalfant, Marty Cooper, Charlie Ahearn, Debbie Harry, Chris Stein, Tom Silverman, Arthur Baker, Bill Adler, Rick Rubin, Lyor Cohen, Ruza Blue and Sal

Abbetiello, among others, were heavily involved in bringing local, national and then global attention to hip-hop culture, allowing it to spread like a wildfire. Even noted culture vultures, such as Malcolm McLaren, were allowed entrance in before the novelty wore off and the next trend to capitalize on became their priority.

Hip-hop also incorporated its travels into the Downtown scene, the modern art world and punk influences with little to no problem. At no point was hip-hop/rap something you had to seek out, put in real effort to participate in or log serious man-hours for in order to gain acceptance. Hip-hop's "exclusive feel" back then was never a deterrent to anyone who wanted to be a part of it.

Though no fault of his own, Yoh didn't experience the stretches between 1981-84, 1986-89 or 1990-92, where rap—and by extension hip-hop culture—made inroads and breakthroughs to the mainstream. There was a time when, in order to be a rap fan, you were also by extension a supporter, participant or contributor to hip-hop culture as a whole. With the passage of time, rap became removed from the wider culture that birthed it, which has removed the need for participants and fans alike to learn its history or study it, unlike other art forms or disciplines where such an education would be required.

The staple breakbeats and records emcees and b-boys employed were from every musical genre imaginable. The artistic influences and references found in aerosol art on trains spanned from classic comic strips, cartoons and comic books to contemporary art found in galleries. B-boys drew inspiration and incorporated moves from kung-fu films, the salsa and merengue they danced to at home, as well as old film footage of tap dancers or whatever dance moves they saw in film or television.

The point is that hip-hop's inclusivity was always one of its strengths. However, those within hip-hop had to learn and study their craft and respect the culture as they were the ones contributing to it. There was a built-in apprenticeship program with checks and balances installed in every single cultural discipline. With those who solely look to profit from the genre, that's never been a concern.

"I only know hip-hop as a massive entity. An inclusive, embracive culture of many doors for easy entry. Before my time there were rules to participation that have vanished—now almost anyone with a functioning microphone can place their art underneath her umbrella," Yoh wrote. This is part of the problem with rap now. Whereas before there were barriers to entry for an artist, a process he or she had to follow just to become nice enough to be considered ready to enter a studio and record a song, in the era of home studios, email and Pro Tools, anything goes. With the passage of time, coupled with advances in both production and communications technologies, this has only gotten worse.

Once an artist could record his or her own music on a laptop and upload it to their SoundClick page and then sell it on their MySpace's SnoCap store, there was no chance rap's Pandora's Box would ever be closed. Based on the previous continuum, between 1979 and 1997, we should've had at least two more golden eras in rap, but there hasn't been one since thanks to major record labels scaling back A&R departments, outsourcing artist development and furthering the mainstream-underground industry divide.

Hip-hop has always been inclusive. If you spoke another language? Incorporate that into your music. If you came from a unique background? Rap about it or reference it in your art/music/production. Play an instrument? Do it. Can you sing? Find a way to work that into your output, too. Hip-hop, much like Jeet Kune Do, stresses expressing yourself honestly through your art and being original so that you could gain acceptance on your own terms rather than by copying others. However, rap was also about influence, inspiration and competition that led to innovation, style evolutions and the overall growth of the genre.

What Yoh recognizes as the "hip-hop" he loves and grew

up with is to older cats like myself a watered down corporate byproduct far removed from the hip-hop we grew up listening to. The hip-hop WE grew up with was only played at night, hated by our elders, located all the way at the back of the record store and didn't even have serious publications dedicated to it until well over a decade into its existence.

If participants were required to study the genre and the culture that birthed it before they could participate in it, the thinking is they'd realize they were part of a proud tradition that deserves to be respected, thus valuing the art form and elevating their voices even more.

When something is acquired for free, it cannot be fully appreciated and will almost always be taken for granted. For hip-hop, that's a recipe for disaster.

Inside 6ix9ine's Outrageous Sentencing Hearing

by Rich Juzwiak

6ix9ine, also known also as Tekashi 6ix9ine and by his government name, Daniel Hernandez, remains a free man by the skin of his rainbow-colored fronts. At Friday's sentencing for his 2015 conviction of use of a child in a sexual performance, Hon. Judge Felicia Mennin conceded that while he had "technically" violated the terms of his plea agreement, she nonetheless would not impose the prison sentence of one to three years, as was recommended by the Manhattan District Attorney's office.

Instead, Judge Mennin sentenced the gravel-voiced rapper to three years probation (technically four, though he's already been credited with one year served of interim probation) and 1,000 additional hours of community service (he already completed 300 as part of his plea agreement). He was ordered to refrain from gang activity and claiming affiliation publicly—he's previously indicated that he's affiliated with the Bloods, though in court today, his blustering attorney Lance Lazzaro rebuked that idea. Mennin also ordered Hernandez to maintain the social media restrictions of his original plea, which bar him from posting sexually explicit or violent images featuring women and/or children, and to "lead a law-abiding life" during his probation. Further, she ruled him eligible for Youthful Offender adjudication, so he will not have to register as a sex offender despite his guilty plea. (The crime occurred when Hernandez was 18.)

Assistant District Attorney Sara Weiss argued to the court that in being rearrested twice between the time of his plea and his sentencing, Hernandez had violated the terms of his agreement. Lazzaro argued, though, that because the agreement had set sentencing at October 20, 2017, his recent arrests were not relevant to the case at hand. Both of those arrests occurred in 2018; one in January for allegedly assaulting a 16-year-old boy in a Texas mall, and one in May for allegedly driving without a license. After the former arrest, he allegedly grabbed an officer by the hand while his handcuffs were being taken off in a Brooklyn police station and was charged for assault.

Lazzaro additionally argued that because the date had never been formally moved on record, despite the case's several adjournments (mostly at the defense's request because 6ix9ine had difficulty meeting the requirement of obtaining his GED)[40], his client had abided by the terms of his agreement. Though Judge Mennin agreed with the prosecution's argument on this matter, she nonetheless did not feel bound by the plea agreement because she did not preside over its ruling—that was Hon. Michael R. Sonberg—and did not think imprisoning 6ix9ine would be "just."

For about an hour, Weiss reiterated the contents of the letter[41] she had sent Judge Mennin in August arguing that 6ix9ine deserved jail time, focusing on 6ix9ine's 2018 arrests, his social media beef with other rappers, and his supposed gang affiliation. At one point, she attempted to show part of a video for 6ix9ine's "Blood Walk," but abandoned it when she wasn't able to bring up the footage on the screen that displayed the People's evidence. With a wince, the judge stated that she'd already watched it.

One new detail emerged, though, regarding the crime to which 6ix9ine pleaded guilty in 2015. In the initial complaint, the most sexually explicit video featuring the 13-year-old girl, which 6ix9ine appeared in and uploaded to his social media, was described as such: "...The child engages in oral sexual intercourse with the separately charged defendant Taquan Anderson, while the defendant, Daniel Hernandez, stands behind the child making a thrusting motion with his pelvis and smacking her on the buttocks. The child is nude in the video."

But in fact, it was even worse than that. In the only time during the sentencing hearing that the child victim was acknowledged explicitly, Weiss told the court about a video in which 6ix9ine is seen fondling the breasts and smacking the butt of a 13-year-old who was being penetrated by two adult males at the same time—orally and vaginally. Weiss quoted 6ix9ine as saying in the video, "This is what we do, this is how we rock." In response to a query about the discrepancy between the description of the video in the complaint and the one in court, a spokesperson at the Manhattan District Attorney's office said in an email, "There are uncharged individuals in connection with this incident."

While Weiss dissected 6ix9ine's social-media image, which has included the brandishing of guns and gleeful response to a shooting[42] allegedly involving a member of his crew at the Barclay's Center, 6ix9ine's combative lawyer Lazzaro portrayed 6ix9ine's online life as "all image."

His statement, as well as that of 6ix9ine that followed, and that of a preacher who has supposedly taken 6ix9ine under his wing, Bishop Lamor M. Whitehead, focused on a theme: 6ix9ine is a fantasy, Daniel Hernandez is the reality. Lazzaro spoke at length of the supposed philanthropy that Hernandez performs, when he does things like handing out wads of cash to school kids and poor people in the Dominican Republic. Many of these examples have been documented on 6ix9ine's Instagram in the past year, during which several hearings in this case occurred and several more were adjourned. Judge Mennin, in fact, highlighted 6ix9ine's "number of acts of unsolicited generosity in service of members of his community" during the sentencing.

Lazzaro made some curious claims, like 6ix9ine is "probably the most-viewed person in the world on Instagram." (He has 14.6 million followers, which is a lot, but not the most.) He described 6ix9ine's Top 5 duet with Nicki Minaj, "FEFE," as "just very, very nice." He referred to 6ix9ine throughout his statement as "Danny."

"I am Daniel Hernandez, to the court I am Tekashi 6ix9ine," said 6ix9ine when it was his turn to talk. He spoke mostly in a hushed, halting manner. "It's become to the point that the bad things are being looked at and the good things are being overlooked." He seemed oblivious to the fact that his government name has never been invoked in public more frequently than in connection to this case, in whose documents it is printed throughout. He said that he wanted to use his platform "to help kids like me," who grew up in poverty. He reiterated his extensively documented good deeds that his lawyer had just enumerated. "This stuff will never be as big because this stuff doesn't make headlines," he groused, which is also incorrect; online hip-hop media breathlessly covers 6ix9ine's goodwill gestures.[43]

While arguing his own goodness, 6ix9ine highlighted his recent Make a Wish Foundation-assisted visit with a six-year-old battling cancer.

"If I was such a bad person, if I was such a monster that the people want me to be, why in the right world would a six-year-old with brain cancer... Terminal 4, his whole right side of his body was paralyzed, why would his last wish be to see me?" he said. (Just a guess here, but maybe because he's six and hasn't read up on what "use of a child in a sexual performance" entails?)

The children, 6ix9ine argued, were what should keep him out of prison. "I have millions, I'm not talking about one million, I have millions of kids, youth ages 11, 12, 13, 8, 4, 2, 1 around the world that look at me, Daniel Hernandez as a role model. I have changed their lives," he said.

"I have millions of kids that look up to me and the last place I want to be is incarcerated," he said a bit later. "They don't deserve it."

Bishop Whitehead reiterated that 6ix9ine's online image is "smoke and mirrors." In a tone-deaf turn of phrase that perhaps speaks to how little regard the proceedings had for the 7th grader featured in the pornographic videos 6ix9ine posted online in 2015, Whitehead said of 6ix9ine: "This kid is not a bad kid...He can touch people that we can't touch."

Whitehead, who is black, cited his own hardships with racism, explaining that, "This coat that I wear and this collar, it costs blood sweat and tears and I'm not going to give it up for smoke and mirrors, or just because somebody's a good rapper." Whitehead was previously accused[44] of inventing claims that he was collaborating with the Brooklyn District Attorney's Office, the NYPD, and the Brooklyn Chamber of Commerce on various initiatives. He spent five years in Sing Sing on multiple counts of identity fraud and grand larceny and was released from prison in 2013. He told Judge Mennin he would oversee 6ix9ine's progress and she requested status updates from him.

When sentencing, Mennin seemed to side with the defense in that the "overblown, exaggerated" public persona of 6ix9ine did not reflect the true humanity of Daniel Hernandez. When she said, "You can't punish a person for how they choose to market themselves," I was reminded of 6ix9ine's initial statement to police regarding the videos he appeared in and posted of a 13-year-old girl engaged in sex acts: "I was doing it for my image." That he was subsequently convicted and sentenced for participating in these videos for his image suggests that in fact, you can punish a person for how they choose to market themselves.

The hearing was over almost two hours after it started. The crowd in the courtroom was largely stacked with friends and family of 6ix9ine—his mother, the mother of his nearly three-year-old child, and his brother, were all there according to his lawyer. When Judge Mennin concluded her sentencing and the hearing was over, applause ripped through the air. 6ix9ine was free and that's what mattered most.

How Do We Stop Black Grief From Becoming A Commodity?

by Sharine Taylor

When Pusha T dropped his vicious Drake diss track "The Story of Adion", amidst the ego-driven bravado of their exchange, the public airing of dirty laundry and line-crossing bars, what caught everyone's attention was the featured image of the song's subject. Taken in 2007, the image depicted the Toronto rapper in Jim Crow-era Blackface. While Drake has since addressed (and not apologized for) the image, mentioning that he intended to highlight prevalence of Black actors being stereotyped and type casted,[45] at its core the image brought a loaded reference of a traumatic cultural period to an audience who might not fully grasp its complexity. In the context of battle rap, sure, the image was a sucker punch to the gut, but its usage also begs the question, who exactly did the image intend to shock.

PhD student and cultural commentator, Huda Hassan, writes,[46] "The threat to black existence and black life has never ended, thus black mourning hasn't ended; and so long as the conditions remain that ensure black people will die for or because of their blackness, so too will black suffering." This is Black grief and in more and more instances, our grief has been upended into commodifiable content. As an outpour of creations emerge—documentaries, music videos, songs, tweets— from both Black and non-Black content creators, I've always been interested in knowing not only who the intended audience is, but who is actually consuming this work. I've wondered why the pain inflicted on our global community is often propelled into the public forum, becoming a free-for-all catalyst for creativity.

What are we to do with Black grief? It is the headlines that populate our feeds, it is the viral videos that display our injustices, it is the retweets and shares and likes and threads and all the posts that explain and re-explain our humanity. The answer is so painfully obvious: we're to heal from it. We are to unplug, talk to our loved ones, get therapy or find alternative means of professional help, but so much happens in a day and in a week, and healing seems to exist in a fleeting distant.

A few weeks ago hip hop became the centre of attention when Kanye West made disparaging comments in the form of tweets about "free thinking" in addition to publicly aligning himself with folks who have said notoriously awful things about Black people, our history and how to cope from intergenerational trauma. What's worse is while the public wrestled with their feelings of confusion and hurt from his actions, other Black artists—many of whom are men—rallied behind him to show their support. Within days, an almost[47] two hour interview between West and Breakfast Club host, Charlamagne Tha God was produced and made available to watch where the artist was seen explaining himself (or attempting to) and even had his statements challenged by Charlamagne.

I had to sit with myself for a minute and ask, "Who were those tweets made for? What conversations were supposed to ensue thereafter?" By way of his tweets, his insistence on wearing a "Make America Great Again" hat and subsequent commentary, under the guise of love, West made himself an alt-right darling and was dubbed "brilliant" and "genius." Yes, the artist has every right to parallel his own beliefs with a political ideology that reflects his school of thought (whatever that is), but I can't help but think that how he's arrived at his conclusions, and very publicly so, is at the expense of Black grief.

In all of what he's done where—claiming slavery was a choice (and later being confronted by TMZ's Van Lathan),[48] calling Donald Trump his "brother" (I do not know any, single person who

63

would even have the desire to openly admitting being brotherly with someone as morally bankrupt as Trump) and other ways he's given voices of the alt-right a platform—he has (significantly) contributed to using Black greif, and the people whose thoughts threaten our lives and livelihoods, for his own personal gain driven by his obsession with attention and celebrity. He even unapologetically addresses the incident on "Wouldn't Leave" and "Ghost Town", two tracks off his newly released album, Ye, that implies that he could have said much worse.

Our intra-community ills are made points of conversation in the public forum and no one or institution is being accountable for the ills imposed on our community.

Unfortunately, he's not the only one. There have been many people who have seen the publicity that can be garnered when there's an international digital outcry against injustices made on our community. This April, director Lauren Brownson premiered her made-for-Netflix documentary, *The Rachel Divide*. The doc was a disturbing look into how Dolezal, a white woman who feigned and benefitted from Blackness and Black woman identity, navigated her life post-KXLY expose. To be frank, the documentary was both poorly executed and spent more time trying to humanize someone who is obviously (and incorrectly) trying to recover from a traumatic childhood and less time critiquing—save for the last few movements of the film—how her act co-opts and trivializes Blackness and specifically Black womanhood.

Again, who was this documentary made for and why does it have to be predicated on the global Black community? It certainly wasn't made for Black folks who'd already decided that her narrative was one that need not receive any further attention. The probability of the doc being made to elicit empathy for Dolezal is a likely, albeit unwarranted, reason, but from what demographic?

Days after West's antics became the subject of conversation, the video for Childish Gambino's new single, "This is America" premiered. The video was intentionally chaotic featuring Black children dancing in the foreground of police chases, shootings and massacres of Black folks that immediately made headlines. It drew on several references including the Jim Crow caricature, as Donald Glover likened his animated facial features and expressions while delivering bars. An immediate observation revealed that the video seemingly suggested that Black folks are the architects of their own demise, blinded by the latest viral dance moves despite the fact that all of the violent acts represented were reflective of white individuals motivated by white supremacy ideology. In "This is America," their identities were nowhere to be found.

The video was polarizing. People rightfully critiqued it[49] while others praised it for its aptness. Surprisingly, the visual got its biggest approval from a largely white audience. A few things factor into this: until recently, his most loyal fans were largely white college kids[50]. While his self-directed and produced, hella Black, F/X television series, *Atlanta*, attracted a significantly larger black audience, it doesn't excuse his spotty articulation of race in the past. The artist has had problems with his fetishization of Asian women, his representation[51] of Black women in his creations, making a career off being the token Black guy and the strange part of a 2012 stand up show where he shared he, "came harder than [he'd] ever come...before" when an Armenian woman told him to, "Fuck me harder with that N-word dick." Despite Atlanta becoming a runaway hit, it also raised questions by critics who questioned was an artist like Glover justified for producing it.

Perhaps there's no resolve, yet. Perhaps we take situations as they come and deal with it the best way we know how: we create or find digital communities, we make light of our grievances and connect with other members of the Black diaspora[52] through

65

memes or hashtags like #IfSlaveryWasAChoice (a response to West's comments on TMZ that slavery was a choice), we create conversations, we take a digital hiatus,[53] we share thoughts and ideas. But it seems like the conversations that are being had often include the wrong people.

How do we make the concerns and experiences of our communities seen and heard without inflicting further violence on ourselves and our collective psyche?

Our intra-community ills are made points of conversation in the public forum and no one or institution is being accountable for the ills imposed on our community. And what about when our grief is leveraged by other Black people? In the midst of everything that was happening with West and Glover, Lakeith Stanfield, actor and Atlanta co-star, stated in a now-deleted tweet that if you wanted to "test your parents(sic) ignorance level" to "bring home a person of a different ethnic background. Specifically a Black woman". Hypothetical or not, people shouldn't be subjected to be experiments, especially given the current social climate regarding race relations and given the mysogenoir that permeates it.

Before entering a public spat with Drake, Pusha T's album artwork for his album *Daytona* uses a $85,000 licensed photo (paid for by Kanye West) of drug paraphernalia in a washroom inside late singer, Whitney Houston's, Atlanta home in 2006. Given the controversy surrounding Houston's death, the multiple film productions that have already and have been reported to take place about her life, as well as new information that has since been made public knowledge by way of the 2017 documentary on the artist, *Can I Be Me?*, I ask again: what are we to do with Black grief and who is this art being made for?

Art should make us uncomfortable. It should make us think critically and give its artists the opportunity to share their experiences on how we live, but where do we draw the line? A thread began to circulate as West continued to post more content onto Twitter that posited that his latest string of actions being performance art. West has been lauded as a creative genius and innovator and it's not like he's ever shied away from making provocative, controversial statements in the past, but under the guise of "art," it seems like it functions as a means to evade accountability and wreak havoc as one pleases, despite the casualties.

Does art need to have casualties for it to attain one of its many transformative possibilities? How do we make the concerns and experiences of our communities seen and heard without inflicting further violence on ourselves and our collective psyche? All of these factors are worth interrogating, especially when they spread and manifest within a digital landscape where clicks are currency and, these days, the only thing that matters.

It's not a foreign concept that our grief be turned into art that transcends boundaries, space and time. The cultural production of Black people is often borne from a state of disenfranchisement and making art despite our conditions, but the difference between then and now is that what was once experienced and enjoyed within our insular community is now being thrusted into the public domain, packaged, marketed and commodified for global consumption. What are we to do with Black grief? Who knows. We can heal from it, we can learn from it but we shouldn't commodify it.

Did Kanye West's "Five-For-Five" Album Release Strategy Hinder Teyana Taylor's *K.T.S.E.*?

by Amir Said

Very few people can be the leader of the creative production behind the music on a given album and the marketing force behind said album at the same time. Normally, these roles are given to multiple people because it's best to split delegation of these duties. Which is what Kanye West should have done with Teyana Taylor's latest album *K.T.S.E.*

In this regard — i.e. another botched album roll out after an ill-fated decision to include Teyana Taylor's album in a forced, multi-album release campaign — Kanye West hindered *K.T.S.E*'s initial potential. While the G.O.O.D. Music album extravaganza may have secured the attention that Kanye wanted, the blind side of such a strategy is that it overlooks the fact that, even with featured production by the same super producer, each artist is unique and therefore not necessarily suitable for a one-size fit all album roll out.

Every artist's album needs its own distinct promotion and marketing campaign, its own breathing room for its initial bow onto the marketplace. A good marketing strategy is one that includes, among other things, the right timing and a singular approach. However, Teyana Taylor's album was not fitted with a singular approach; instead it was packaged as part of a summer-set of Kanye West-powered album releases. As such, the album was tethered to the success or failure and expectations of the group as a whole. In this case, *K.T.S.E.* deserved its own space.

One could make the argument that if *K.T.S.E.* was not tethered to this string of five albums in five weeks, even fewer people would have cared. But marketing aside, albums have to do their own talking. Less elbow room for *K.T.S.E.* meant that it was going to be received through the same prism of the "five for five" marketing scheme. You market projects this way when you want to showcase your label's new talent, not when you want to spotlight individual artists who already have brands and strong followings. You also mount this kind of campaign when there's a weak link that needs to be masked. *K.T.S.E.* was certainly not a weak link.

Further, I don't believe that fewer people would have cared if *K.T.S.E.* was detached from the "five for five" roll out. Teyana has her own thing. A reality show on Vh1 ("Teyana & Iman"), a visible NBA Husband (who by the way, is actually nice with the rhymes), and a great New York backstory. That's more than enough to drum up a distinctive marketing campaign, especially if you allow/trust the right people to help you.

Certainly, Kanye West's value add in terms of production and music direction greatly benefited *K.T.S.E.* But while Kanye West receives praise for his willingness (and humility) to work with others to produce the best possible records, might it be that he also deserves criticism for his unwillingness to give up the reigns to the marketing approach to five albums that he just oversaw? Depending on market trends and the temperature of a given climate, sometimes it's wise to move up the release dates for products, and sometimes it's prudent to push them back. This is especially true in today's world of music releases. That Kanye West, ever in love with the spotlight and any spectacle that can potentially show off his supposed genius, failed to recognize this basic point is terribly unfortunate for Teyana Taylor.

Even worse than tying Teyana Taylor's album to an ill-fated, forced multi-album marketing campaign; even worse than another botched roll-out is this: The decision to go ahead and release

69

Teyana Taylor's album one week after Beyoncé & Jay-Z shocked the world with their surprise (and widely lauded) album, and days after the murder of XXXTentacion. There just really wasn't enough oxygen left in the room by week's end. If there was ever a time for an album to be pushed back, even as little as one week, it was now.

It also seems like Teyana Taylor actually wanted her album pushed back at least a week. In a an interview on "Big Boy's Neighborhood" this past Tuesday, Taylor made a number of telling remarks:

- That she was "rushed"
- That "if it was the way that I wanted it to be, y'all probably wouldn't have gotten it until, like…"
- "…I'm willing to wait for whatever [it comes right]."
- "…we're fixing that" [as in things expected to be on the album were missing.]

Taylor also mentions that sample clearances issues were a part of the problem: "'Wait, does that mean they were able to get everything cleared?' It was really just an honest misunderstanding of me thinking maybe some shit happened overnight." But "samples not cleared" is the new "it's politics;" an easy way to excuse an incomplete product. And samples never get cleared "overnight". So for Taylor, putting part of the blame on sample clearance issues allows her to express her feelings about the rushed rollout of the album without actually throwing Kanye West (her label head and executive producer) under the bus.

To be certain, Teyana Taylor's album is a good album that will catapult her higher regardless. But when the product is a delight, as is the case with *K.T.S.E.*, you can afford to push it back a little to make sure that the climate is ripe for release, or at least more conducive to the best possible reception. So I can't help but wonder that if Kanye West didn't insist on being both the man behind the boards and the man behind the marketing would the initial rise of *K.T.S.E.* been higher?

When initially planned for 6/22, nobody knew that Beyoncé & Jay-Z were going to drop a joint album. And who could have predicted the murder of XXX. But a leader's job includes absorbing late-breaking news and developing stories, and offering up a wise response. Sometimes making the decision to simply stay the course, despite a dramatically different landscape, is the wrong course of action. I think that was the case here. Kanye has the power and the goodwill to make a such a delay. He's made delays before, and I mean the guy implied that slavery was a choice that enslaved Africans had made — and many people still waited for his new music with baited breath.

No matter how you look at it, though, the timing of the release of *K.T.S.E.* was going to be a lose-lose. But I arrive at this assessment from two angles. One, the "five for five" marketing scheme bet the house on the collective package and essentially ensured that the album would be rushed out. Two, the release date (albeit pre-planned) was sandwiched in between two totally unpredictable conversation-shifting events and the very predictable "new Drake album" factor.

If someone else was steering the G.O.O.D. music marketing ship, would they have recognized this and advised that *K.T.S.E.* be pushed back? Maybe. But for all intents and purposes, Kanye West is the face of and brains behind G.O.O.D. Music. Which means he's likely afforded the healthy number of yes-men that you would expect for someone in his position. So even if Kanye did receive such a warning (and perhaps someone did speak up), would he have listened? Would he have scrapped the last piece of his heavily marketed "five for five" release scheme just to preserve the best possible setting for one of his artist's albums? I don't think so. Let's be clear here, to Kanye the G.O.O.D. music label was higher up on the marquee than any of the individual acts. It seems to me that Kanye was more concerned with delivering the package deal that he promised and promoted, rather than assuring a better lift off for Teyana Taylor's *K.T.S.E.*

Lastly, we can't overlook that the planning and execution of this "five for five" marketing scheme was one aspect of the overall problem. The record was not finished. And since it wasn't done anyway, the smart thing would have been to take the loss there and postpone the release of *K.T.S.E.* Part of the commentary that underscores what I write is this op-ed is that, given the fluidity of how albums can be released and pushed out to streaming companies, and given the reality of listener fatigue vs. new releases, I'm not convinced that going ahead with the release date as planned was the better loss to take. And it's pretty clear that at least one person at G.O.O.D. Music agrees.

The Greatest Year in Hip-Hop History
by Christopher Pierznik

Of all the conversations and debates surrounding the best of the best in hip-hop—MC's, groups, producers, labels—perhaps the most difficult to ascertain is what is the greatest year in hip-hop history.

This is not a new question, of course, but I thought I'd bring a new angle to it by determining the best through a 16-slot bracket tournament.

Before we get to the matchups, a few notes on the seedings and inclusion of years:

The impact of the year goes beyond the music released. It also includes cultural impact as well and historical importance. Important strides like mainstream media acknowledgment, television presence, and inclusion in awards shows matter, but the music carries the most weight by far. The general consensus is that hip-hop started in 1973, but no one owns an album from that year, so it was not included.

Nothing is a classic overnight and perspective needs time. That's why an athlete must be retired for five years before being included on a Hall of Fame ballot. The same is true here but because of the ever changing nature of the genre, I expanded it to a full decade so that nothing after 2008 is eligible.

The tournament is slotted the same way as NCAA March Madness, with the highest seeds facing off against the lowest seeds in the first round, then the winners moving on to the next round. Teams are not re-seeded in each round, so a George Mason-esque Cinderella run is possible.

The impact of the year goes beyond the music released. It also includes cultural impact as well and historical importance. Here are the first round matchups:

(1) 1993 vs. (16) 1984

(2) 1988 vs. (15) 1985

(3) 1994 vs. (14) 2001

(4) 1996 vs. (13) 1992

(5) 2000 vs. (12) 1986

(6) 2003 vs. (11) 1999

(7) 1995 vs. (10) 1987

(8) 1998 vs. (9) 1997

Last Four Out: 1989, 1991, 2004, 1990

To be fair, this should probably have been a 24-slot tournament, but at what point does it end? An important year was bound to be snubbed and 1989 should have probably made the cut. Maybe it'll be just the motivation needed to win the NIT.

On to the games...

Sweet 16 [First Round]

Matchup

(1) **1993** vs. (16) **1984**

Analysis

1984 is important to the growth of the culture. It was the year of the first hip-hop tour, the "Fresh Fest," it introduced the concept of diss records with UTFO's "Roxanne Roxanne" and Roxanne Shanté's reply "Roxanne's Revenge," and, most importantly, it was the year Russell Simmons and Rick Rubin formed the greatest label in hip-hop history, Def Jam Records. However, '84 is like the mid-major that had a great run in the conference tourney and is just happy to be in the Big Dance. 1993 is a team from a major conference that is loaded with future pros and nearly went undefeated. '93 is the team that can attack from any angle. East Coast hardcore: *Enter the Wu-Tang (36 Chambers)*, *Enta Da Stage*, *Bacdafucup*. West Coast hardcore: *Doggystyle*, *It's On* (Dr. Dre) *187um Killa*, *Strictly 4 My N.I.*.*.A.Z.* Southern hardcore: *Till Death Do Us Part*. Smooth: *Midnight Marauders*, *Reachin' (A New Refutation of Time and Space)*, *Buhloone Mindstate*. High-energy from the East: *Here Come the Lords* and the West: *93 'til Infinity*. Even the soundtracks were dope: *Judgment Night*, *Menace II Society*. And we haven't even mentioned *Black Sunday*, *Return of the Boom Bap*, *21 & Over*, *Slaughtahouse*, or the monster *19 Naughty III*.

Result

The founding of Def Jam does all it can to keep '84 in the game, but there's a reason '93 is the number one overall seed. It's a rout by halftime and bench players like Del the Funkee Homosapien even get some playing time.

Final score: **1993:** 111 – **1984:** 67

Matchup

(2) **1988** vs. (15) **1985**

Analysis

The second overall seed, 1988 brought diversity to the genre through a combination of "gangsta rap," conscious rhymes, sociopolitical themes, complex lyricism and empowered females. It is a lethal combination of groups releasing groundbreaking albums—N.W.A's *Straight Outta Compton*, Public Enemy's *It Takes a Nation of Millions to Hold Us Back*, Jungle Brothers's *Straight Out the Jungle*, EPMD's *Strictly Business*, Boogie Down Productions's *By Any Means Necessary*, Eric B. & Rakim's *Follow the Leader*, Run-DMC's *Tougher Than Leather*—and classic LPs from solo artists—Slick Rick's *The Great Adventures of Slick Rick*, Big Daddy Kane's *Long Live the Kane*, Eazy-E's *Eazy Duz It*, Ice-T's *Power*, MC Lyte's *Lyte as a Rock*. Even more importantly, the music continued to make inroads within pop culture, most notably with the birth of Yo! MTV Raps. Conversely, 1985 is like the inexperienced version of the '88 team with plenty of raw talent and promise, but still a few years away. The bankruptcy of Sugarhill Records, the first viable hip-hop record label, hurt the team, but the music was entering a new age with LL Cool J's debut *Radio*, Too $hort's sophomore album *Players*, and Run-DMC's record-breaking second album *King of Rock*.

Result

Freshman phenom LL and future Hall of Famers Run-DMC keep it respectable, but '88 is an all-time great team with a deep bench and their ferocious full court press is too much for the young team to handle.

Final score: **1988:** 93 – **1985:** 74

Matchup

(3) **1994** vs. (14) **2001**

Analysis

At first, it appears that the (3) vs. (14) matchup is one that could result in an upset. 2001's low seed is due to its lack of depth, but it still boasts Jay-Z's *The Blueprint,* Nas's *Stillmatic* and the battle in which the two engaged at the end of the year. D12's *Devil's Night,* Cormega's underground gem *The Realness,* and two soundtracks—*The Wash* and *Training Day*—help, and while big names like Ludacris (*Word of Mouf*), Ja Rule (*Pain is Love*), and even Wu-Tang Clan (*Iron Flag*) didn't supply their best projects, they still have memorable moments. On the other side, 1994, stacked with young talent from all over the map, was the year that hip-hop was reborn. There were groundbreaking albums from New York—Nas's *Illmatic,* The Notorious B.I.G.'s *Ready to Die,* Method Man's *Tical,* and Jeru the Damaja's *The Sun Rises in the East,* O.C.'s *Word...Life*—California—Warren G's *Regulate...G Funk Era,* 2Pac's group *Thug Life Volume 1*—Chicago—Common Sense's *Resurrection*—and Atlanta—Outkast's *Southernplay-alisticadillacmuzik*—as well as strong sophomore efforts from Redman (*Dare Iz a Darkside*) and Pete Rock & CL Smooth (*The*

Main Ingredient)—and anchored by veterans Beastie Boys (*Ill Communication*) and Gang Starr (*Hard to Earn*). With the decline of grunge rock, '94 was also the year that hip-hop emerged as the genre of the future, making hip-hop artists platinum-selling superstars.

Result

While Jay-Z was making some of the best music of his life and Nas was returning to his roots in '01, they are no match for a squad made up of the raw talent of B.I.G., Common, André 3000, Redman, and a younger Nas. 1994 runs the 2001 veterans off the floor in a game that wasn't as close as the final score makes it appear.

Final score: **1994: 99 – 2001: 87**

Matchup

(4) **1996** vs. (13) **1992**

Analysis

All Eyez on Me. It Was Written. The Score. Reasonable Doubt. ATLiens. Ill Na Na. Hard Core. Hell on Earth. Muddy Waters. Da Storm. Illadelph Halflife. The Coming. Ironman. Nocturnal. Endtroducing. Legal Drug Money. Through the first half of the year, 1996 was undefeated and appeared to be a lock to become the number one overall seed. Then, one night in September, it all crumbled. 2Pac's death changed everything overnight and, though not related, lackluster releases by Snoop Doggy Dogg (*Tha Doggfather*), Dr. Dre (*Dr. Dre Presents... The Aftermath*), and

Chuck D (*Autobiography of Mistachuck*) saw '96 limping into the New Year. Still, the year saw classic debuts from Jay-Z, Busta Rhymes, Foxy Brown, Ghostface Killah, and Lil' Kim, spectacular follow ups by Mobb Deep, The Roots, Redman, and blockbuster releases by Fugees, Nas and 'Pac himself (twice). While it faded towards the end, '96 still has a nearly impeccable résumé.

Meanwhile, 1992 was a transitional year between two classic mini-eras. Dr. Dre's The Chronic changed the music and Pete Rock & CL Smooth's *Mecca & the Soul Brother* was a classic, but they were alone. Redman (*Whut? Thee Album*), UGK (*Too Hard to Swallow*), and Common Sense (*Can I Borrow a Dollar?*) unveiled their promising, yet uneven, debuts, while '80s legends Eric B. & Rakim (*Don't Sweat the Technique*) and EPMD (*Business Never Personal*), as well as Ice Cube (*The Predator*) dropped albums that were strong, but a notch below their previous works. It was also the year that hip-hop in various forms became ubiquitous on radio, so it was the first time that sounds like G-Funk and hardcore hip-hop were played alongside more commercial acts like Arrested Development and Kris Kross.

Result

While Dre and Pete Rock, along with Diamond D off the bench, do their best to keep it close, 1992's lack of direction is magnified by a roster that is a mixture of too old and too young, especially when compared to the way 1996's talent coalesced at the perfect time, even in spite of 2Pac's departure.

Final score: **1996:** 84 – **1992:** 70
Matchup

(5) **2000** vs. (12) **1986**

Analysis

A clash of two completely contrasting styles, 1986 is a traditional, New York-centric squad, while 2000 incorporates the South and the Midwest into their game plan. Neither team has much depth, but '00 is a higher seed thanks largely to a career year by Eminem (*The Marshall Mathers LP*), an almost perfect output by Ghostface Killah (*Supreme Clientele*), and strong showings by Outkast (*Stankonia*), Slum Village (*Fantastic, Vol. 2*), Wu-Tang Clan (*The W*), Jay-Z (*The Dynasty: Roc La Familia*), as well as the innovative stylings of Nelly (*Country Grammar*). On the other side, Run-DMC and Aerosmith form a combination never seen before ("Walk This Way" off Raising Hell) the Beastie Boys (*Licensed to Ill*) bring both boundless energy and funky originality, and Schoolly D (*Schoolly D*) influenced an entire generation of gangster rap, but the rest of the year is outdated and forgettable, and though the future is bright with superstar recruit Rakim, it would be another year until he would unleash an album on the world.

Result

Run-DMC is at the top of its game, giving '86 a chance to win, but '00's versatility proves to be too much.

Final score: **2000: 69 – 1986: 65**

Matchup

(6) **2003** vs. (11) **1999**

Analysis

An argument could be made that 2003 is the most intriguing year in hip-hop history, at least in terms of albums released. The game's biggest name, Jay-Z, was (supposedly) retiring, 50 Cent was the most anticipated new artist since Snoop, and Outkast crafted a genre-bending double album that won a Grammy for Album of the Year. In addition to *The Black Album*, *Get Rich or Die Tryin'*, and *Speakerboxxx/The Love Below*, there were gems courtesy of newer artists like T.I., Freeway and Obie Trice, veterans such as Gang Starr, and less commercial MCs including Brother Ali, Immortal Technique, Jaylib, and Little Brother. The most recent year in the tournament, 2003 was the final year of hip-hop the way it had been. Beginning in 2004, those that had dominated in recent years—Jay-Z, Eminem, Dr. Dre—took a step back and new artists—Kanye West, Lil' Wayne—and different regions—Houston, Memphis—became the focal point.

In contrast, 1999 was only four years earlier but in many ways feels as if it's a different era. It was the year Dr. Dre made his triumphant return (*2001*), Eminem introduced himself (*The Slim Shady LP*), The Roots gained massive exposure (*Things Fall Apart*), Mos Def made a classic (*Black on Both Sides*), Nas confronted hatred (*I Am...*), Rawkus became a household name (*Soundbombing II*), and Jay-Z (*Vol. 3...Life and Times of S. Carter*) continued his meteoric rise. It was also the year of Prince Paul's brilliant concept album (*A Prince Among Thieves*), Method Man & Redman's stellar collaboration (*Blackout!*), Mobb Deep's strong return (*Murda Muzik*), Kurupt's ode to G-Funk (*Tha Streetz iz a Mutha*), as well as the only worthwhile posthumous project by

81

The Notorious B.I.G. (*Born Again*). More importantly, 1999 was also the year that hip-hop was confronted with the future. Though they would do battle in two years, Nas and Jay-Z shared a common enemy in '99: bootleggers. For Jay, it was a friend and business partner who leaked his album to the street vendors and was stabbed as a result (Jay pleaded guilty and received three years probation). Nas, on the other hand, became the first major hip-hop artist to become a victim of next generation of bootlegging in the form of mp3 file sharing. While this is now expected and it's almost shocking when an album doesn't leak, this was viewed as a crisis at the time, so much so that Nas decided to scrap the original project (a double album entitled *I Am… The Autobiography*), record several new songs and release one single album. While *I Am…* was good (and the original is great), the long lasting impact is that this was the first salvo in the music industry's war on piracy, a war that it kept losing until it completely changed its way of doing business. Much of it began in 1999.

Result

In the first upset of the tournament, 1999 knocks off 2003 in convincing fashion. The stars carried each team, with '03 Jay-Z outplaying his younger self, Dr. Dre overpowering Outkast, and 50 Cent and Eminem playing to a near draw, but it was '99's bench play, as well as its varied styles and its impact on the music that proved to be the difference.

Final score: **1999: 83 – 2003: 73**

Matchup

(7) **1995** vs. (10) **1987**

Analysis

1987 was the year that hip-hop started to mature. Up to that point, lyrics had been secondary as DJ's were often the focal point while MC's yelled basic, monosyllabic rhymes that were often call-and-response interactions with the crowd. Then, a new class of freshmen walked on campus and changed everything. Ice-T brought the lavish life of a California gangster (*Rhyme Pays*), Chuck D and his sidekick Flavor Flav brought an intriguing mixture of fiery sociopolitical rhymes and goofy fun (*Yo! Bum Rush the Show*), KRS-One brought stories from the streets of the Bronx (*Criminal Minded*), and Rakim brought a sophistication to lyrics that had never been seen or even imagined before (*Paid in Full*). They, along with DJ Jazzy Jeff & The Fresh Prince (*Rock the House*), an evolving LL Cool J (*Bigger & Deffer*), and even an unpolished N.W.A (*N.W.A and the Posse*), ushered in a new era of the music almost immediately, creating a clear distinction between what came before and what came after. Hip-Hop may have matured in '87, but it exploded in the 1990's and 1995 was not only the midpoint of the decade, it was also the year in which the culture started down a path that would end in violence and confusion. While there had been rumblings about discord between artists from the two coasts, it was on full display at The 1995 Source Awards in New York. Dr. Dre and Snoop were booed upon accepting an award, Puff Daddy announced "I live in the East and I'm gonna die in the East," and Suge Knight took a not-so-veiled shot at Puff when appealing to young artists. It began a two year standoff that would lead to the deaths of two of the culture's biggest stars. Outside of the drama, though, there was some great music from all

83

over the map. From California came 2Pac's *Me Against the World*, Tha Dogg Pound's *Dogg Food*, Tha Pharcyde's *Labcabincalifornia*, Tha Alkaholiks' *Coast II Coast* and Cypress Hill's *III: Temples of Boom*. Atlanta, Philly, and Cleveland received some long overdue shine thanks respectively to Goodie Mob's *Soul Food*, The Roots' *Do You Want More?!!!??!*, and Bone Thugs-n-Harmony's *E. 1999 Eternal*. And a slew of New York artists released quality material. Three Wu-Tang members released classics—Raekwon's *Only Built 4 Cuban Linx...*, Ol' Dirty Bastard's *Return to the 36 Chambers: The Dirty Version*, and GZA's *Liquid Swords*—Mobb Deep shook everyone with *The Infamous*, and The Notorious B.I.G. oversaw his protégés, Junior M.A.F.I.A., and their *Conspiracy*. AZ (*Doe or Die*), Smif-n-Wessun (*Dah Shinin'*), Big L (*Lifestylez ov da Poor & Dangerous*), Kool G Rap (*4, 5, 6*), and Showbiz & A.G. (*Goodfellas*) also kept speakers blasting.

Result

The game was tight throughout. Rakim was sensational, the best player on the floor, but 1995's collective talent, aggression, and assorted styles finally won out, carried down the stretch by The 1995 Source Awards, one of the most influential moments in hip-hop history.

Final score: **1995: 87 – 1987: 82**

Matchup

(8) **1998** vs. (9) **1997**

Analysis

It stands to reason that the two most evenly matched teams of the first round are the eighth and ninth seeds. These two years may have occurred consecutively and they may be matched almost equally, but that does not mean that they are the same. Not even close. The hip-hop landscape of early 1997 was vastly different than that of late 1998. The murder of The Notorious B.I.G. in March, merely six months after the killing of 2Pac, cast a pall over the entire culture, but the music endured. Bad Boy dominated the year with a trifecta of classics—B.I.G.'s *Life After Death*, Puff Daddy's *No Way Out*, and Mase's *Harlem World*. Wu-Tang also returned in full with their own double album, *Wu-Tang Forever*, that broke sales records. Jay-Z (*In My Lifetime, vol. 1*) and Nas (The Firm group album) released albums that had both strong and weak moments, but new artists like Capone-n-Noreaga (*The War Report*), Company Flow (*Funcrusher Plus*), and Missy Elliott (*Supa Dupa Fly*) introduced new styles, Will Smith returned to the mic (*Big Willie Style*), Master P broke through to the mainstream (*Ghetto D*), and the world saw its first of seemingly countless projects of old 2Pac songs (*R U Still Down? [Remember Me]*). The following year, there was a void within hip-hop. Two figures that had taken up so much space and attention were gone and there was plenty of room for others to take some of the spotlight. Much like 1987, 1998 was a year in which new and previously overlooked artists took the opportunity to shape and mold hip-hop in their own image. DMX took hip-hop by storm, releasing two number one albums (*It's Dark and Hell Is Hot* and *Flesh of My Flesh, Blood of My Blood*) in the same year and his peers, including

85

Big Punisher (*Capital Punishment*), Mos Def & Talib Kweli (*Black Star*), Noreaga (*N.O.R.E.*), and The LOX (*Money, Power & Respect*) were not far behind. It was also the year Jay-Z became a superstar (*Vol. 2…Hard Knock Life*), Snoop became a No Limit Soldier (*Da Game Is to Be Sold, Not to Be Told*), Outkast released another gem (*Aquemini*), and Lauryn Hill crafted a masterpiece (*The Miseducation of Lauryn Hill*).

Result

Undoubtedly the best game of the first round, it was full of momentum swings and lead changes as the teams went back-and-forth. '98 Jay-Z outplayed his '97 self, but the reverse was true of Master P, effectively canceling one another out. Ultimately, 1997 prevailed, thanks to Bad Boy and Wu-Tang, as well as the overall impact of B.I.G.'s murder.

Final score: **1997: 94 – 1998: 92**

Sweet 16 [First Round] Analysis

Not too many surprises as the top five seeds advance, but 1999's upset creates an interesting second round matchup against 1994. The heavy favorites have been 1993 and 1988 and nothing in the Sweet 16 did anything to change that.

Elite Eight [Second Round]

Matchup

(1) **1993** vs. (9) **1997**

Result

Even the emotional boost of losing their captain and a virtually unstoppable performance by Puff Daddy isn't enough for 1997. 1993 is better at every turn, with classics from both coasts and starmaking turns by numerous members.

Final score: **1993:** 104 – **1997:** 95

Matchup

(2) **1988** vs. (7) **1995**

Result

1995 is a year that is difficult to top, but 1988 managed to do so in convincing fashion, as the fab five of Chuck D, Ice Cube, KRS-One, Slick Rick, and Rakim frustrated the youngsters. Two interesting game notes: (1) 1995's aggression and frustration combined to set a record for technical fouls and (2) the game was delayed twice after players slipped on Eazy-E's jheri curl that had dripped onto the floor.

Final score: **1988:** 88 – **1995:** 73

Matchup

(3) **1994** vs. (11) **1999**

Result

1999 surprised many by their first round victory, but Cinderella's shoe suddenly became very tight when it came time to face off against 1994. '99's various styles were all helpless as Nas and B.I.G. played like vintage Jordan and Pippen, their combined production speaking for itself and their legacies hounding 1999 the whole time.

Final score: **1994:** 91 – **1999:** 70

Matchup

(4) **1996** vs. (5) **2000**

Result

2000 was never in contention. Eminem and Ghostface did all they could, but it wasn't nearly enough as 1996's distinct talent advantage was too much to overcome.

Final score: **1996:** 104 – **2000:** 87

Elite Eight [Second Round] Analysis

All chalk as the top four seeds march on to the Final Four.

Final Four

Matchup

(1) 1993 vs. **(4) 1996**

Result

Two teams loaded with stars and influence, they were virtually equal throughout. In the end, the combination of Wu-Tang, Snoop, and Tribe overcame 2Pac and Fugees.

Final score: **1993:** 94 – **1996:** 89

Matchup

(2) 1988 vs. **(3) 1994**

Result

A contest of two disparate styles, this was also a great matchup. Down the stretch, though, the combination of Chuck D and Ice Cube proved to be unstoppable.

Final score: **1988:** 82 – **1994:** 76

Final 4 Analysis

The two best years advance to meet for the title. As it should be.

Championship

Matchup

(1) **1993** vs. (2) **1988**

Result

An instant classic between the two golden ages of hip-hop, with each team matching the other. Every *Straight Outta Compton* or *The Great Adventures of Slick Rick* was met with an *Enter the Wu-Tang (36 Chambers)* and *Doggystyle*. The albums of 1988 have a bit more of a lasting impact, but there are more great albums in 1993, thus canceling each other out. In terms of just music, '93 had the advantage and thus appeared to be on its way to the crown, but the impact and influence beyond the music, such as the premier of Yo! MTV Raps and the emergence of other regions and styles, pushes 1988 over the top in overtime.

Final score: **1988:** 95 – **1993:** 93

After being awarded the trophy and cutting down the nets, the entire team, including Jerry Heller and Rick Rubin, all broke into the Ed Lover Dance to celebrate.

1988 IS THE GREATEST YEAR IN HIP-HOP HIS-TORY!

Notes & References

1 Mcbride, Ian, "Why Do The Juno Awards Hate Rap?," *Noisey*, https://noisey.vice.com/en_ca/article/64yk3w/why-do-the-juno-awards-hate-rap.

2 CBC, "Inside the Junos, episode 2: why Rascalz refused their 1998 award,'" *CBC*, https://www.cbc.ca/music/junos/news/inside-the-junos-episode-2-why-rascalz-refused-their-1998-award-1.4532216.

3 Patch, Nick, "Kardinal Offishall: Junos disrespected Drake," The Star (May 6, 2011) https://www.thestar.com/entertainment/2011/05/06/kardinal_offishall_junos_disrespected_drake.html

4 Watters, Haydn, "The Strumbellas, Leonard Cohen win big while Drake gets snubbed at Junos gala dinner," *CBC* (April 2, 2017) https://www.cbc.ca/news/entertainment/juno-awards-gala-dinner-1.4051712.

5 "2017 CANADA MUSIC YEAR-END REPORT,'" Nielsen (January 4, 2018) https://www.nielsen.com/ca/en/insights/reports/2018/2017-music-canada-year-end-report.html

6 Peach, Rob "Rap Music as "Coded Language": A Short Note on Tricia Rose's "Black Noise"," Reflect Black (November 18, 2014) https://reflectblack.wordpress.com/2014/11/18/rap-music-as-coded-language-a-short-note/.

7 Cote, Martha "Loud Lary Ajust Can't Win Quebec's ADISQ Because of a Stupid Technicality," Noisey (June 9, 2015) https://www.nytimes.com/2015/03/22/arts/music/kendrick-lamar-on-his-new-album-and-the-weight-of-clarity.html.

8 Dombal, Ryan "15-10-15-20: Pusha-T," Pitchfork (July 14, 2011) https://pitchfork.com/news/43058-5-10-15-20-pusha-t/.

9 Goldensohn, Rosa "They Shared Drugs. Someone Died. Does That Make Them Killers?" New York Times (May 25, 2018) https://www.nytimes.com/2018/05/25/us/drug-overdose-prosecution-crime.html.

10 Kuznia, Rob, "Her fiance gave her heroin. She overdosed. Does that make him a murderer?," The Washington Post (May 8, 2016) https://www.washingtonpost.com/national/her-fiance-gave-her-heroin-she-overdosed-does-that-make-him-a-murderer/2016/05/08/f9a9e79a-f29b-11e5-a2a3-d4e9697917d1_story.html?utm_term=.bdd6ca8d06e2.

11 Chesman, Claire-Donna "What Kendrick Lamar's Pulitzer Prize in music means for hip-hop," Revolt (April 25, 2018) https://revolt.tv/stories/2018/04/25/kendrick-lamars-pulitzer-prize-music-means-hiphop-0700838c24

12 Martinelli, Marissa "This Year's Other Two Pulitzer Finalists on Losing to Kendrick Lamar" Slate (April 17, 2018) https://slate.com/culture/2018/04/pulitzer-finalists-michael-gilbertson-and-ted-hearne-on-kendrick-lamars-win.html.

13 Rosenberg, Alyssa "What the Classical Music World Can Learn from Kendrick Lamar's Pulitzer Prize," The Washington Post (April 18, 2018) https://www.washingtonpost.com/news/act-four/wp/2018/04/18/what-the-classical-music-world-can-learn-from-kendrick-lamars-pulitzer-prize/?noredirect=on&utm_term=.a354799e83df.

14 Sisario, Ben, Alter, Alexandra, Chan, Sewell "Bob Dylan Wins Nobel Prize, Redefining Boundaries of Literature," New York Times (October 13, 2016) https://www.nytimes.com/2016/10/14/arts/music/bob-dylan-nobel-prize-literature.html?mcubz=2&mtrref=www.nytimes.com

15 Dylan, Bob "Bob Dylan – Banquet speech," *Nobel Prize* (2016) https://www.nobelprize.org/prizes/literature/2016/dylan/25424-bob-dylan-banquet-speech-2016/

16 Watson, C. Elijah "Kenny Beats Wants To Be Rap's Quincy Jones [Interview]", OkayPlayer (2018) https://www.okayplayer.com/originals/who-is-kenny-beats-rico-nasty-777.html

17 "DOES THE MUSIC INDUSTRY'S DEFINITION OF 'CATALOGUE' NEED AN UPGRADE?," *Music Business Worldwide* (December 5, 2017) https://www.musicbusinessworldwide.com/music-industrys-definition-catalogue-need-upgrade/

18 "Song Revenue Chart," Hits Daily Double (September 14, 2018) http://hitsdailydouble.com/song_revenue_chart

91

19 Knopper, Steve "A Hip-Hop Signing Frenzy Sends New Record Deal Prices Soaring," Billboard (March 29, 2018) https://www.billboard.com/articles/business/8272682/hip-hop-signing-frenzy-record-deal-prices-soaring

20 Knopper, Steve "Brockhampton's RCA Deal Worth $15M: Sources," Billboard (April 2, 2018) https://www.billboard.com/articles/business/8280751/brockhampton-rca-record-deal-worth-15-million

21 Beauchemin, Molly, Gordon, Jeremy "David Lowery Files $150 Million Lawsuit Against Spotify," Pitchfork (December 9, 2015) https://pitchfork.com/news/62685-david-lowery-files-150-million-lawsuit-against-spotify/

22 Dredge, Stuart "Paperchain aims to crack the challenge of 'royalty black boxes'," Music Ally (August 2, 2017) https://musically.com/2017/08/02/paperchain-aims-crack-challenge-royalty-black-boxes/

23 Starr Bonin, Liane "What's The Deal With Black Box Royalties?," Song Trust (June 7, 2018) https://blog.songtrust.com/whats-the-deal-with-black-box-royalties

24 Hernandez, Manny "The Anatomy of a Music Publishing Split Sheet," Medium (March 9, 2017)https://medium.com/@TMPRecordsllc/the-anatomy-of-a-music-publishing-split-sheet-cd9d1a22c057

25 Hogan, Marc "Don't Give Spotify Too Much Credit for Adding Credits," Pitchfork (February 5, 2018) https://pitchfork.com/thepitch/dont-give-spotify-too-much-credit-for-adding-credits/

26 Setaro, Shawn "The Musicians Behind Your Favorite Songs Are Coming for Their Credit," Complex (July 30, 2018) https://www.complex.com/music/2018/07/musicians-behind-favorite-songs-coming-for-their-credit/

27 Baynes, Chris "London stabbings: Six teenagers attacked in 90 minutes during night of violence on capital's streets," The Independent (April 6, 2018) https://www.independent.co.uk/news/uk/crime/london-stabbings-six-teenagers-attacked-violence-knife-crime-david-lammy-sadiq-khan-israel-ogunsola-a8291181.html

28 Baynes, Chris "London stabbings: Six teenagers attacked in 90 minutes during night of violence on capital's streets," The Independent (April 6, 2018) https://www.independent.co.uk/news/uk/crime/london-stabbings-six-teenagers-attacked-violence-knife-crime-david-lammy-sadiq-khan-israel-ogunsola-a8291181.html

29 Thomas-Beaumont, Ben "Is UK drill music really behind London's wave of violent crime?," The Guardian (April 9, 2018) https://www.theguardian.com/music/2018/apr/09/uk-drill-music-london-wave-violent-crime?CMP=aff_1432&utm_content=ESI+Media+-+The+Independent&awc=5795_1551714890_5012fce2b17dbfbfd13c765216b4ae6e

30 Press, Associated "Beyonce's 'Daddy Lessons' Rejected by Grammy Country Committee," Billboard (December 7, 2018) https://www.billboard.com/articles/news/grammys/7604485/beyonce-daddy-lessons-rejected-grammy-country-committee

31 Caswell, Estelle "How the triplet flow took over rap," Vox (September 18, 2017) https://www.vox.com/2017/9/18/16328330/migos-triplet-flow-rap

32 Divita, Joe "RECORDING ACADEMY SENIOR VICE PRESIDENT: BEYONCE GOT ROCK GRAMMY NOMINATION BECAUSE OF JACK WHITE GUEST SPOT + LED ZEPPELIN SAMPLES," Loudwire (December 12, 2016) http://loudwire.com/recording-academy-senior-vice-president-beyonce-rock-grammy-nomination-jack-white-led-zeppelin/

33 "Global Music Report," (2018) https://www.ifpi.org/downloads/GMR2018.pdf

34 Kristensen, Jared "The Rise of the Genre-less Music Fan," Audience Republic (January 28, 2018) https://audiencerepublic.com/blog/the-rise-of-the-genre-less-music-fan/

35 Walker, Rob "The Song Decoders at Pandora," New York Times (October 14, 2009) https://www.nytimes.com/2009/10/18/magazine/18Pandora-t.html

36 Pelly, Liz "Discover Weakly," The Baffler (June 4, 2018) https://thebaffler.com/latest/discover-weakly-pelly

37 Zellner, Xander "Migos Tie The Beatles for Most Simultaneous Hot 100 Entries Among Groups," Billboard (February 5, 2018) https://www.billboard.com/articles/columns/chart-beat/8098099/migos-the-beatles-simultaneous-hot-100-hits

38 Phillips, Yoh "Hip-Hop Needs to Be an Inclusive Art Form—Not an Exclusive Culture," DJ Booth (February 28, 2018) https://djbooth.net/features/2018-02-28-why-hip-hop-shouldnt-return-to-exclusivity

39 Adams, Dart "Hip-Hop Turns 40," NPR (August 11, 2013) https://www.npr.org/sections/therecord/2013/08/11/211115072/hip-hop-at-40-is-a-shell-of-its-younger-self

40 Juzwiak, Rich "Sentencing in Rapper 6ix9ine's Child Sex Case Delayed Because He Failed His GED," Jezebel (January 30, 2018) https://jezebel.com/sentencing-in-rapper-6ix9ines-child-sex-case-delayed-be-1822557621

41 Juzwiak, Rich "D.A. Says 6ix9ine Has Violated Plea Agreement, Recommends Prison Time," Jezebel (August 10, 2018) https://jezebel.com/d-a-says-6ix9ine-has-violated-plea-agreement-recommen-1828238915

42 II Coleman, Vernon, C. "6IX9INE CREW MEMBER ACCUSED OF FIRING GUN AT ADRIEN BRONER AND JESSIE VARGAS FIGHT," XXL (April 2018) http://www.xxlmag.com/news/2018/04/6ix9ine-crew-member-accused-of-firing-shot-adrien-broner-jessie-vargas-fight/

43 Preezy "6 EXAMPLES OF 6IX9INE DOING GOOD DEEDS," XXL (September, 2018) http://www.xxlmag.com/news/2018/09/6ix9ine-doing-good-deeds/

44 Gonen, Yoav "Ex-con using Eric Adams ties to push youth program's bogus claims," NY Post (October 17, 2016) https://nypost.com/2016/10/17/ex-con-using-eric-adams-ties-to-push-bogus-claims-over-youth-program/

45 Billie-Blais, Braudie, Kim, Michelle "Drake Explains Blackface Photo From Pusha-T's "Story of Adidon"," Pitchfork (May 31, 2018) https://pitchfork.com/news/drake-explains-blackface-photo-from-pusha-ts-story-of-adidon/

46 Hassan, Huda "The State of Black Mourning," Hazlitt (April 24, 2017) https://hazlitt.net/feature/state-black-mourning

47 Burton, Jack "Here's everything you need to know about Kanye West's new interview," On the A Side (May 2, 2018) https://ontheaside.com/music/heres-everything-you-need-to-know-about-kanye-wests-new-interview/

48 Harrison, Kitanya "The Difficulty in Defining Donald Glover's 'This is America'," Medium (May 7, 2018) https://medium.com/s/story/this-is-america-dont-catch-me-slipping-8f1072f730e9

49 Collazo, Richey "Why You Shouldn't Be Supporting Atlanta, Or Donald Glover," Affinity Magazine (2017) http://affinitymagazine.us/2016/11/09/why-you-shouldnt-be-supporting-atlanta-or-donald-glover/

50 Yue, Victoria "DOES CHILDISH GAMBINO HAVE AN ASIAN PROBLEM?," Hyphen Magazine (December 29, 2011) https://hyphenmagazine.com/blog/2011/12/29/does-childish-gambino-have-asian-problem

51 Collazo, Richey "Why You Shouldn't Be Supporting Atlanta, Or Donald Glover," Affinity Magazine (2017) http://affinitymagazine.us/2016/11/09/why-you-shouldnt-be-supporting-atlanta-or-donald-glover/

52 Parham, Jason "Say What You Meme, Meme What You Say," The Fader (April 2017) https://www.thefader.com/2017/04/27/memes-black-twitter-diaspora-essay

53 Elder, Sajae "Why Unplugging Is Especially Important for Black Women," Flare (January 31, 2019) https://www.flare.com/news/avoiding-racism-on-the-internet/

Part 2
PROFILES/
RETROSPECTIVES/
REVIEWS

The Perfectionist:
Mac Miller Is Finally Making
the Music He's Always
Wanted to Make.

by Craig Jenkins

Mac Miller died on Friday, September 7. This profile was reported in mid-August.

Mac Miller is nervous. He's pacing, running scales and planning outfits in the Late Night With Stephen Colbert green room during a Monday taping where he's the musical guest. It's a windowless white space with two extraneous doors that don't appear to move or lead anywhere; like a Scooby-Doo trap room. Wardrobe deliberations go on longer than you'd expect; and the room is making everyone loopy. The Pittsburgh rapper — normally relaxed and easy-going — is growing wiry from anticipation. After trying several crisp shirt and pant combos, Miller ends up onstage in his publicist's sunset-hued Stussy sweatshirt, where he runs through an airtight performance of his new album *Swimming*'s funk-rap highlight "Ladders," backed by the stellar house band, Jon Batiste and Stay Human. Inside the room, a sea of shiny, bald heads suggests that the crowd is considerably older than the late-stage teens and 20-somethings that comprise Mac Miller's fan base. Colbert tickets sell out well ahead of the guest announcements; it's possible that no one in the audience knew they were seeing Mac, or the episode's flamboyant first guest Nicki Minaj, until days before, if at all. It becomes clear that Mac isn't anxious about playing the room. He's anxious about winning it.

I met up with Mac Miller in the lobby of the Bowery Hotel

the day after Colbert with a plan to wander around and talk shop in lower Manhattan. Out back, there's a cozy patio with a vaulted glass ceiling made doubly breathtaking by the onset of a fast-moving afternoon thunderstorm, the worst in a two-week stretch of late summer rain. The storm complicated our plan to cruise the streetwear shops up Mercer but offered a scenic backdrop for indoor reflection. Mac was still pondering the performance from the day before and wondering what he could have done better, even though the general consensus among the chorus of internet rap diehards who watched the video was that he did a great job. "I have a tendency to kinda brood about stuff and cook in it," he says. "I'll wake up and just sit here and think about it for hours."

This is partly because Mac hears sounds even a keen ear might miss, and while this causes a potentially unhealthy level of self-reflection it also keeps him in a close orbit of jazz fusion guys like Thundercat, the funk apostle Dam Funk, and rap technicians Vince Staples and Kendrick Lamar. Listening to the playback of "Ladders" on site in the mixing room at Colbert, Miller caught an almost imperceptible rhyming misquote in a backing vocal and asked staff to adjust the levels subtly so it blended in better. It's not preciousness so much as a studio rat's high bar for professionalism.

That attention to detail isn't limited to the studio. Having a smoke on a bench on Bowery, Mac glanced up the street and then quickly popped back inside the hotel. He'd worked out that a gentleman peering at him from behind a bush was communicating with another in a vehicle across the street. Paparazzi were waiting for him outside Colbert the night before, and this looked to be more of the same. Photographers show up to Mac Miller's scheduled appearances all the time, but hiding behind shrubbery outside his hotel feels cartoonishly weird. When the weather cleared, and the gentlemen watching from outside disappeared, we strolled up Great Jones and stumbled on the building where Jean-Michel Basquiat worked and lived. Mac looks for pointers on how to live and work as an artist in the work of performers of every stripe, from within rap and well beyond it; back at the hotel he gushed about HBO's new documentary *The Zen Diaries of Garry Shandling*: "He was always writing the words, 'Just be Garry.' 'Just be Garry.' And that shit struck a chord with me because that's the goal, to get better and to try to make this shit the most of a reflection of who I am."

As we walked, elderly gentlemen from a local men's shelter recognized the rapper from reruns of his MTV show *Mac Miller and the Most Dope Family*. A steady trickle of excited rap fans stop him to say hello. The few that linger to talk longer all seem to want something; one wanted a feature for his mixtape, and another asked the rapper to check out his SoundCloud page, graciously sparing us the spectacle of a street cipher. Mac is cordial and patient with people even when he appears to smell a pitch coming. The most striking fan interaction happened when two deaf girls asked for autographs outside the hotel. Mac was quietly floored by this. He rejects the notion that he's all that famous, but the truth is that he earned respect among hip-hop fans through years of sweat and hard work. Most rap careers open big and crumble over time, but this one is a long game.

That stormy middle-August stretch marked the eighth anniversary of Mac Miller's *K.I.D.S. (Kickin' Incredibly Dope Shit)* mixtape, an hour of capable flows and peppy if pedestrian lyrics he wrote when he was 18. By 20, he'd scored a platinum single and topped the *Billboard* 200 chart with his debut studio album *Blue Slide Park*. "When I first started, I thought I was going to be the biggest thing in the world," he says. "There was this time when I was the most Googled thing on the internet. It was like 'diet, carrots, and Mac Miller.'" With attention came withering criticism. He's relaxed about it now — he called *Blue Slide*'s rare 1.0 Pitchfork score "legendary" in retrospect — but he has admitted to being profoundly affected[54] by the early pans, and he has tried a little harder to express himself more clearly with every project since.

Mac Miller grew up playing music, and he listens to more than he lets on. In 2015, a lengthy Billy Joel kick led to the release of a cover of The Stranger's "Vienna"; on the walk in lower Manhattan, he broke unexpectedly into sections of ELO's "Mr. Blue Sky" and the Carpenters' "We've Only Just Begun." He thinks the best Beatle is Lennon, but he's begun to to appreciate McCartney's softness as he gets older. His earliest experience playing an instrument came from piano lessons at 6. Later, he picked up guitar, bass, and drums. He's bashful about his talents because of the company he keeps; it's easy to feel like an amateur on bass when you've got Thundercat on speed dial. (At the *Swimming* listening party in July, he noted that he wrote horn parts for "Ladders" when I asked about the beat, but he isn't listed as an arranger in the album credits.) Mac's voice is the instrument he's most keen on improving. In the falsetto counter-melodies of "Self Care" and the tender, Auto-Tuned outro of "Jet Fuel," *Swimming* builds on the gains as a vocalist that coalesced on *The Divine Feminine*. He's still thinking about a vocal coach.

The chief drawback of blowing up young is the lack of room for error. Because Miller's music is frank about his struggles, and because those struggles periodically involve drug use, he lives in the constant shadow of questions about his well-being. There are people who think he's a round-the-clock reckless, depressive party animal. Really, he spends his days relatively upbeat and preoccupied with music, and also with working out and balancing his diet. He's not above mistakes and indulgences: Last May, Miller caught a DUI after crashing his Mercedes-Benz G-Class in Southern California and summarily went silent on social media. Your mind works through the worst with the guy who made *Faces*, the 2014 mixtape full of ominous lyrics about hard drugs and musings on premature death. "I used to rap super openly about really dark shit," he says of that time in his life and artistry and the mark it has left on the way audiences connect the facts of his life with the themes of his music, "because that's what I was experiencing at the time. That's fine, that's good, that's life. It should be all the emotions." As a result, he knows what everyone thinks about him, and now he has to teach himself not to care.

You grow up in the public eye when you become famous in your teens. Your mistakes get more scrutiny than the normal person's. You slip up, and it could end up in a newspaper. Is that unnerving?

There's pressure. A lot of times in my life I've put this pressure to hold myself to the standard of whatever I thought I was supposed to be, or how I was supposed to be perceived. And that creates pressure … It's annoying to be out and have someone come up to me and think they know. They're like "Yo, man, are you okay?" I'm like "Yeah, I'm fucking at the grocery store." You know? It's the job. This is what I signed up for. So, you just have to not. You have to have your own reality and that has to be the driving force of your life. Do I wish that every single thing I did when I was 19 wasn't a discussion? Sure.

I feel like the public sense of who you are differs from the reality. What does that do to your thinking?

You know what's funny? I feel like the public perception of me varies on who you ask. But there's a bit of a freedom in knowing that people are going to think all types of shit, no matter what. It actually makes me less stressed about how my actions are perceived. It's out of my control. I mean, to a degree…I could control it. I could live this squeaky clean life and everything. I could try to control the media. But I've been finding freedom in just living and letting people say whatever the fuck they want. Like, do I really care what Hollywood Life is saying? If I read a headline, and I'm like, "Wow, that's completely untrue..." I'm like, "That's as far as it goes. Okay, cool. So a bunch of kids now think that." Fine. As long as I have people that are hearing my music, and there's still that relationship...all that [other] shit lasts a day.

That's interesting. There are artists who absolutely do try to exert control over their image, not necessarily by changing their lives but by getting out front and trying to shift perceptions and kill stories. Is it not worth it to do that?

Maybe I'm wrong. Maybe that's just a game that I haven't gotten into playing. But it just seems exhausting to always be battling something...to always be battling for what you think your image is supposed to be. You're never going to be able to get anything across. It's never gonna be the real...No one's gonna ever really know me. You know what I mean? That's okay. The people that have the best chance of knowing me, that would like to, would just be by listening to my music. Even friends that I've lost touch with, if they ask how I've been, I'm like, "That's the best way to know how I'm doing."

But people reading too much into your music can also create its own misconceptions. If people hear sad songs, they think, "This guy's fucked up." And it leads to "Are you okay?" on the street.

I have noticed that, as far as headlines and people listening to the music and taking them into account, and applying them to the music. But...I've also not talked about what songs mean, what's this or what's that. I've just kind of left it up to interpretation. I don't know if it's the right or the wrong way or if it helps people digest my music properly or if it doesn't. I just feel like I worked so hard to make something, and then when I take the kids to college, I have to let them kind of...Whatever happens.

You don't have control over them once you release them.

Yeah. But here's the thing: I probably do. I probably do more than I realize. I probably could do more to control the perception of me.

What would that look like?

I have no idea.

Would you have to be a more literal songwriter?

I think that — I've seen a lot of different takes on what the music is. And that's what I like. I like different responses. You know? Everyone's not being like, "This song is obviously about *this...*"

That mentality is out there.

For sure. There's different takes...I guess I'm just not as concerned with that as I am with having a relationship with music in general.

Hearing *Swimming* in the shadow of Mac Miller's recent press gave some listeners and critics the impression that the music was fallout from crashing his car and breaking up with the singer Ariana Grande, in the same way that people assumed that The Divine Feminine was about the same relationship, when the concept and a chunk of the music actually predated it. "It's not that I mind," he says of the popular misgivings about the meanings of his songs. "What can I do? Stand on a mountaintop and say, 'I wrote these songs at this point in my life'?" Really, the birth of *Swimming* happened two years ago with the creation of the album opener "Come Back to Earth." As Mac began toying with the song — he worked through ten different versions before settling on the first — he got restless about his process, which, historically, involves booking several weeks at the nearest recording facility

101

and camping out there until an album is completed. This time around, he worked in Southern California, both at home and at Los Angeles's famed Conway Recording Studios, and in different locales around the Pacific Ocean: "I did two songs in Hawaii. 'Hurt Feelings' was done in Hawaii, and 'Wings' was done in Hawaii. 'Perfecto' was in Chile." The change in geography gives the record a warmth and a depth that feels like a new direction. Mac albums are rarely as contented in quietude as this one is. The songs lure listeners in with slow, delicate grooves and drop them off with a word about perseverance.

Swimming also gets its character from its collaborators. Mac is the main voice throughout the album, but if you comb the credits, you catch J. Cole, Flying Lotus, Dam Funk, and Thundercat in the list of players and co-producers, and Snoop Dogg, Dev Hynes, and Syd from the Internet as guest vocalists. In the past, the range of outside producers who pitched in work on Mac Miller albums sometimes gave the sequencing of the record a bit of a jolty feeling. *GO:OD AM* and *Watching Movies* both ping-pong between reflective songs and rowdier rap tracks, but Swimming feels both cohesive and expansive. (A great group of guests is as much a feat of magnetism as luck; Hynes told me he ended up on "Self Care" thanks to a habit of dropping in on friends' studio sessions whenever he's in their city.) Some of this is surely thanks to co-producer Jon Brion, a mainstay in pop, indie rock, hip-hop, and film scores with collaborations with Fiona Apple, Aimee Mann, and director Paul Thomas Anderson in the '90s.

Mac Miller sought Jon Brion's assistance as a fan of the producer's score for screenwriter Charlie Kaufman and director Michel Gondry's futuristic rom-com *Eternal Sunshine of the Spotless Mind*. A chance encounter in a jam session led to a deeper musical connection, and, as sessions for *Swimming* drew to a close, Mac asked Brion to come work his magic. "I called him, and I was like, 'Yo, we're down to the final week. This is kinda where the album ended up going. Just come to the studio.' He brought a semi-truck of instruments and filled all of Conway up. We went through the record, and he started playing things on every song." Miller remains awestruck by watching Brion work: "He taught me a lot about putting together stereo sound, using all of the space in the speakers and what that does to texture." The album title came from a running gag between the two. Brion would tease the rapper for constantly asking for "water sounds." On his last birthday, Miller woke up and resolved to call his "water" album *Swimming*.

The new music nestles in a sweet spot every Mac Miller project since 2013's *Watching Movies With the Sound Off* touches but rarely dwells on. Miller's best records are songs of grizzled perseverance. The doleful Watching Movies tracks "Objects in the Mirror" and "REMember" talk about weathering loss and adversity. *GO:OD AM*'s "Weekend" and "Rush Hour" find solace in rest and strength in pure ambition. *Divine Feminine*'s "Stay" powers through a tight spot in a relationship. From the wounded repose of "Come Back to Earth" ("I just need a way out of my head") to the tranquil, therapeutic "Self Care," *Swimming* seems most concerned with quieting stress and seeking out lasting peace. It's not specifically about localized, reactionary depression, but instead about heeding quiet epiphanies and training his brain to weather natural lows. "I really wouldn't want just happiness," he says when I ask about how he manages hurt feelings and negativity. "And I don't want just sadness either. I don't want to be depressed. I want to be able to have good days and bad days...I can't imagine not waking up sometimes and being like, 'I don't feel like doing shit.' And then having days where you wake up and you feel on top of the world."

May might've looked like a low, but Mac Miller's August was a peak. *Swimming*'s hushed, unfussy musicality paid off as the album landed at a strong No. 3 on the *Billboard* 200 in a week stacked with quality rap releases. (It might've been No. 2 if not for the surprise drop of Travis Scott's *Astroworld*, which surged past *Swimming* and Drake's *Scorpion* to No. 1.) Mac is happy with the outcome: "I'm less concerned with being king of the hill than being able to put shit out." His teenage dream of being top dog has settled into a steady drive to stick around the rap business as long as it'll have him. The patient evolution of his art will keep him in the conversation as long as he's careful. "Now I'm in the clouds, come down when I run out of jet fuel," he raps on *Swimming's* "Jet Fuel," "but I never run out of jet fuel."

Thank You, Mac Miller

by Donna-Claire Chesman

I did not want to have to write this, or anything like this, ever. Now that I am writing, I cannot imagine doing anything but, and that is a gift you gave me. Ever since you were Easy Mac with the cheesy raps, ever since you flashed brilliant grins on Blue Slide Park, you gave me the gift of language and poetics in a way no one else ever has. I was 17 and scared in a hospital bed and you had my back, man.[55] You and your punchlines and Big L impersonations, and parties on 5th Ave took my mind off brain tumors and possibilities of chemo and spinal taps and surgeries. You took me to Pittsburgh and you rolled me a blunt, and you made me happy again.

I was 17 and thought my life was over, and with *Blue Slide Park*, you showed me all the ways life could be lived. I was woefully depressed and didn't know the first thing about proper therapy channels, medication, admitting I had something deeply wrong with me, and you got me excited about life again. In the hospital, and no one knows this, but since we're one big Most Dope family now, I would watch videos of you freestyling and try to craft my own 16s whenever my room was empty. It was so grounding and therapeutic. When I hit the flowstate while the nurses were away, man I thought I was finally anxiety-free. Here's the thing about me rapping, though—I wasn't very good, but you sure were.

And then the surgery happened, and I was okay, and you were okay. I played *Blue Slide Park* as we left Columbia Neurology behind us. And we kept smiling like we do, like you said. And then the winter of 2015 rolled around, and I shut myself up in my bedroom and drew the shades and wrote a letter, and you know how it goes. On the emotional readiness scale, I would consider

105

myself Tinkerbell. I feel too much too fast and then I implode. The beauty of *Faces*,[56] then and now, was that it was 24 laborious and abstract, and deranged songs. You went from tripping to screaming to breaking down love and drugs. You had the words for me when I was my most confused.

In the winter of 2015, I had this itch to kill myself, but I also had this convoluted spirituality. I wear a Kabbalah bracelet and a Star of David, and you must get it because you titled your album *The Divine Feminine*. In 2015, I wasn't sure if I was supposed to live or die, so I would test myself. I would put myself in dangerous situations and through dangerous acts and drink dangerous amounts just to know. If I was supposed to die, I would. I made it into a game because I had to. I gave myself "the Faces-rule." The tape comes on and I give my mortality a stress test.

This was all terribly ritualistic and I was at my lowest, but every time the project came to a close, I was still alive. I had vivid, graphic nightmares and stopped sleeping. *Faces* gave words and sounds to my nightmares and when I realized I could finally explain myself, I realized I could survive. Thank you, Mac, for reaching out from whatever plane you were on when you made *Faces* and showing me there was a life left for me to live in a kindred, cosmic sense that will only make sense to us.

I lived, man; we did it.

Even soundless, Mac, you gave me my words. You gave me my life, man. I wrote myself out of 2015 with *Run-On Sentences: Vol. 1* on in the background. It was February and I was still sitting in pitch darkness, but I was finally back at that poetry business. I was writing the best poems of my life, and the first publication credit I ever earned was for a piece I wrote to "Birthday." The poem was about living, somehow—just like all of your music and your legacy will be about living, somehow.

I lived, man; we did it.

In 2016, my life was feeling like it was mine again, and like clockwork, your music was right there with me. It was uncanny—it is uncanny—how we've managed to live through everything together year-to-year. It's a Jewish thing, I think. In 2016 I was in and out of love and you were very much in, and I was feeling on top of the world somewhere in Bushwick and you had it all figured out, too.

And then when life didn't ask and pulled the rug out from under me, in the pockets of *The Divine Feminine*, you were still there and you still understood. I returned to *GO:OD AM*, I learned what fight and recovery sounded like. All these years, man, and you kept teaching me what life could sound like if I just gave it some time and elbow grease. When I began to settle into the reality of my depression, to accept that this is how I am going to have to live every day, *Watching Movies With The Sound Off* was the record that showed me exactly how sadness could be beautiful and beyond reproach without being glamorized. Your language was always fucking thrilling, but *Watching Movies* unlocked something in me that colors everything I write to this day.

You made "I Am Who Am," which I've vowed to get tatted down my arm just as soon as I know this writing thing is going to work out. You made a song about the Jewish Diaspora and how you don't want to be chosen you just want to be left alone. You made a song talking to a void, while talking to yourself, while talking to me, while I talk to myself, and it was slick and avant-ish and brilliant. You made my favorite song, Mac, the one I play people who want to get to know me.

In 2017, my grandfather passed away. The same day I found out about his passing, and again, no one knows this, but that was when I bought a three-foot painting of you because I was distraught and that seemed like a reasonable coping method. As

I'm writing this, I have that piece of art framed in my living room right beside me. I look up at it whenever I have a writer crisis of faith. Some people have an everything-artist. Some people have a mentor-artist. Shit, Mac, you were a light. You were transcendent to me.

Then there was *Swimming*.[57] You didn't release that album, Mac, you gifted it to me. 'Nother year, same shit. One-to-one, you and I. It's 2018, and I'm fucking terrified, man. I'm scared and I'm excited, and I'm at peace. All at once. I wake up in the middle of a panic attack damn near every day; some days I don't know how to help myself. *Swimming* is the first album I put on every morning. I mumble bars to myself when the breathing gets tough. All of the nameless evil that plagues me lives on *Swimming*, in this stunning, heavenly package I could have never articulated without you. People might think you saved my life, but you did something so much more important: you showed me exactly how I can save myself.

In 2018, I found out you read my writing—a lot of my writing—and you liked it. That means the world to me. At the time of writing this, over 30 people have reached out to me personally to see how I am. I'm happy to be part of your legacy in that way, to be known in my corner of the internet as That Mac Miller Girl, while you go down as a legend who touched so many people's lives.

Thank you, Mac. Thank you for your love, and for reading my writing. Thank you for teaching me that I can keep living so long as I keep writing, so long as I keep creating. Thank you for explaining the Jewish Diaspora to me in song. Thank you for *Macadelic*, an album that sounds like my specific brand of day-to-day. Thank you for growing with me and showing me that I am not crazy at all. I promise on everything I am going to write my heart out for you, just like you showed me time and time again for a decade.

There truly has never been a motherfucker iller, Mr. Miller.

Bad Bunny: Life in Puerto Rico for a Refreshingly Weird Latin Trap Star

by Julianne Escobedo Shepherd

The ice-blue infinity pool with the built-in barstools gently laps into a skyline so dreamy you can barely distinguish it from the ocean. The yard is built on a steep incline among a dense clutch of trees, where red ginger crops up wild. There's a barrel near the pool, under a gazebo, of the sorts carted into corporate-sponsored parties to let people know who's paying. It reads BACARDI-BACARDI-BACARDI, its logo a faded yellow.

This sprawling mansion, in a semi-gated community on el campo in Vega Baja, Puerto Rico, has obviously been used before for lavish parties: there's a serving station in the back where bartenders can set up and administer drinks. The house doesn't even have an address — to find it, someone has to drop a pin. But its purpose right now is semi-permanent, and symbolic of a come-up. For years, growing up on the other side of Vega Baja in the tiny, close-knit neighborhood of Almirante Sur, Benito Antonio Martínez Ocasio and his friends would drive through this area, eyeing houses and dreaming. This was the one they liked best, and, by a stroke of luck, in June it came up on Airbnb, so they snatched it up, fulfilling some sort of impossible feat. There's some money now, and a reason to use it.

The world knows Martínez Ocasio as the Puerto Rican rapper Bad Bunny[58], a 24-year-old Latin trap king with a distinctive, slackened baritone and a wardrobe full of tiny sunglasses and outrageously patterned, button-down shirts. This particular week, the first in July, "I Like It," his Nuyorican party smash with Cardi B and J Balvin, has climbed triumphantly to No. 1 in the United States, and it's widening his reach to an ever-growing English-

109

speaking audience. Ask him about the milestone of having the top summer jam in the States and he casts down his eyes and grins, flashing teeth that belong in a Whitestrips commercial and revealing an unlikely facet of his offstage disposition: for someone in possession of such obvious charisma, el conejo is a shy one. "I think if I keep working in the way that I am, from the heart and from passion and with love, well, the fruits of that will keep coming," he says in Spanish, his voice low but direct.

Bad Bunny has already witnessed abundance: in a little under two years, he has become an unequivocal superstar across Latin America and the diaspora. His irreverent, emotional, trumpet-like verses have been dominating on near-ubiquitous features with some of rap and reggaetón's biggest names — Ozuna, Arcangel, Farruko, Alexis y Fido, Daddy Yankee, Nicki Minaj and, soon, Drake, who sings his verse in Spanish — and on his own songs, which notoriously started out as SoundCloud singles he uploaded while he was attending the University of Puerto Rico at Arecibo as a communications student interested in radio, moonlighting as a bagger at the ECONO grocery store.

But he has yet to release a proper album, and that's why Bad Bunny is here, in the wish-fulfillment Airbnb. Though his life has been a near-constant tour across Latin America, the U.S., and Europe, in July he has a rare month off that he's calling his "vacation," but it's hardly that. Upstairs, away from the pool and a kitchen stocked with rum and pizza boxes and bags of Charms Blow Pops, he's set up a makeshift studio where he's hunkering down and trying to finish his first full-length, La Nueva Religión, an album he hopes will broaden his renown as well as his stylistic range.

"I know what it is to be a normal kid, I know what life is like for young people." —Bad Bunny

Bad Bunny's friends are crashing here too, a phalanx of young men and one woman, some of whom he's known since middle school, all of whom he tries to be around as much as possible. There's also his little brother, Bernie Martínez Ocasio, age 21, who has the same long, lanky body, and is traveling with Bad Bunny on his next tour to help. (Their youngest brother, Bysael, is 16 and still in school, but maybe not for long — he's a baseball talent besting players years older than he is, and his next move is, ideally, training camp for the pros.) They all move as one unit, and Bad Bunny is reliant upon them to keep him grounded. Today in the mansion are eight young men, eating pastelitos de guayaba and chatting, and if it weren't for the fact that their leader is upstairs painting his nails and choosing his looks for this photo shoot (he declines to work with stylists), you could mistake the place for a boarding school dorm. Its contents are quite dudeinous: wet towels on the floor in the bathroom; empties in the recycling; a bong on the counter; *Un Nuevo Día*, the Telemundo talk show, blaring at a low din on the television, even though no one's watching it.

The familiar, average guyness is also, perhaps, a reflection of the crossroads where Bad Bunny now finds himself: a fairly regular twentysomething from a modest barrio in PR now learning to navigate astronomical fame, a fact that he and all his friends seem rather bewildered and blinkered by. (By way of explaining, his friend Jeddel Ashbiel Rosado recounts succinctly what it's like for them to go to the club now: "Una foto... nah, trés fotos..." and so on.) The Martínez Ocasio familia, on the other side of Vega Baja, have been powerless since Hurricanes Irma and Maria: Their home is running on three generators, a fact that would ground anyone, but might have added gravity for Bad Bunny, who personally distributed water, food, and generators to his hometown last year. And so he is taking care to relish every minute of his success, even as he's looking toward the promise of even more substantial wealth and fame.

That's where "Estamos Bien" comes in, the lush, triumphant trap single Bad Bunny released a few days before, which would eventually become another 2018 summer banger, hitting almost 100 million YouTube views in just a few weeks. Translating, basically, to "We Good," it is truly a document of his appreciation for his new circumstances; though his voice naturally has a somewhat mournful quality due to its low weight, he perhaps has never sounded happier than when he sings "el dinero me llueve" — translated roughly, "the money is pouring" — but the song is much deeper than that, full of heart. It was, in fact, inspired by the very house in which he is staying, as was the self-directed video, which was mostly shot there and on the beach in Vega Baja. "It occured to me, when we got this house, that we should go buy a little camera," he says. " At first my plans for it weren't clear, but the idea for the song came to me and shooting the video with the camera came later. But we just got it to record the summer... It was just for us to remember this time."

His friends are all in the video — that's Jeddel in the backseat of the convertible, the cute, grinny fellow with the curly fade and yellow sunglasses — and it also very likely shows a young man in the twilight of normalcy before he becomes even bigger. He knows how he got here, clear in a verse sung an octave lower than the rest:

Aunque pa casa no ha llega'o la luz
Gracias a Dios porque tengo salud, eh, eh (amén)
La vida no tiene repetición
Después que mami me eche la bendición, yeh

When the video was done, Bad Bunny sent it to his mom over WhatsApp. She cried with pride, like she always does. "My mami and papi love my music," he says. "They're always listening to the radio waiting for one of my songs to come on. And when it does, they turn up the volume — and turn it back down when it's over.

Benito Martínez Ocasio knew he wanted to be a singer from the age of 5. His father was a truck driver; his retired schoolteacher mother, like so many Latinx moms, encouraged his education in the ways of Jesús. "My mom is very religious — Catholic — and from a young age they brought me to the church. I've always liked to sing, [so] people in the church invited me to be part of the children's choir." He quit by the time he was 13 — "I said, 'Nah, now I'm too old for this'"— but he'd already started experimenting with different styles and vocal tones, idolizing reggaetoneros on the radio like Daddy Yankee, as well as salseros like Héctor Lavoe, who are as essential to the cultural fabric of Puerto Rico as the humidity.

By the time he reached high school, he'd begun freestyling to entertain his classmates, little rhymes that dunked on people and made them laugh. "I knew he always had something special," says DJ Orma, who has known Bad Bunny since 10th grade and now tours with him as his DJ. "He would always rhyme and even if it was just making fun of people, not everyone could do that. I always knew he had potential."

Given time to overcome his initial bashfulness, Bad Bunny's sharp sense of humor comes through in person, too, but underneath that is the all-encompassing drive of an artist. "I did those freestyles joking around," he says rather modestly, "but only a few people knew I actually made tracks... [When] I started freestyling, everyone liked it and it was very funny, but in private I did it for real. Then people started to motivate me saying, 'Why don't you put out music, put it online, put it here, put it on Facebook, whatever whatever' and I went, 'No no no.' But little by little, something was working in my mind and I said, 'It's true, I need to put something out.'"

Still in college, he began posting his tracks on SoundCloud. In 2016, he garnered a runaway hit with "Diles," a simple, self-produced synth-trap track over which Bad Bunny's voice drips

113

honeyed, weeded, sensual nasty talk about dat ass. It caught the ear of DJ Luian, a reggaetonero with clout, connections, and a record label called Hear This Music; soon Bad Bunny was being heralded as the leading voice of the then-still-coagulating Latin trap genre, which recognizes and honors the outsized influence of Black Atlanta but also expresses cross-cultural fealty to español.

"Diles" was an early indicator of what is so compelling about Bad Bunny as an artist: though he tends to keep his flow and tone in the low bass-y zone, the versatility of his voice is truly impressive, and you can hear the history of his influences within it. He emotes like a salsero can, weepy and biting on a breakup track like "Soy Peor," then cocksure and stunting on the weeded "Krippy Kush." "My songs are always a mix of things I feel and think; things that I know are happening, things that have happened to friends, things that I know personally," he says. "When it comes down to it, when I talk about me I'm not talking about a huge difference [from the general public], because I know what it is to be a normal kid, I know what life is like for young people."

He posts Instagram videos of himself just dicking around and singing with the projection and depth of an opera singer; in another life he could also sing corridos with a Mexican banda. But Bad Bunny is self-aware enough that he understands what his talent can do. "Realistically speaking, yes, in two years I've turned into a star, and that tells me that I can do a lot," he says. "If in two years I made myself a star, well, I expect that in two [more] I'll be able to make a mark. My only goal here is that the people will always remember my music and that they enjoy my music 10 years, 20 years from now. That people have great memories of these songs, and that they won't die. For real. I'm ready to make songs that don't die."

We're sitting poolside on some wicker chairs when he says this, his brown eyes looking true. On cue, we hear a car in the distance blasting "Te Boté (Remix)," the savage breakup track packed with reggaetón superstars on which Bad Bunny's verse dominates. He grins, points to his chest and proudly says, "Ese soy yo," as if I don't know — as if the track's not playing in at least 437 places at once on the mainland and in Puerto Rico at any given moment.

He's wearing a choker made of metal skulls, the kind one might find at a Hot Topic or even a Spencer Gifts circa 1997, and he's paired it with an L.L.Bean logo T-shirt and a Supreme baseball jacket. The sleeves are leather but he seems not to be sweating. He smells hella good, too, like some fancy oil cologne they mix up fresh in a boutique scent store, but it's not — it's Unpredictable by Glenn Perri, something he picked up at The Mall of San Juan after the woman working in the perfume shop chased him down with it.

Nothing from the album is quite ready to be heard, he says, but he does agree to play two guide tracks from songs he's working on that he thinks will challenge his fans, but not too much. He doesn't want to freak anyone out, but he's ready to get weird. He spends much of the day bleating, "I CAN'T FEEL MY FACE!" in English, transmuted into a soprano that sounds more "sped-up hook on a Juelz Santana single" than "The Weeknd." He says, "Since childhood, I've been a clown. I've always liked being very funny or trying to make people laugh. It's my original self."

The first track he plays is mid-tempo, faster than anything he's released before. The house music-alluding outro on "Estamos Bien" may have been intended to ready his fans for this because it sounds like '90s hip-house, but not in a corny or nostalgic way. The second track sounds like trap music as filtered through Marilyn Manson and The Matrix, and he says he wants Diplo to remix it. Both are wild."In reality, I'm still working on this," he says, not shyly but as a caveat that perhaps two unfinished tracks cued up on his iPhone aren't even a sketch of what his debut album will sound like. But it's something. "The reference tracks are really premature, but like, what I want for this record — the sounds, the vibe, the

115

ambiance — are more of the things I like, more of me, more of what I am, and more of what I think is my generation, those born in the '90s and the '00s. From childhood, I've had a lot of goals of things that I want to do in music. When I release my record, there are going to be more songs to give people an understanding that my musical concept can be different — but also me."

"If in two years I made myself a star, well, I expect that in two [more] I'll be able to make a mark." —Bad Bunny

Bad Bunny's personal style is refined and, like his music, spans a wide spectrum and is a little bit funny. In the "Krippy Kush" video, he wears a yellow windbreaker and Vans and spaced-out white sunglasses; he looks somewhere between Miami trap kid and the featured raver in a Happy Mondays video from 1991. In the clip for "I Like It," he's toned down for Cardi B, perhaps as a sign of respect, wearing a Puerto Rico baseball jersey and his signature cat-eye shades. More recently, he showed himself painting his fingernails a nice lavender in the "Estamos Bien" video, which led a horde of rather closed-minded commenters to speculate on his sexuality; he responded in a quite dirty tweet that as punishment he would impregnate those dudes' wives and then make the husbands raise his children. "He doesn't look like a regular trap artist right now, because he's so hipster and so strange, and I think he's being innovative," says DJ Orma. "Back then [before his fame], he didn't have the money to dress like this, but he had the ideas. Here in Vega Baja, almost nobody used to wear shorts above the knee, because people thought they were 'gay' or something. But in the skater community, that's normal. He likes that skate swag."

Among Bad Bunny's millions of rabid fans are the traditionalists: those whose reception to the way he bucks tradition and rigidity in urbano music demonstrate the problem of changing hyper-machismo culture across the Americas (recall how some fans and fellow artists initially responded to A$AP Rocky and Young Thug wearing "dresses"). His retort to such conservativism is typically funny, nasty, and open — recall another Twitter thread in which he advocated for women to cease shaving their pubic hair as a form of freedom — and it's precisely his unique sensibilities that seem to sail him through such close-mindedness without seeming to scathe him personally.

But as he seeks a more global fanbase, there's another close-mindedness he may have to encounter. Though English-speaking audiences have seemingly become more open to music in Spanish — thanks largely to Luis Fonsi's career-resurrecting 2017 mega-hit "Despacito"— rap en español has very infrequently engaged non-diasporic audiences in the English-speaking world (with a few exceptions, including a couple of reggaetón booms, if you're counting). With the runaway popularity of "I Like It," Bad Bunny's already got a leg up — and his verse includes two bars that constitute the first time he has rapped publicly en inglés. He's gradually bettering his English, although he makes it clear it's the English-speaking world that needs to catch up to the Spanish-speaking one — the "Latino gang gang"— and not the other way around. "Sometimes I [forget] there are people that think I represent a town, a hood, a country. When I land [in Vega Baja], it feels super dope, but it's also a responsibility — people expect the best from you. That's why, every time, I try to be like, I am just me. I'm being me, and if what I am [is what] you like, well, good. If not, there will be someone else who will come and do that for y'all."

Growing up, Bad Bunny spent a lot of time at the small skate park at the Complejo Deportivo Tortuguero in Vega Baja, and every year his crew takes a group photo there, near a halfpipe graffitied with a giant pink octopus. On a Thursday afternoon, they all decide to hop in a car caravan and drive over to take some more flicks. Bad Bunny stays in the car, straightening out his 'fit, but everyone else unloads with the video camera and wanders around. There are two boys of about 17 sitting atop the halfpipe, looking glum, until Bunny gets out of the car, unmistakably tall and gangly, wearing Barbie-sized sunglasses with a red tint to them.

"¡Ay, conejo!" one of the kids exclaims, the sight of his fave rapper cutting through his teen malaise. Bad Bunny greets them generously and takes selfies with them. This is his home, and he remembers what it's like to be a fan because he still is one: another dream he recently fulfilled, and perhaps an early instructor for his outsize persona and flamboyant sartorial instincts, was seeing some live WWE matches.

Bad Bunny's fascination with wrestling started when he was a kid; ask about it, maybe after he's smoked a blunt, and his face lights up. "Papi would watch wrestling all the time, when I was little like 5 or 6 years old, but I didn't watch it, I would stay playing with cars and things. Like two years later, because of some cousins of mine, I started to watch it, and since then I've been a huge fan of WWE," he says, animated. "I was huge fan of the wrestling here too, the IWA, and papa would take us to fights. So it's always been a dream of mine to go to WrestleMania or at least a pay-per-view match. Because I hadn't been to any, other than the small fights they had here, and it was now, thanks to God, that I could go to WrestleMania. Twice!"

For his "Chambea" video, in which he struts around in a floral Gucci suit and raps about being a hard-ass motherfucker, Bad Bunny hired Ric Flair to give him a rousing intro. Back at the house, he sits on a leather couch and pulls from a Phillie. "[Making the video], I kept saying, something's missing. Then it occurred to me, like damn, let's put a legendary wrestler in here. When I got to the video I was nervous—real nervous—and I didn't know if he was gonna be humble or more like the persona. But he's a super, super good dude and we became friends! He invited me to WrestleMania later, and he introduced me like a friend to all of the wrestlers. I met John Cena!"

"It's like fulfilling your childhood dreams, not as an artist or career dreams, but your kid dreams. I've never felt jealous in my life, but the only time I've ever felt jealousy was when I saw the photo of Post Malone with The Undertaker. Brooo, I almost cried! You saw he did the choke-slam on him?"

It's slightly surreal to see a burgeoning global superstar gush about another star the way millions of others would gush about him, but maybe that's the crux of Bad Bunny, and why he's resonated so strongly with so many people. He doesn't take what he has for granted, and even strong weed can't tamp down his emotions. Back at the Airbnb, as nighttime sets, there's the knowledge that in one week, he'll be back on tour — first across Europe, beginning in a small outdoor arena in Badajoz, Spain, through to the U.S. and Canada, and back home somewhere around November, a punishing four months on the road. Bad Bunny takes another hit off the Phillie and passes it to his boys; the air is thick and alive. Even with a celebratory tenor in the room, there's a wistful sense, too, an expectation of the loneliness that accompanies fame. He's having the time of his life, and he's savoring it. He knows it might never be like this again.

Tu Pum Pum: The Story of *Boricua Guerrero*, the Hip-Hop & Reggaeton Album That Paved the Way for Latin Trap

by Eduardo Cepeda

Ask an older hip-hop head – or young romantic of the genre – and they'll tell you that to be in New York in 1997 was to bear witness to hip-hop wizardry. The genre was basking in the warm afterglow of golden age rap, and had yet to succumb to the excess of the jiggy era. And though many will always argue about which era was the best (just wait, one day you'll wax poetic about the mumbliest of mumbles to your kids), one thing is clear: by 1997, the art form's infectious sampling, lyrical decimation, and depiction of life in New York's outer boroughs made tunnel banger hip-hop something to truly behold.

For over 25 years, Unique Recording Studios operated on the top three floors of the now-razed Cecil B. DeMille building in New York, and once served as the lifeblood of rap in the city. The birth of recorded hip-hop can be traced to those very rooms, in the form of productions by Arthur Baker and Tommy Boy Records. The list of artists who used those studios to leave their legacies on the world is endless.

In 1997, DJ Playero and Nico Canada holed themselves up in a New York City hotel room for two months, hoping to capture some of that magic, and in the process, preach the gospel of dembow to a new audience. The fruit of their efforts resulted in a rallying cry declaring that Puerto Rican reggaetoneros had arrived. *Boricua Guerrero: First Combat* exposed underground/reggaeton stars and up-and-comers to a wider U.S. audience by joining forces with some of hip-hop's elite. It helped crack the door open, creating the space for an eventual reggaeton takeover – and the entire first disc didn't even have a single dembow riddim.

Though underground thrived in Puerto Rico, and mixtape series like the Playero compilations and DJ Negro's *The Noise*[59] often showcased reggaeton stars spitting rhymes on boom-bap backbeats, *Boricua Guerrero: First Combat* took future reggaeton stars like Winchester Yankee (soon to rebrand as Daddy Yankee) and put them in the studio with some of hip-hop's biggest artists, like Q-Tip, Nas, Busta Rhymes, Fat Joe, and Big Pun to name a few. This was the biggest collaboration between Puerto Rican and mainland rappers at the time. One might even say Boricua Guerrero: First Combat was the most ambitious crossover event in history.

Boricua Guerrero: First Combat – Mission I Rap is the mouthful namesake of the first disc in the compilation, and the album's intro serves as a sort of declaration of war, outlining the myth of borders, and refers to Puerto Rico and the mainland U.S. as two nations united by the collaboration. Throughout the record, Playero and Canada's production features the kind of New York-style, mid- to late 90s hip-hop beats that were popping at the time – beats that would have felt equally at home at a cypher, on a Big L record, or as a backing track on a Stretch and Bobbito show freestyle. And the Puerto Rican rappers held nothing back as they went toe to toe with hip-hop's brightest.

Right out of the gate, Javiah and Busta Rhymes' "Loco Como Rodman" sets the tone for this near-hour of tunnel bangers. And there's no shortage of standout moments throughout. Eddie Dee holds it down solo on "Sube Y Baja," the late Mexicano's sandpaper flow perfectly complements Fat Joe's effortless delivery on "No Mas Tregua." Plus, "Listo Para Morir," by Miguel y Kalil and Akinyele, could be a classic in its own right. But perhaps one of the most surprising moments is when Daddy Yankee – then Winchester Yankee – snapped on "The Profecy." His now long-abandoned backpacker flow might come as a shock to the legions of fans who know him for his lighter, less severe subject matter and delivery, like rapping about gasolina or hula hoops.

It's impossible to overstate the impact the album had, and how costly the project must have been. "Even now, I dare say there's been no CD that cost this much to make," Playero told El Diario de San Juan[60] on the 10th anniversary of the project. "We were the first to fuse Borinquen rappers with United States rappers," he said, echoing the sentiment the album begins with. But the exorbitant cost paled in comparison to the long-lasting effect the project had on Puerto Rican, mainland U.S., and to an extent, global culture.

This was a pivotal moment for the genre's trajectory – perhaps its first breaking point. It legitimized Puerto Rican rappers to mainland audiences. But it was so much more than just an exercise in lyrical flexing. This wasn't about showing off bars. This was about showing the world that Puerto Rico had an entire urbano music community that needed to break. And the way to do that was through disc 2, *Mission II Reggae*, the Trojan Horse of the project.

Disc one captivated hip-hop audiences and proved that Boricuas could hold their own against already well-known rappers. It served its purpose, grabbing the listener's attention. Then, the 21-track dembow assault on disc 2 introduced the same audiences to Playero's secret formula. Though this was still mostly underground-style reggaeton, before its transformation to mainstream pop,[61] the production and execution on these tracks was far superior to earlier Playero mixtapes. And the word "reggaeton" occupied substantial space on various tracks. This was reggaeton's cotillion.

But despite the effect it had on reggaeton's growth, this wasn't some cheap ploy to trick audiences into learning about the genre, and it surely wasn't some third-rate attempt at emulating New York hip-hop. "Boricua Guerrero felt like its own genre, and like it had more flavor in comparison to other rap records of that time," Nico Canada told El Diario.[62] There's something magical about the interpolation of rapid-fire bars coming from the likes of Don Chezina and Winchester Yankee alongside hip-hop royalty like Q-Tip – no matter how far-removed it is from the Yankee we hear on the radio in 2018. And perhaps most importantly, it's part of a long history of musical collaboration and partnership between Puerto Ricans and African-Americans, a reality we see manifested in genres like Latin trap today. Without the inroads made by Boricua Guerrero, there would be none of the crossover collabs that emerged during reggaeton's mid-2000s explosion,[63] nor the groundbreaking contemporary link-ups we've seen since "Despacito," like the Travis Scott and Nicki Minaj remix of "Krippy Kush."

There's still a few days of summer left, and with them, surely a couple of beach days. Cop that .rar file, unzip that shit, and upload it to your iTunes. Then, take a trip way back to when tunnel bangers met up with dembow at the bodega.

Bhad Bhabie Isn't Going Anywhere
by Meaghan Garvey

It's 10:30 a.m. in Brooklyn and Danielle Bregoli is eating olives for breakfast. Just olives—a selection of green and kalamata from the oily Key Foods salad bar; the only snack that piqued her interest after wandering the aisles, uninspired. Lingering outside the store afterwards, we scan 5th Avenue for a salon that can attend to her acrylic claws, as she doesn't feel like herself when her nails are short. It's clear from the jump that Bregoli doesn't open up to strangers right away; my amusement at her breakfast of choice is met with a shrug, as if to say, "And what?"

I've never been more anxious to meet a 15-year-old. Frankly, I'm not sure I've ever spent much time with a 15-year-old since high school, let alone one who's best known for stealing cars and roasting the elderly (i.e., anyone over 30). But it's hard to feel intimidated by this barely five-foot presence spitting olive pits onto the sidewalk in a white tee and jeans, with her squeak of a Florida drawl and a baby-like giggle that initially catches me off guard. Instead, I feel weirdly protective, scanning the sidewalk for lingering eyes or wayward shouts of the three words no one wants to hear: *"Cash me ousside!"* But it's early, and the only person who's bothered Bregoli so far is a red-eyed drunk who loops back three times to beg for a photo only to get shot down three times by her hulking bodyguard, Frank. "Please?" the guy slurs, waving a mini vodka bottle. "I'll let you pour this in my mouth!" Frank re-positions his nearly seven-foot frame: "Sir, you're speaking to a child."

The initial plan was to meet Bregoli and her team—her manager Adam, her other manager Dan, her publicist Ariana, and Frank—for a fancy lunch and spa manicure in Midtown, but

Bregoli shot that down immediately. Instead, we meet at Atlantic Terminal Mall in Brooklyn, a setting she's deemed more fitting. From there, we wander towards nearby Park Slope in search of a nail salon, the "less bougie" the better. Bregoli begrudgingly approves of a spot, and I settle in next to her for a manicure as she monitors, eagle-eyed, the length of the plastic tips being applied to her tiny fingers. The technicians hover nervously, warning her that the nails will easily break if they're too long. Bregoli rolls her eyes: "I've been getting nails this length since I was 10 years old."

"I DON'T KNOW IF I LIKE THE FEELING OF BE-ING IN TROUBLE, OR IF I JUST LIKE THE FEELING OF YOU KNOWING THAT I JUST TRICKED YOU."

Disclaimer, dear reader: this next detail's boring but important. There are two basic types of fake nails: acrylics, the cheaper, old-school option you typically see with super-long claws, and gels, which are more natural-looking but less durable. Practically speaking, the difference has a lot to do with class and race. In Park Slope, populated by Cool Dads pushing luxury strollers, you're probably going to get a gel manicure; in Crown Heights, whose community is largely Afro-Caribbean, you're more likely to find acrylics. Realizing that her in-progress manicure is the former, Bregoli jumps up, her irritation finally bubbling over. "These are just gonna break!" she yelps over her shoulder to Ariana. "I need acrylics! We need to go somewhere more hood!"

The only other patron in the salon, aside from the six of us, is an older West Indian woman whose feet are submerged in a pedicure bath. At the drop of the word "hood," the room's energy shifts. "It's 2018!" the woman shouts disgustedly at Bregoli, who immediately seems to retreat inside herself, falling silent. "You want 'more hood'? Oh, I'll show you more hood!"

Ariana seems to grow a foot taller in the moment. "No, I'll

show you more hood!" she warns. "You are yelling at a child right now!" The salon workers look on in horror. Everyone is shouting except Bregoli. I'm pretending to be invisible, wet nails captive under the air dryer, midway through what is easily the most stressful shoulder massage of my life. "Um, it's okay, you don't have to..." I whisper, planning my escape as Frank barks, "I'll beat your son's ass!"

The rest of us duck outside as Ariana throws down her credit card. Immediately, Bregoli proceeds to violently rip off her raw plastic tips. Her nail beds begin to bleed profusely. "That's why you don't eat olives for breakfast," she deadpans, blood dripping onto the sidewalk. It's not even noon.

If you're reading this, you probably know[64] how we got here. Bregoli debuted in the public eye in a September 2016 episode of Dr. Phil, alongside her apparently distraught mother Barbara. "I Want To Give Up My Car-Stealing, Knife-Wielding, Twerking 13-Year Old Daughter Who Tried To Frame Me For A Crime," read the episode's fairly straightforward title. None of this totally explains Bregoli's near-instant viral appeal. Daytime television isn't exactly lacking in the "troubled youth" department, but with a few infamous words—"Cash me ousside, howbowdah?" she threatened the audience in her comically thugged-out South Florida drawl—Bregoli became a star, or at the very least, a meme.

Bregoli returned to Dr. Phil a few months later for a stint at Turn-About Ranch, where she was entrusted with the care of a little horse named Chief. The footage shows Bregoli bonding with Chief and sweetly embracing her cowboy mentors. "I just feel okay with who I am now," she told the camera with a serene smile. But face-to-face with Phil in the studio for a second time, Bregoli's tone had changed. "I made you, just like Oprah made you," she smirked, and she wasn't exactly wrong. (Has a Dr. Phil episode gone viral this side of 2010—or ever, really?)

These days Bregoli doesn't like talking about the show too

much, other than to emphasize that her and her mother's relation-ship was never as dire as it seemed. "The show just wanted views," she tells me, matter-of-factly. Her awareness of her own role in a cynical content machine strikes me for the first of many times throughout our day together; I can't tell if I'm relieved or sad.

That nearly a year after the episode aired, The Artist Formerly Known as the "Cash Me Ousside" Girl was officially re-introduced as Bhad Bhabie, rapper extraordinaire, wasn't particularly surprising news in itself. Nor did it seem especially unusual that "These Heaux," her first single, entered the Hot 100 at No. 77 last September, making Bregoli the youngest woman to debut that high in Billboard history. After all, it was 2017—the year streaming data officially turned the Billboard charts into a teen-driven free-for-all, and the year we seemed to collectively decide we liked memes more than music. Still, it's rare that one person gets two shots at virality—and even rarer that they finesse that virality into a career. But later that September, Atlantic Records issued a press release announcing that they'd signed Bhad Bhabie to a multi-album, multi-million dollar deal. And though most of the media coverage was snarky, accompanied by the expected State Of The Industry hand-wringing, the power dynamic was obvious: the blogs needed the hate-clicks more than Bregoli needed the blogs.

I'd prepared myself for the inevitable onslaught of stray "Cash me ousside" shouts, doubtful if anyone who'd recognize Bregoli on the street would know the name "Bhad Bhabie," if they knew she was rapping at all. But not once during our day in Brooklyn were those three words uttered. When people recognized her—and they did, everywhere we went, a bizarre majority of them grown men—all I heard, over and over, was: "Hey, you're that little rapper girl!" It was as though the gnarly reason for her fame had been wiped from our collective minds, leaving only the fame itself.

Post-fame Bregoli does pretty much the same stuff pre-fame Bregoli did—namely, listen to rap and get her nails done. Back in

Park Slope, after wrapping her bloody fingers in a napkin, we hop in an Uber to Crown Heights, where Ariana has found a salon on North Flatbush much more to Bregoli's liking. Her mood brightens as soon as her acrylics are underway, and Dan runs to a bodega to fetch her yet another confusing meal—a bagel with cream cheese and bacon, an unspeakably off-putting combination.

As Bregoli's technician works, she and I chat until we're interrupted by a man in his mid-thirties with short braids and a "BROOKLYN" flat brim, selling earrings out of a velvet-lined case. Bregoli buys a small silver pair for $5. "You know, you look like that rapper girl," he muses off-handedly, and Bregoli grins, her eyes flashing mischievously. Realizing who it is, the man suddenly breaks into a rendition of "These Heaux," politely censoring "hoes" into "girls": *"I ain't nothing like these girls! Don't compare me to no one!"* He knows every word; everyone seems pleasantly stunned, Bregoli included. "That song's hot, though!" he says, posing for a photo. "Keep making them hits!"

Later, I mention to Bregoli that she seemed relieved he didn't say, "Cash me ousside." "Because I'm not a sentence," she says, eyes fixed on her white-painted talons. "And I'm doing more than just a sentence now."

"WHAT IF PEOPLE JUST THINK [MY MUSIC] IS A JOKE? WHAT IF IT DOESN'T BLOW UP? I WAS SCARED. LIKE, FOR REAL. BUT IT TURNS OUT, LIKE, B*TCH, I'M A RAPPER, OKAY?!"

"These Heaux" was a little formulaic, maybe, but hardly the dumpster fire Bregoli's critics might've liked to imagine. (Upon its release, the song overtook Taylor Swift's No. 1 spot on the Spotify Viral 50 chart. "Congrats to @taylorswift13 on that #2," Bregoli tweeted; if you couldn't get behind the song, you could at least appreciate the schadenfreude.) But by the release of Bhad Bhabie's second and third songs, which arrived tacked together in a single video—perhaps because their run time was less than two minutes each—I quickly came to terms with a jarring realization: "Hi Bich / Whachu Know" was a banger. Produced by SoundCloud rap's go-to guy Ronny J, "Hi Bich" was especially addictive; with bratty, stutter-step bars like, "I ain't worried 'bout no basic bitches/All y'all look like you still fly Spirit," Bregoli already seemed exponentially more comfortable on the mic. If you weren't told the artist's name, you'd probably love it.

The proof was all over YouTube, in an endless ouroboros of reaction videos—and reactions to reaction videos, and reactions to reactions to reaction videos. Bregoli's Youtube channel is overrun with all sorts of these reaction videos, which far outnumber her actual songs. Not that this is saying much: at the time of our interview, there were a whopping three Bhad Bhabie songs in existence, aside from a handful of unofficial remixes. Today that total is up to seven; the video for her latest, "Gucci Flip Flops" with Lil Yachty, depicts a Pleasantville-type universe infiltrated by SoundCloud rap values. (There's a David Spade cameo, if you've ever wanted to see him in a durag.)

I have long tried to parse the grim world of the YouTube celebrity, a futile endeavor that generally leaves me feeling approximately 3,000 years old and ready to move to a cave. But Bregoli's videos, I must admit, tend to be genuinely entertaining and often laugh-out-loud hilarious. As a rapper, Bregoli is capable (in a recent *Complex* interview with Peter Rosenberg, she rates her own music a very fair seven out of ten); as a YouTube comic, she is a star. For many artists these days, the content helps sell the music; with Bregoli, it seems to be the opposite.

My favorite video on Bregoli's channel has a fairly unenticing title. "Danielle Bregoli reacts to BHAD BHABIE 'HI BICH / WHACHU KNOW' roasts and reaction vids" doesn't exactly scream, "What a fantastic way to spend nine minutes of your dwindling life!" But it's the best indication I've seen of Bregoli's truest talent. In an infinite landscape of shockingly dull 22-year olds showing off Sephora hauls to millions of subscribers, the scathing wit of Bregoli's videos is almost refreshing. You really have to watch it to get the full effect, but the best part is when Bregoli responds to a deeply uncool Perez Hilton video, wherein the 40-year old man named after a Republican socialite brays about how stupidly Bregoli spells "Bhabie." "Hasn't he been around since, like, the '70s? No one even reads blogs anymore!" Bregoli says witheringly, curling her mouth around the word "blogs" as though she's talking about a rotary phone. By the end of the video, almost every one of the YouTubers have begrudgingly admitted that the song's kind of fire, Perez included.

Preparing for our meeting the night before, I'd assumed the crucial mission of my day with Bregoli and company would be to somehow pierce through the inevitable veil of Atlantic-coached PR spin: that Bregoli had dreamt of being a musician since first hearing Trina's "Da Baddest Bitch" (which was released—oh god—three years before Bregoli was even born), or some other smokescreen that stressed how organically all of this unfolded.

"Did you know you wanted to rap as a little kid?" I ask the tiny person barely past childhood, as her acrylics take shape. "No, I had no idea," Bregoli answers without pausing. "I didn't know I wanted to rap at the beginning of 2017 either." "Really?" I respond, startled by her transparence. "So what was the moment you realized you wanted to be a rapper?" "I think it was kind of like, I have this platform, being famous. I can see how I want to use it," she continues casually, picking warily at her bacon/cream cheese bagel with one hand. "So I went to a studio and they were like, Oh, my gosh, you're not bad at it. You have the ability. And then [Atlantic] was like, we wanna sign you. And I was like, okay!"

Going through Bregoli's YouTube later, I found a video that seemed more vulnerable than any of the "content" I'd seen from her, even if it was more "reacting to reactions." In it, she describes her first-ever recording session in April of last year. "I was kinda scared," she said, imagining the worst possible response. "What if people just think it's a joke? What if it doesn't blow up? I was scared. Like, for real. This is real life. But it turns out, like, Bitch, I'm a rapper, okay?!" With that, Bregoli laughs wildly and sticks her tongue out. It's the face of someone who's just gotten away with the biggest finesse of her then-14 years of life.

"I WAS BAD, BUT I WAS ONE OF THE KIDS THAT NEVER GOT CAUGHT. IF ANYONE EVER KNEW I DID SOMETHING, IT WAS BECAUSE I TOLD THEM. 'CAUSE I'M A REALLY GOOD LIAR."

Danielle Bregoli was born in 2003 in Boynton Beach, Florida. Her father, a sheriff's deputy for the Palm Beach Police Department with whom Danielle is currently estranged, separated from her mother not long afterwards. Her mother, Barbara Bregoli, was diagnosed with breast cancer when Danielle was four. In a 2009 article[65] in the *Palm Beach Post*, Barbara recalls her daughter rubbing aloe on her chest to soothe her radiation pains and making friends with the hospital staff; in photos, an angelic-looking Danielle tenderly rubs noses with her mom; her ponytail almost as long as it is today. In our conversation, Bregoli describes her part of Boynton as the quieter side, but her school—"for troubled girls," she says—introduced her to the other side of town.

"I wasn't stealing cars at like, six," she assures me, as though that was a possibility I was entertaining. "But I've always been bad. I used to drive this little Barbie car and tell random people, 'Fuck you!' and flip them off." She giggles. Although she never considered being a musician, or tried to write a song, she describes herself as creative all the same. "I used to be a good story writer," she recalls, amused. "I could make up a story with like, eight people in it and tell you where they all lived, what color their houses are."

But her truest talent, Bregoli freely admits, eyes gleaming, was deception. "Yeah, I was bad, but I was one of the kids that never got caught," she says. "If anyone ever knew I did something, it was because I told them. 'Cause I'm a really good liar, so I end up snitching on myself." She points to my phone. "I could really get you to believe this is a fake iPhone." Why would she want to snitch on herself, I ask—did she like the feeling of being in trouble? "I don't know if I like the feeling of being in trouble, or if I just like the feeling of you knowing that I just tricked you," she answers with a smile.

In school, Bregoli fit in with everyone, even if she never got too close. "The school was tiny, and you'd sit with a bunch of different girls at a bunch of different tables," she recalls, as though it were ages ago. "They all had their own personalities, the tables: the emo girls, or the regular girls, or the mean girls. And I was able to sit at every table. They all loved me. Even the tables that didn't like each other, I could sit at both of them and blend right in." Was it because you were nice to them, I ask? "It was because I can relate to so many different situations," Bregoli replies. "Or at least I think I can." Or maybe, I offer, she was such a good liar that she could mold herself into whoever they wanted her to be. "Exactly," she nods.

As far as close friends, Bregoli has only ever had one, but they don't talk anymore. Among her small handful of tattoos, the name "Zandalee" is scrawled across her left ring finger. "She was a prostitute; I met her at the school," she tells me. "That girl would do anything for money. When I became famous, she partnered with my dad, because my dad said that if they ruin my fame, he'll give her money. You know how they say shit goes sour after you tattoo someone's name? This happened within like 24 hours of the tattoo."

These days, Bregoli tells me, her best friend—and only friend, really—is Frank, who grew up nearby in Broward County and started working as her bodyguard at the beginning of 2017. Her phone background is a photo of his newborn son who, along with Frank's seven-year old daughter, she adores. Despite their 20-year age gap (and two-foot height gap) their relationship is genuinely sweet, and he is intensely protective of Bregoli, perhaps to an extreme. In an Uber later, while Bregoli rambles along to whatever comes on the radio into her Instagram livestream, he silently monitors the incoming comments. When one appears that reads something along the lines of "Kill yourself," Frank begins typing furiously.

"What'd you say?" asks Adam. "I'll beat your brother's ass," Frank admits, laughing but not remotely joking, and snatches Bregoli's phone from her manicured claws, putting her on time out. Keeping Bregoli out of trouble is a constant part of Frank's day. You can see him trying his best to de-escalate a recent face-off between Bregoli and Woah Vicky, a clearly white 18-year-old Instagram star who claims Ancestry.com results show she's African-American; but Bregoli darts around him to land a couple blows.

But despite Frank's good intentions, I can't help but feel a little sad that Bregoli appears to have no one even close to her age to talk to. And though she carries herself maturely in conversation, with her quick wit and low tolerance for bullshit, she behaves in her element like I'd imagine any 15-year old would. Throughout the day, Bregoli sporadically breaks into her own rendition of Lil Pump's "Gucci Gang," re-styling its hook as, "Poopy gang, poopy gang, poopy gang!" As our Uber from Crown Heights to Midtown dragged, she grew increasingly hyper with her phone privileges revoked, shriek-laughing and tangling herself in her seatbelt as if it were a straitjacket. She begs to stop at McDonald's each time we pass one; Frank tells me the biggest change in her spending habits, since getting rich, is the hundreds of dollars in McDonald's she Postmates each week.

As for Bregoli's favorite rappers, the list goes: Lil Pump, Trippie Redd, Smokepurpp, XXXTentacion, and Kodak Black. Four out of those five are from Florida (excluding Trippie Redd, though he may as well be); two of those five (XXXTentacion and Kodak) have serious sexual assault or battery charges attached to their names. Early last year, Bregoli starred in Kodak's "Everything 1K" video, perched atop a Rolls Royce in a "Cash Me Ousside" T-shirt; the second Bhad Bhabie track ever released was a remix of Kodak and XXX's "Roll In Peace." She's friends with most of her Top 5 in real life, too; she tells me she wants her next tattoo to be a small "K," for Kodak, on her finger.

To expect a 15-year old to be aware of this music's baggage would probably make me delusional; I don't know if there are any easy answers. And it's just as complicated to try and pinpoint whose responsibility, exactly, might it be to step in here. Bregoli's estranged father, Ira Peskowitz, has spoken to the press at length about his concern over his daughter affiliating with these popular men with harrowing criminal records, and his disgust at the adults who've seemed to condone it. "Danielle bonds with anybody who shows any type of care for her," he said last year. "When someone comes and puts their arm around her, she's vulnerable, she just opens up to them." But it's impossible to tell from the outside if Peskowitz's comments are born from genuine concern for his daughter's well-being, sheer greed, or something deeply complicated in between. Bregoli responded to his statements with a single, scathing tweet: "please stop interviewing this piece of shit before his people call me AGAIN asking for 10k or they gon' keep talkin to press."

"Aww, is she on the Disney Channel?" the security guard asks when we finally arrive at *Complex*'s midtown office for a photo shoot, the final item in our day's itinerary. Dan laughs: "Imagine the opposite of that."

At the shoot, Bregoli is obviously tired, hitting restless, unsmiling poses with her gaze fixed on the images popping up on the photographer's screen; it's clear she's a little self-conscious about the way the portraits are coming out. Ariana huddles up in an attempt to lift her client's sinking spirits. "Something I always tell my artists when they're doing photo shoots: sometimes it helps to put your own music on in the background," Arianna says gently. "It just boosts your confidence." Bregoli looks baffled. "No, not my music!" she yelps. "Play Pump!" "Gucci Gang," once again, fills the room, and Bregoli gets back in the zone, covering her face with her hands and glaring out through the cracks.

While she changed from a white tee and jeans to a hoodie and jeans for the shoot, her manager Adam addresses me candidly: "I always tell people: don't blame her, blame me." He doesn't specify what exactly he means by "blame," but we both know anyway. He tells me he called up Bregoli the day after the Dr. Phil episode ran. Signing established social media stars or reality TV personalities with a built-in network appears to be Atlantic's M.O. these days, from Cardi B to Walmart Yodeling Kid. The label doesn't seem concerned with spending time and money building an artist's fanbase when they can get one pre-fab. In other words, no matter what you think of Bregoli's rap career, it's clear she's more symptom than cause.

Earlier at the nail spot, I'd asked Bregoli if she thought she wanted to be a musician for the long run—if this rap thing was a vocation now. "If that's what the world wants out of me, then yeah, I might," she said calmly, without hesitation. "If my albums sell, I'd be more than happy to. But I'm not desperate to do anything. I could go back to Boynton if I really wanted to. Don't get me wrong, I'm grateful for everything, but I don't wanna make it seem like I wouldn't be able to survive without fame. 'Cause I did it for 13 years." She pronounces the number as though it's an eternity. "My goals for the next part of my life: Whatever I'm handed, I'm gonna make the most of it. If it's good for me, I'm gonna take it."

"I Don't Remember the Samples I Use. Hell No."
–The Story of *Madvillainy*
by Gino Sorcinelli

Prior to becoming a household name with a fan base that boasts Common, Snoop Dogg, and Kanye West, the historic indie label Stones Throw Records consisted of a bunch of broke dudes living together in LA and trying to get founder Peanut Butter Wolf's brainchild off the ground.

With Wolf, former Stones Throw manager Egon, and art director Jeff Jank sharing the same living space during the label's formative years in the late 90s and early 2000s, their collective path towards success took an important turn when super-producer Madlib joined them as an informal fourth roommate. "It was the three of us just winging it, no plan, no money," Jeff Jank recalled in a 2011 interview with *Ego Trip*. "Madlib moved in unofficially, first set up shop in the living room, then into this '50s-era bomb shelter downstairs with 18-inch concrete walls."

It was in the Bomb Shelter studio that Madlib's obsessive pursuit of musical mastery reached a new plateau. With a new workspace finalized and ready for use, his now-legendary ability to work on music for days on end was on display right away. "He made music all day on a consistent schedule that really impressed me," Jank told *Ego Trip*. "All the much more impressive that his three breaks a day were to smoke giant mounds of green bud."

"A lot of the beats on '100 Beats', you can't use, 'cause I'm just fucking around and freestyling. Some of 'em might be so way out, 'cause I'm just using what I have."—Madlib

137

Stones Throw had grown in both size and stature by the time the first few years of the new millennium rolled around. Madlib transformed into the label's flagship act, with his relentless instrumental output leading to seminal projects like Lootpack's *Soundpieces: Da Antidote*, Quasimoto's *The Unseen*, and a remarkably tasteful and well-executed Blue Note remix project titled *Shades of Blue* in June of 2003.

Yet despite their commendable track record, the label's future was uncertain. Even though Stones Throw had gained some widespread recognition for their achievements, the late 90s and early/mid-2000s marked a long, difficult period for the entire music industry. Physical sales were declining at a steady clip and labels were still figuring out how to harness and monetize the power of the internet. In other words, achieving stability was a frequent uphill battle for all independent record labels.

Adding to the uncertainty of Stones Throw's future was the creative rut that Madlib found himself in prior to the release of *Shades of Blue*. Despite his unstoppable output, the label's rising star seemed burned out on rap music, which was still Stones Throw's primary focus at the time. "I was looking to do anything to kick start his interest in hip-hop," Egon said in a 2014 *Pitchfork* feature.[66] "We had the chance to do a reunion album of [Madlib's first group] Lootpack. I got them weed, booked studio time, and it fizzled out."

"Cuts like 'Raid' I did in my hotel room in Brazil on a portable turntable, my (Boss SP) 303, and a little tape deck."—Madlib

While Madlib tried to re-ignite his interest in rap music, MF DOOM was going through his own difficulties outside of the Stones Throw ecosystem. The mysterious, masked MC had found a second act to his career six years after the tragic death of his brother and fellow KMD member Subroc in 1993. After achieving cult hero status with his 1999 album *Operation: Doomsday* on Bobbito's Fondle 'Em record label, it seemed like he had a bright future ahead of him in the rap game. But his renewed success was brief—Fondle 'Em folded a mere two years after DOOM's reemergence, leaving his career in a state of free fall.

With both DOOM and Madlib's future's looking somewhat murky, their paths began moving slowly towards a point of intersection. Madlib started making beats for rap albums again, then he name-dropped Dilla and DOOM as two artists he wanted to work with in an *LA Times* interview—marking the first mention of a possible MF DOOM/Madlib collabo.

Egon hoped to use the perspective joint effort as a way to ignite new a creative fire within Stones Throw's star act. Realizing he had a mutual acquaintance who knew DOOM and lived in Kennesaw, Georgia—DOOM's home base at the time—Egon decided to try to make a connection. "I told my friend that Madlib's been making beats and I needed to get them to DOOM to get Madlib back into rap again," Egon told *Pitchfork*.

"I know how I want it to sound, and if you liked how it sounded (on the beat CD), well, take the beat or not. Once it's done, it's done."—Madlib

Egon provided his acquaintance with some of Madlib's earlier work to pass along to the elusive MC. DOOM was blown away by what he heard once he gave it a thorough listen. After some haggling and a few terse negotiations with one of DOOM's managers, the masked rapper flew out to LA for an initial meeting.

Though DOOM and Madlib said very little to one another, it was determined that there was enough unspoken chemistry to pull something off. Both men started recording demos together, marking the beginning of a creative odyssey that would span the next year and beyond. By the summer of 2002, Stones Throw

139

Records announced that the two artists were working on a project with "no title or projected release date."

Having set the wheels of creation in motion, another watershed moment took place when Madlib went to Brazil with Cut Chemist, Egon, and J.Rocc of The Beat Junkies to participate in some Red Bull Music Academy events in late 2002. Inspired by the crazy, incredibly rare records he found during his visit, the trip sparked a creative frenzy. According to Madlib, he was so in the zone during his time abroad that he made entire beat tapes out of single records. "I was digging with Cut Chemist and all them in Brazil," he told *Scratch Magazine* in 2005. [67] "I was pulling out whatever, crazy-ass records, and n****s was like, 'There ain't gonna be nothing on that record.' I made a whole beat tape, they was tripping."

Throughout his stay in Brazil, Madlib's creative spell couldn't be broken—even when his travel companions tried to lure him out to bars, clubs, and parties. He resisted, opting instead to punch out an endless string of beats on his trusty 303. "I was keeping Brazilian time, sitting in my room smoking some terrible weed and sampling shit, while everyone else was out partying and getting drunk," he told *Pitchfork*.

In the aforementioned *Scratch Magazine* interview, Madlib went on to explain that he made the majority of the Madvillainy beats in a hotel room during his trip. Utilizing a laughably bare bones makeshift studio, he somehow created the bulk of the instrumentals for an album that wound up being a landmark release for Stones Throw. "Cuts like 'Raid' I did in my hotel room in Brazil on a portable turntable, my (Boss SP) 303, and a little tape deck," he told *Scratch Magazine*. "I recorded it on tape, came back here, put it on CD, and DOOM made a song out of it. N****s be sleeping, thinking they need all this gear." Stones Throw also noted in a 2004 website post[68] that "Rhinestone Cowboy" and "Strange Ways" were recorded in the same fashion.

Seeing the fruits of Madlib's hotel studio labor proved to be an unforgettable experience for those close to the project. Stones Throw's trusted engineer Dave Cooley—who later mixed the vocals and beats on *Madvillainy* with his carefully trained ear—recalled Madlib's absurd workflow during and after the Brazil trip with awe. "He had hundreds of 2 track beat snippets on CDs," he said in a 2017 interview with the website *Grown Up Rap.* "In one month of reclusive producing he had a CD made up called *100 Beats.* Two weeks later, he had another CD made up called *Another 100 Beats.*"

"I was keeping Brazilian time, sitting in my room smoking some terrible weed and sampling shit, while everyone else was out partying and getting drunk."—Madlib

According to Coooley, Jeff Jank designed custom covers for the CDs—which were given to artists on Stones Throw and used to pitch beats to MCs not on the label. Although the beats included on *100 Beats* and *Another 100 Beats* were likely heard by a slew of non-label artists, many of the instrumentals ended up staying in-house and laying the foundation for several of Stones Throw's most important releases. "Most (if not all) of the material for *Madvillainy,* Jaylib's *Champion Sound,* and I think Dudley Perkin's first album was sourced from that one month's worth of Madlib beats!" Cooley told *Grown Up Rap.*

It's remarkable that such a wealth of material was culled from these two CDs, as many of the beats were freestyled. Samples were rarely tracked—that would only slow down Madlib's furious pace of completion. And his beatmaking pace during the Brazil trip was so manic that even Madlib himself felt many of the *100 Beats* instrumentals were too outside the box for any sort of practical application. "A lot of the beats on *100 Beats,* you can't use, 'cause I'm just fucking around and freestyling," he said in a 2004 interview with *Wax Poetics*.[69] "Some of 'em might be so way out, 'cause I'm just using what I have [in front of me]. Whatever. I don't remember the samples I use. Hell no."

Though Madlib's roughshod, straight out of the 303 method has been questioned a time or two before in interviews, it seems like he utilized this style for reasons beyond mere convenience. After having over-zealous engineers mess up some of his beats during his early years in the industry, the difficult to alter 303 instrumentals seemed like the perfect solution to avoid future tampering. "I don't want people fucking it up making their mix," he told *Scratch Magazine*. "I know how I want it to sound, and if you liked how it sounded (on the beat CD), well, take the beat or not. Once it's done, it's done."

"I never knew you could make an entire album without hooks and have it sound that good. That album showed me that music has no rules."—Danny Brown

Madlib's distrust of engineers is something he has repeated elsewhere, but he did OK some sound alterations to the *Madvillainy* beats from the ever-dependable Dave Cooley. In addition to helping salvage Dilla's *The Diary* many years after his passing, Cooley gained a seller reputation at the Stones Throw for helping several key releases achieve their optimal sound. Cooley seemed to "get" Madlib's vision—often improving the producer's rawest creations with slight tweaks while preserving the integrity of his original beat CD. It's a difficult tightrope walk that few people besides Coooley seem capable of.

A 2005 *Remix Magazine* interview[70] with Madlib and Dave Cooley provides some helpful insight into how the roughest tracks from *Madvillainy* were likely coaxed into being ready for the general listening public. "Madlib likes to shoot from the hip, so sometimes it's a deliberate and intentional choice on his part to go with the most rough-hewn version of a mix he can get," Cooley told *Remix*

Magazine. "But if he and Wolf want to take a stab at making the track boom a little bit more in certain places, that's where I come in." To get a sense of the work Cooley might have put into a single track—which in the *Madvillainy* era was mostly 303 beats recorded to a 16-track Roland VS-1680 digital workstation—take the example of how he used some clever fiddling to make a mono snare drum sound like a stereo drum recording. The process included making a copy of the original SP-303 beat in Pro Tools, boosting the midrange where the snare drum happens in the beat, using the copy of the original to key a gate, putting stereo reverb on the snare gate, and much more sonic trickery that should be read in-depth via the *Remix* article for a fuller understanding.

"They were like, 'Fuck it, I'm done. Madlib started on other stuff, and DOOM, well, you never know what he's doing." —Jeff Jank

With the bulk of the *Madvillainy* beats done after the Brazil trip, it came time for DOOM to lay down some more verses. Though DOOM recorded his lines on *Madvillainy* at the Bomb Shelter with Madlib, both artists have stated numerous times that there was very little interaction during the recording process. "The process wasn't really a big deal," Madlib explained in a 2016 interview[71] with *Red Bull Music Academy.*[72] "We just hung out, went to clubs, got drunk. I'll hand him a beats CD, I go to sleep, he'll work on some music, he'll go to sleep. I'll wake up, I'll make some more beats, listen to what he did."

If the two artists were feeling particularly adventurous and wanted a change of pace, they partook in some psychedelics. "We might take some shrooms together if we awake at the same time, and then listen to the music when it's done," Madlib told *Red Bull Music Academy.*

DOOM recalled the process much in the same way during his

2011 *Red Bull Music Academy* interview. Though the pace of work was often furious due to familial obligations for DOOM, making quality music remained a priority throughout. "I'm staying in LA and I'm trying to get back to my children," he said. "So I'm working as fast I can without sacrificing the quality."

DOOM also confirmed that he and Madlib rarely spent large chunks of time together, sometimes going for days at a time without interacting. "He's always in the Bomb Shelter and I'm up on the deck writing," he told *Red Bull Music Academy*. "He'd give me another CD and I'm writing, and he's back in the Bomb Shelter, so I would hardly speak to him. We might stop and he'll burn one and we'll listen to the beat and then that's it, and then the next two days I probably won't see him."

Much in the same way Dilla and Madlib had a quiet friendship that seemed to transcend the English language, DOOM and Madlib often used music as their primary mode of communicating. "We spoke through the music," DOOM told *Red Bull Music Academy*. "He'd hear a joint and that's my conversation with him. Then I'd hear a beat and that's like what he's saying to me."

Unfortunately, as effortlessly as recording without speaking seemed to be going, the album was almost derailed when a demo tape was taken from Madlib's room in Brazil and leaked online. With online leaks destroying the success of several albums released around the same time, the harsh news was like a gut punch to both artists. They assumed the worst, fearing a disastrous commercial performance for their first project together. "They were like, 'Fuck it, I'm done,'" Jeff Jank told *Pitchfork*. "Madlib started on other stuff, and DOOM, well, you never know what he's doing."

"All that other stuff? Sugar coat. Extra. Totally extra. Stay focused. Cut and dry. The beat is dope, the rhyme dope? Record it, let everybody hear it."—MF DOOM

Despite the temporary setback, the duo trudged on and decided to finish the album. It wasn't long, however, before another potential obstacle presented itself. When DOOM brought the partially finished version of the original album home for a listen, he decided he didn't like how he'd laid down his vocals. This led to a rash and alarming decision. "DOOM took the semi-final material home and upon review decided that he had put everything down with "too much energy" in the vocal takes," Dave Cooley explained[73] in his *Grown Up Rap* interview. "So all those takes were scrapped!"

Known as a reclusive and difficult to pin down artist, DOOM's decision to blow up his vocals and start from scratch likely struck fear into the hearts of many people involved with the *Madvillainy* project. Now, with the gift of 20/20 hindsight, it seems like he made the right decision. "He ended up re-recording the vocals with a super laid back delivery, on a rough mic, and those became the finals…I think to the betterment of the record," Dave Cooley told *Grown Up Rap*.

Scrapping the original vocals to record with a low quality mic seems like a fitting touch for two artists who pride themselves on testing the limits of lo-fidelity recording. "Put the rhyme over it, that's it," DOOM told *Wax Poetics* in 2004 while describing the group aesthetic. "Vocal too loud? Turn it down. All that other stuff? Sugar coat. Extra. Totally extra. Stay focused. Cut and dry. The beat is dope, the rhyme dope? Record it, let everybody hear it."

"I ain't have a record player. I bought it on vinyl just to stare at the album. I stared at it and I just kept going, 'I understand you.'"—Mos Def

From the two-track, cassette deck 303 beats to the re-recorded vocals, it all worked out in the end. Released in March of 2004, *Madvillainy* received an almost instantaneous positive response from both critics and fans. *Pitchfork* rated it a 9.4/10[74], *The Village Voice*

145

gave it an A-, and the album currently holds a 93/100 average[75] score at *Metacritic*. The praise wasn't limited to mere high ratings, as Eric Henderson of *Slant Magazine* heralded the album[76] as a "masterpiece" and said that it " alone validates the artistry of sampler culture."

In addition to critics and fans, the album spoke to many peers. For Danny Brown, whose career had just started when *Madvillainy* dropped, the record introduced a new way of structuring songs and taught him how to be a fearless rule-breaker. "I never knew you could make an entire album without hooks and have it sound that good," Brown told *Complex* in a 2013 interview.[77] "That album showed me that music has no rules. Before that I thought you needed 16 bars and hooks to make a good song."

Others like Mos Def turned to *Madvillainy* for regular inspiration and a sense of connection. Saying that DOOM "rhymes as weird as I feel" in a 2009 video interview with FR Lab, Mos Def went on to say "Dude, I swear to God, when I saw that Madvillain record, I bought it on vinyl. I ain't have a record player. I bought it on vinyl just to stare at the album. I stared at it and I just kept going, 'I understand you.'"

"He'd hear a joint and that's my conversation with him. Then I'd hear a beat and that's like what he's saying to me. And still to this day that's how we do it."—MF DOOM

Since introducing Stones Throw to a broader audience with *Madvillainy*—the label's most commercially successful rap album to date—there has been much discussion of follow-up effort. Madlib told *Red Bull Music Academy* that the duo has 20 tracks recorded, but remains evasive about an actual release date. Though he projected his usual nonchalant attitude about a sophomore effort, he also seemed concerned that a Madvillain project might not be received with as much warmth today as it was 15 years ago. "People are expecting too much and they're complaining about certain things that this

DOOM record isn't going to have anyway, mastering and mixing," he told *Red Bull Music Academy*. "We like our stuff dirty. I think people are on a different level now."

Could the approaching 15 year anniversary in March of 2019 convince the beloved, ever elusive duo of DOOM and Madlib to actually put out an official second release? Though this prospect is unlikely, it seems like they might relish in the reaction such an unexpected stunt might generate. Having described their first album together as being "like a conveyor belt of creativity" in a 2016 interview with *Bonafide*,[78] hopefully they will finalize their existing songs into a formal release and treat their loyal fan base to some new material when March rolls around.

Whatever their final decision, we should always consider ourselves fortunate to have *Madvillainy* to revisit at any time. A remarkable combination of gritty beats and dome-splitting verses, DOOM and Madlib's handiwork still sounds ahead of the curve a decade and a half later.

Let's Take A Moment
and Care for Saba

by Alec Stern

One minute and fifty-two seconds into "American Hypnosis", the eleventh track on his 2016 album *Bucket List Project*, Saba raps "I hated my life until I played the piano". It's a line that speaks about identity; how a single small moment can completely separate one's life into a concrete "before" and "after". In the same way, this is often how we look back on our lives after we lose someone close to us. Like *Bucket List Project*, Saba's newest album, *CARE FOR ME* emerged from a place of grief, and in both cases, it was familial. Even the album's title, stylized in all caps, reads as a plea for rescue from the pain and burden of simply surviving what others have not. It's the sound of someone who's reached the "Acceptance" stage of grief, yet sees none of the clarity that was promised in getting there. But there is something bigger at work with this record, and I could feel it from the first moment I put it on. Over the last several years, I have come to understand that loss is far more complex than most paint it to be. There's more going on than simply grief, and even grief itself has layers of abstruse humanity buried within it. *CARE FOR ME* is unquestionably a record about loss, yet within that simple concept, so much about the experience of life emerges through its cracks.

CARE FOR ME caught me off-guard with its humanity. In returning to it over-and-over again the last few months, I've often wondered if other people see as much of themselves in this record as I do. I've questioned if it could mean as much to people outside of Chicago as it means to our community. I've wanted to know, given the slew of new music available at our fingertips every day, how many people even knew the record existed. It was following these curiosities that led me to want to write this piece. Yet the real reason is that I, like Saba, find writing to be the most effective and cathartic way of working through the thoughts and feelings I simply cannot shake. Something about this record just needed to come out of me, even if I didn't know what that thing was. It wasn't until I was deep into writing, weeks of putting my thoughts on the page, that I came to the realization that in a sense, I had been linked with this record since it's very beginning.

The first time I saw Saba was at the Metro in Chicago on February 9, 2017. It was the second night of Noname's Telefone tour, a celebration of the recent release of the Chicago rapper's debut album of the same name. There are two things I distinctly remember about that show. The first was, despite the album being released only days prior, the entire crowd on the floor of the Metro, comprised of almost all high school and college-age kids, sang along to every. single. word. There is something about a homecoming show, or even more, a concert for a hometown hero as he or she embarks on the road to eventual stardom, that brings out something special in everyone involved. The energy and excitement in that room made it clear: no matter what happened to Noname after this night, she would always represent Chicago proudly, and we in-turn would always have her back. That's just something about Chicago that I know to be true. The second thing I remember about that performance is the tears. Throughout the performance, Noname would drop the mic to her side in order to collect herself; to wipe the tears from her eyes, or to take a much-needed moment of pause. The crowd and I ate it up, and ecstatically cheered every time she did so. It was such a beautifully intimate and human moment to share: all too rare to see from an artist on a major stage. In that moment, she was both the best of us and just like us at the same time, and it was profoundly moving to see how emotional this moment had made her. It wasn't until

149

the end of the set, however, that we learned the true reason for her tears. After performing the album in its near entirety, she quietly approached the microphone, and with a shaking voice, told us that she was sorry, immediately draping the room in a heightened and fragile quiet. The band came together at the side of the stage and looked on as she composed herself. The room was smaller, more approachable now. With a heavy sadness in her voice, she told us about a friend of hers who had died just one day before. Someone she had known for a long time. He had tragically, and senselessly, been killed after a fight on the train. As we all knew Noname, real name Fatima Nyeema Warner, was a born-and-raised Chicagoan, it was clear to all in the room that this fallen friend had been one too. We had lost one of our own, whether we had known him or not. It was then, after a respectful moment of silence in his honor, that she brought out her friend Taj, or Saba, to help her with the final song of the night. The song was called "Shadow Man", and fittingly, it was about a funeral.

Within thirty seconds of *CARE FOR ME*, you hear the words "alone", "awkward", "peer pressure", and "depression". The music itself is hazy, diluted, and reflects the black, white, and grey of the cover photo of Saba in his grandmother's kitchen. As you press play on the first song, "BUSY / SIRENS", the music sounds as if it is waking itself from a slumber. It rubs its eyes and hunches up to sit, and then takes a small inhaled breath before Saba speaks the opening line: "I'm so alone". These words come at you whether you are prepared for them or not, whether you know Saba or not. He's reflecting on friendships, and the awkwardness he feels in his own skin while trying to maintain a closeness with those around him. He even expresses trouble coping with the fans he's gained as a rapper, as it hasn't gotten him any closer to any tangible human connection, despite what his peers all assume. It is here that the central theme of the record is presented, and the tone and content of it come into focus. Saba's friend and cousin, John Walt, or Walter, has been killed. More specifically, he was killed "for a coat". He says the word with utter disgust, as if he hopes to never see or wear one again. The senselessness of someone dying over such an object becomes even more heightened when paired with the words that precede it, as Saba pours salt in his own wound by reminding us all that "Jesus got killed for our sins". As in; Jesus died for Something. My friend died for Nothing. This is hip hop as reflecting pool; songwriting as diary entry and vice-versa. And it's very painful.

Hip hop as a form of storytelling has always maintained two distinct paths for artists to take: one that moves beyond reality, and one that doubles down on it. While there will always be a need for escapism and entertainment in music, perhaps especially for a genre that is rooted in the reality of disenfranchisement and the brutality favoring black communities of America, there will also always be a need for art to reflect the world as it exists. Within this framework, *CARE FOR ME* has emerged as a new masterwork in a long-list of classic rap albums, especially of late with the Obama years, and the reckoning of the post-racial lie that his victory prophesized. Famed Chicago Poet Kevin Coval borrowed Dave Egger's famous title when dubbing it a "Heartbreaking Work of Staggering Genius". It's stunningly cohesive, compelling, and refreshingly bold in its aims and execution. It's remarkably timeless and universal in theme, yet it's sonic pallet is singularly rooted in the sounds of Chicago. But it's the perspective shown on the album, through each of its ten beautifully rendered songs, that gives the record its power and potency. *CARE FOR ME* is a multifaceted exploration of loss, and how intense and excruciating it can be when paired with love. It's about the realities of being black, and being feared, and being lonely. It's about family, and insecurity, and the police, and writing, and smiling. Perhaps above all, it's about young men's lives in Chicago, and how they feel, and matter, whether they live and tell their stories or not. Because for

151

every life passed, there has to have been a life lived.

The record opens with "BUSY / SIRENS", which sets the tone for the feel and stakes of the record right away, it's 5:30 runtime practically an epic within today's landscape of sub-two minute Soundcloud bites. The vibe is slow and downtrodden, yet thoughtful, as we are exposed to the frustrations, anxieties, and depression Saba feels with the people around him. The song's hook is sung by theMIND, who is quickly becoming the Nate Dogg of Chicago's rap scene. His vocals are remarkably distinct, and seem to always act as the perfect complement or counterpoint to the featured artist he is collaborating with. His words are simple and poignant, and his lyrics on "BUSY / SIRENS" contain some of the most profound ideas on the entire record. On the main hook, he sings, "I seen that skies were grey, I hope to God you're safe", in a prescient statement that is both highly superstitious and deeply protective at the same time. In the song's bridge, he sings the following passage with heartbreak, soul, and a palpable hint of bitterness at a reality he knows too well.

"My biggest fear,
is that I have to say goodbye another time.
So I skip town on our moment, hopefully prolonging this.
I don't need nobody new to miss."

This concept, a flip on the idea that it is better to have loved and lost than never to have loved at all, is almost unbearably sad yet completely understandable to anyone that has actually said goodbye to someone in the permanent sense. Those moments of grief and longing, the ones that feel that they might never end, and life will never go back to the way it once was, are the headspace Saba and theMIND are inviting us to with "BUSY". In the world they live in, these moments are all-too familiar, where the prospect of death or imprisonment is a reality for themselves, their friends and their family. "SIRENS", the second piece of the opening track, explores this theme, particularly the concept of being feared by the community and law enforcement simply because of your body: the experience of a woman clutching her purse "'cause of my dreadlocks" or a white person crossing the street "'cause I'm with my friends". Or how the police will automatically assume one is "deservin'" because they "think my cellphone's a weapon". To underscore the record's prophetic and credible worldview, one needs to look no further than Stephon Clark, who was fatally shot multiple times in his grandmother's backyard for the same "misunderstanding" a mere 15 days before the album's release.

The concepts of death and unjust imprisonment as a constant lurking presence continue on the song "LIFE", where the chorus meditates:

"I got angels runnin' way, I got demons huntin' me
I know Pac was 25, I know Jesus 33.
I tell Death to keep a distance, I think he obsessed with me
I say "God, that's a woman", I know she would die for me"

It's one thing to fear death, or to worry about going to jail, but it's another thing entirely to see a systematic force diligently working to make your demise or imprisonment a greater reality. This has been the story of black life in America since the very beginning, with 250 years of slavery, to its modern form of segregation, the growing wealth gap, police brutality, and mass incarceration. These themes are addressed on *CARE FOR ME* in a powerful and ultimately more accessible fashion; by telling a specific story, broader strokes are unraveled. By saying "like a problem won't exist if I just don't exist", he is replacing a statistic for a living, breathing, feeling human being. By saying "a lot people dream until they shit or get shot", he is turning the unnamed and

153

unknown causality into someone who had a present worth living for and future worth dreaming about. It's telling, however, that he ends this line with two words that, when taken together with this context, can sound utterly foreign or chillingly familiar based on the listener's skin color: "that's life."

The suite of songs that come next further detail Saba's complexities, and shed light on his past and present. "CALIGRAPHY" details the way in which so many of us work through our demons; through writing. Saba is a product of Young Chicago Authors, the highly influential creative writing and performance youth organization that has been largely responsible for many of the city's most notable artists of late, including Chance the Rapper, Jamila Woods, Eve Ewing, Malcolm London, and Noname. The city's deep poetry scene is hugely responsible for this recent artistic renaissance period, providing a space for young creatives to express the realities of their lives, something particularly needed in a city like Chicago. Young Chicago Authors sessions famously begin by asking its attendees and students the simple, yet loaded question, "Where are you from?", and on "SMILE" Saba tells us about his life in Austin, Chicago through stories of family.

If you Google Austin, Chicago right now, odds are that the three allotted "Top Stories" on the page will be related to shootings. This is the type of space many neighborhoods on Chicago's South and West Side operate in within the media, both citywide and nationwide. While the South Side is the segment of the city most will mention when discussing gun laws and crime statistics, several neighborhoods like Austin on the West Side struggle with the same issues. In fact, in 2016, Austin held the distinction of the most recorded homicides of any neighborhood in the city. Yet, in terms of coverage, the West Side is rendered rather invisible when compared with the South Side. Same problems, but no attention. Saba sheds light on this later in the album by saying, "we from the part of the city that they barely mention".

Through their very existence, accounts like *CARE FOR ME* are so often what is needed to change these narratives. For places like Austin, and for other largely black neighborhoods around the country, communities are regularly written-off within a larger cultural framework as the sum of their worst parts. But for all the people lost in this viewpoint, the people that laugh, and cry, and dream, and make mistakes like everyone else, tracks like "SMILE" act as vital tributes. Here, Saba attempts to show a more multifaceted take on the place he calls home, by giving small, loving recognitions to his family and the place he grew up. The opening lines of the track are rapped with pride; fittingly, you can literally hear a smile on his lips as the words come through.

"Sweet west side Chicago, two-flat apartment
Red brick and garden, that's been forgotten
Grass all splotchy, vacant lot splotchy, bank account splotchy
And we talk like we from the south"

A few tracks later is "GREY", a title that could easily be the name of the record itself given the sonic pallet and multidimensional, "somewhere in-between" stance of many of the record's ideas that are so often presented as black and white. The song, which ponders some of the pressures and issues of being an artist and the music industry as a whole, ends with a jazzy outro of horns, shuffling drums, and twinkling piano, and a freeform verse that concludes with shouts of "Everything is grey. Everything is grey. Everything." What is most stark about this manic conclusion is how it segues into something completely controlled and carefully presented as the next song begins. Although there are only two proper tracks left on the album, there is a clear moment of distinction happening here, as if the course of the album is about to shift. The moment "PROM / KING" begins, with its ominous and compelling first line "This remind me of before we had insomnia",

155

it is clear that we have stepped into new territory as listeners.

On the date of *CARE FOR ME*'s release, mere minutes before it would be officially available for the world to absorb, Saba took to twitter for one final thought:

"Make sure on the first listen of #CAREFORME you are alone. You have to listen to it by yourself to fully understand".

There is something underappreciated about being alone with a piece of music, especially one that demands as much from the listener as this does. Certain albums or songs are more of a one-on-one conversation than a shared experience really calls for. It's like being at a party, surrounded by strangers and friends alike, but constantly looking for a chance to take that one person aside for a brief moment alone. There is so much humanity in intimate moments like these, and in today's constantly-connected environment, they are more vital to us than ever. Saba is well aware of this feeling, and for creating an album that gives so much, all he asks is for his music to be received with the proper space and care. Even at the album's official listening party in Noble Square the night before the release, all guests were treated to a pair of noise-cancelling headphones rather than the typical loudspeaker setup. I still remember the space I was in when "PROM / KING" began, and even without reading Saba's tweet before listening, I found myself thankful to be alone in that moment.

"PROM / KING" is a masterclass of emotional journalism. It's the centerpiece of the album that takes everything we've heard up to this point, and imbues all of its perspectives, textures, and characters into one succinct, multi-layered, and deeply affecting story. The first time I heard it, when it faded to a close after nearly eight emotionally intense and significant minutes, I could feel that we had just inched one step closer to the apex of what songwriting- storytelling set to beats and articulated through melody and rhyme- can accomplish. Like the best oners, a term that describes a long and intricate scene in a film that is shot, or disguised to appear to be shot, in one fluid take, it isn't until near the end that you realize the enormity of what is unfolding.

"PROM / KING" begins with a flashback to Saba's senior year of high school, and the events that crystalized an eternal bond between him and his cousin Walt. The story is told with equal skill and charm, as well as the happy/sad feeling that nostalgia brings. It has all the hallmarks of a coming-of-age moment: a prom request that isn't reciprocated, risky choices made out of wanting to get laid, an altercation at an after-party, a reunion of family, and so much more. It's the small details, like calling the corsage the croissant, or pretending to send a text when alone at a party, that put you in Saba's shoes as an insecure, searching teen. And it's in his cousin Walter that he finds a true companion and collaborator in music and life. After seven deeply personal and introspective songs about Saba, we are starting to get to know Walt. The most effecting aspect of this song is that with every detail about Walt that is revealed- his dimpled smile, his basketball dreams, his overprotective nature- we become more invested, and the more invested we become, the more it hurts to know what is coming. All of a sudden, theMIND's "I don't need nobody new to miss" makes so much sense in a way it didn't just minutes before.

The song begins with a small heartbreak and ends with a crash collision. What is so tragic is that despite Saba's best efforts (including the John Walt Foundation made in his honor), Walt will now primarily be known for his death, the way so many young black men are, whether their names are put on record or not. That may be why, for all seven-and-a-half minutes of beautifully and heartbreakingly rendered details on "PROM / KING", the one thing we don't actually get spelled out for us is Walt's death, as the song ends with a shadowy recording of Walt's voice. He sings,

"Just another day in the ghetto
Oh, the streets bring sorrow
Can't get out today with their schedule
I just hope I make it 'til tomorrow"

The last line rings and rings, like a telephone call to no one. Spoken from a man whose tomorrows were all cut short, this moment is devastating, haunting, and profoundly moving. It's enormously empowering for Walt to have the final say in this song. It almost leads you to believe that in some other world, he never got on that train, or got in that fight, and somehow lived through it all. It makes it all feel a bit like a dream.

In real life, however, Walt was no stranger to the lurking presence of death, and seemed to comprehend his reality and environment well enough to know that simply hoping for a tomorrow wouldn't be enough to make it there every time. Five minutes into "PROM / KING", a brush-up with death, months before his eventual murder, is detailed. On a cross country phone call with Saba in California, Walt horrifically recounts getting shot at by total strangers. Deeply frightened and searching for logic, Saba questions what he possibly could have done, whose line he must have crossed, to be met with a hail of gunfire on the highway in broad daylight. However, it quickly dawns on him that it doesn't really matter; that where he's from, there doesn't always have to be a "reason" for something like this to happen. Neither of them were safe from the random nature of violence in their hometown. It is then, under the crushing and inescapable weight of helplessness, that Saba says,

"Sometimes I fucking hate Chicago cuz I hate this feeling"

The beat continues, the story continues unfolding, but

everything is different after this line. In an album filled with uncompromised honesty and reflection, this sentiment, performed with tangible defeat, cuts deepest. Perhaps its impact is felt most when considering Saba's larger body of work, most specifically the song most know him for. At this point, it's fair to assume almost everyone has heard Chance The Rapper's *Coloring Book*, and with that, heard Saba's voice, whether they realize it or not. Odds are, you've sung in unison with his voice on the chorus of the album's first single "Angels." The chorus goes:

"They was talkin 'Woo this do wap da bam'.
City so damn great I feel like Alexand.
Wear your halo like a hat, that's like the latest fashion
I got angels all around me, they keep me surrounded"

The power of most choruses comes from their universality. A great chorus is one that could be sung by anyone, regardless of circumstance and geography. However, the magic of this chorus is that there's no mistaking which city is being referenced, yet it's no less inclusive. Chicago is painted on this song as a real city with problems, but one that stands a little bolder than any other. Even being associated with the city is enough to make one feel like Alexander The Great: an invincible, mythic figure capable of wonders. The chorus' last line both reinforces this idea- the surrounding of supernatural forces that propel one forward- while also hinting at the reality of what it is to live there.

If you are from a certain part of this city, you know angels. More pointedly, you know death, and the promise of an afterlife that comes with it. As sung on "BUSY / SIRENS", you know the sight of someone "lyin' where the angels lay", and how that is so often the reason for hearing "sirens on the way". One of the most beautifully rendered aspects of Saba's writing is his duality of perspective: his way of reflecting the harsh truths and emotional weight of the most damning elements of life that are brutally unfair and unjust, while also fighting to perceive these things as building blocks to a more enlightened way of life. That is why his voice, particularly when rapping about Chicago, is so essential. On "CALLIGRAPHY", Saba details an obituary, undoubtedly Walt's, that hangs by the dresser in his bedroom. This memorial, purposefully hung in a place where it could be seen at the beginning of each day, is likely his way of summoning the angels he needs for guidance and strength to continue to live his life in a way that is purposeful, beautiful and true.

Angels appear often throughout *CARE FOR ME*, and Saba raps from the perspective of one of these angels on the album's closer "HEAVEN ALL AROUND ME". After the closing lines in "PROM / KING", there is silence. We are, for a moment, allowed to breathe, to recalibrate, to mourn. What comes next is a faint and hazy stroke of color, which stands out from the greys of everything that came before. We hear a beautiful melody of bells, and before long, a windup of harp strings. It's not unlike the very final moments of *Kid A*, the silence and blissful panorama that follow the album's closing line "and I will see you in the next life". These choices in instrumentation and arrangement that open *CARE FOR ME*'s final song clue us in that we are no longer in Saba's shoes, but in Walter's, who has passed on to the other side.

In "HEAVEN ALL AROUND ME", Walter sees the events after his death unfold, but more specifically, sees all of the people his death has impacted, from the paramedic who tries to revive him, to the friends he desperately wants to touch to convince them, and himself, that he's still there. I'd imagine of all tracks on the album, this one was the most significant to Saba to get right. It's filled with truths he desperately wants to believe- that Walter didn't die for nothing, that he's not really gone at all, that he's in a truly better place now- and by putting it down on wax, he in a way makes it real. That is one of the many powers of making a record: it validates.

CARE FOR ME is a record filled with wisdom, with lessons learned and battles persisted. It understands the complex and messy truths of losing someone- how it's possible for a loss to both push you forward and push you back at the exact same time. It's extremely human in that way, which is why it is already being hailed with the accolades it has received. But more importantly, it already feels like the kind of record that will be tuned to by many in times of need, the kind that changes the course of lives. On "FIGHTER", Saba ends the second verse from the perspective of a girlfriend who, during an argument, says "I know you think you listenin', but you just waitin' to talk." *CARE FOR ME* is one of those albums that hears you while speaking to you. Through these recorded stories, we project our own memories, our own trials, our own environments and loved ones. All of us are constantly in a state of trying to get better, to be happy, to make the most of our lives, and like all of us, this album isn't the product of having overcome in the past tense. Life's not simple like that, and neither is this record. It's all about the process of overcoming.

On February 9, 2017, a few hundred fans in Chicago braved the winter cold to watch Noname perform. In looking back, I cannot believe she actually performed that night, holding in the pain in her heart for her fallen friend. That friend of course was John Walt, who, as fate would have it, was planning on performing with her at that very show. I had never heard of John Walt before that night. For all purposes, to me, he would have been just another victim of a senseless murder, in a city known for senseless murders. But through that show, he became so much more. Although I didn't know it coming in, that night was, in a sense, his vigil.

"Shadow Man", the last song of her set, opens with the following words:

"How do you see me?
How do you love me?
How do you remember me?"

Saba came out to perform his verse on the song, which was written for his uncle: a man who, after being released from years in prison, died in his sleep. He was twenty years old when he recorded this verse, and two years later, would be performing it about his cousin just one night after his murder. At the song's end, Saba and Noname came together at center stage, arms wrapped around one another, peering out at all of us in the crowd. I can't help but wonder how it all felt in that moment, looking out at of us strangers gathered together. After all, they had likely envisioned that night to be one of the best of their young lives. All I know is what I felt being in that room as the lights went up. I felt I had just been a part of something rare in its humanness. I felt a community that had just grown a little more resilient through the bravery of artists we considered our own. It was the feeling of seeing the barely-there rainbow after a storm; a glow in place of shadow. It felt a lot like healing.

I can't shake how surreal it was that that concert happened on that night, in this city. We all left the show with someone new to miss, but more than that, with a new life to remember and celebrate. It was the music of this city that brought us all together, that made this possible. As we stepped out into the cold Chicago air, we could all feel it: there was heaven all around us.

Review: 21 Savage Shows Tremendous Growth On *I Am > I Was*

by Eric Diep

21 Savage's maxim of "I Am Greater Than I Was" is growth, understanding that as an artist and a public figure, you must push yourself to make some changes within.

To be "game changing > clout chasing" is to actively do good in your community with your fame and success. This year, 21 Savage has lessened his creative output to focus on his philanthropy, hosting his third annual Issa Back to School Drive and announcing the 21 Savage Bank Account Campaign to teach kids about financial literacy. With multi-platinum singles ("rockstar," "Bartier Cardi") and a high-profile breakup with Amber Rose in his rearview, 21 Savage continued to stay true to himself and East Atlanta, resulting in his new fans to join him on his leap from street talker to motivational speaker and hitmaker.

The road to *I Am > I Was* was the Saint Laurent Don strategically teasing his album through ambiguous release dates and "forgetting" to drop his album on Dec. 7, but finally coming through on Dec. 21, the weekend before Christmas. *I Am > I Was* is a late contender for Best Rap Album of 2018 simply off 21 Savage's evolution as an MC who sets a high bar for real street rap in the mainstream.

I Am > I Was stands as a much tighter project than Issa in terms of flow and non-skippable tracks, *I Am > I Was* sticks to 21 Savage's promise of "going back gangsta." He has refined the idea by balancing the dark and chilling aura found in his previous projects with mellower backdrops. He chooses to not list his guest features for unexpected surprises, and the A1 players are all here: J. Cole, Yung Miami of City Girls, Offset, Post Malone, Lil Baby, Gunna, ScHoolboy Q, Project Pat, Childish Gambino, and Young Nudy. 21 Savage covers familiar themes – like running in the streets, why he's always rapping about guns, and dealing with his celebrity – and his collaborations strengthen those messages through their loose and organic chemistry.

One of those much-talked about collaborations is 21 Savage and J. Cole's "a lot," which is powered by DJ Dahi production and a sample of East of Underground's "I Love You." Cole, 33, and Savage, 26, may have an age difference, but his thoughts on the very real blessings and curses of his career is universal. Plus, Cole, who has been on a run of guest verses lately, delivers some headline-making lines on fake streams and rappers making memes, as well as empathizing for 6ix9ine's legal situation: "Pray for Tekashi, they want him to rot/I picture him inside a cell on a cot/'Flectin' on how he made it to the top/Wondering if it was worth it or not."

In another major collaboration, 21 Savage and Childish Gambino reflect on the toxicity of the music industry on "monster." Gambino has hinted retiring the moniker altogether, and his verse supports that decision with him rapping, "might pull out, the game so weak." As for 21 Savage, it's one of many moments of introspection, especially since he practices what he preaches. Wealth and notoriety aren't necessarily part of 21 Savage's agenda anymore; he recently took a vow to not wear jewelry and wants to influence the youth to invest in real estate.

I Am > I Was is 21 Savage becoming more of a man. As a teenager, he lived through poverty and violence by becoming numb to the pain. When he raps on "break the law," "My brother lost his life and it turned me to a beast/My brother got life and it turned me to the streets/I been through the storm and it turned me to a G/But the other side was sunny, I get paid to rap on beats," you can't help but salute the changes he's made in his life. On "ball w/o you," a heartfelt track about relationships, he talks about rather having loyalty than love, and on "letter 2 my momma," he showers his mother with praises for raising him as a single parent. It's a constant reminder of his maturity throughout the album, leading by example through his personal experiences.

He also doesn't take himself too seriously. Many of the tracks feature emotive lines that range from his 12-car garage obsession ("Why you got a 12-car garage? /'Cause I bought six new cars") to threats ("The chopper can hit all of y'all/Your brother, your goldfish, and dog) to recognizing his G ("Y'all was in the house playin' Mario/I was sellin' weed and went hollow"). It's what makes 21 Savage such a skilled rapper: he's ruthless, humorous, and deceptively clever when conveying his feelings. The lyrics become instant Instagram captions and tweets, continuing to feed the 21 Savage meme craze.

What also makes *I Am > I Was* such a cohesive listen are the producers. Metro Boomin' only appears twice ("break da law," "asmr") while Kid Hazel, DJ Dahi, Cardo, Wheezy, TM88, Louis Bell, and others give the album more depth. It's equal parts nostalgic and on trend with hip-hop today, where Three 6 Mafia homages ("break da law," "a&t," "good day"), the flute fad ("can't leave without it"), and drawn sword sound effects are all present. Each track attempts at going the distance of showing new sides of 21 Savage. Everyone plays off each other's strength, letting 21 Savage's deadpan delivery and singing be the stars.

I Am > I Was deserves all the recognition for 21 Savage becoming a better version of himself, and it's a much-needed proclamation that he's willing to work on his craft. At 15 songs and 51 minutes long, it's an enjoyable listen with good pacing, filled with the right amount of vulnerability, heartache, menace, and savagery. A year of anticipation and mystery, 21 Savage's sophomore album proves he's a versatile and gifted rapper who

165

has a lot to say.

He'll only make a stronger impact from here.

Album Review: *DAYTONA*

by Zach Quiñones

When Kanye announced via Twitter in late-April that Pusha T's long-awaited album would be dropping May 25th, there was both excitement and skepticism. It wasn't just the controversy surrounding Ye at the time but also the fact that fans had been teased with a new Pusha album since 2013 but left empty handed*. Inclusively, no singles or any attempt at marketing had really been employed for the album.

It wasn't until days leading up to the release did Pusha and his team confirm that the album was indeed dropping and that its title had been changed from *KING PUSH* to *DAYTONA*. The other aspect of the record that was confirmed was the 7-song tracklist. Initial response was a bit of wary and disappointment as many fans felt they were being shorthanded after such a long wait. Regardless, it seemed the wait was finally over and fans were ready to be served up a fresh project from the GOOD Music camp.

In a swift and ruthless 20-minutes, *DAYTONA* slaughters the contemporary music landscape in a fashion that would leave Genghis Khan in awe.

In the current market where the focus is accumulating the highest streams possible, many artists are engaging what has been dubbed "data dumping". This is when an artist releases an album with 18–25 songs in order to loophole the system. It's basic mathematics—an 18-track album is going to get more stream counts than a 10-track album. This lends to record-breaking stream reports but says nothing about the actual quality of the album. Ultimately, these data dumps are the equivalent of a significantly

167

photoshopped and filtered Instagram model.

DAYTONA goes defiantly against the market. A 7-track album that clocks in at a scant 20-minutes, a decision influenced by Mr. West who also produced the album from top to bottom. Ye convinced Push to commit to the daring move under the belief that "if we can't kill you in seven songs, we really don't need to be doing the music."[79] It was quality over quantity. Cut all the fat out and deliver the leanest work of art possible.

From the opening track "If You Know You Know" to its closer "Infared", *DAYTONA* is a carefully crafted wave of ferocity harboring a blitzkrieg of laser sharp raps backed by what is arguably Ye's most expertise production.

Pusha explained that its title represents the "luxury of time"—he can create art at his pace with no mandatory label deadlines to meet. It's also a direct reference to Rolex Daytona watches, which of course are luxury brand watches. The other aspect of this luxury concept is its minimalist presentation, high-end cost (in regards to the samples and artwork), and maximized experience— it may be a 6oz piece of steak, but it's filet mignon cooked up by a Michelin star chef.

Every fiber of *DAYTONA* is given pristine attention; not a single rhyme or sonic movement is delivered without conviction. The sample-heavy production is mean and lean, moving from track-to-track in sleek jolts. If one could correlate that with imagery, it's like Barry Sanders in his prime juking through defensive lines with disgusting ease. In many cases, it almost seems as if Kanye had Push rap acapella then constructed the beats around his vocal performance. It's that seamless.

The song structures play to no contemporary standard or formula but never feel disjointed or messy. Even with obstructive transitions (within and between songs) the overarching groove keeps things airtight. The sonic landscape of *DAYTONA* is a hybrid of the strongest aspects of *Yeezus* and *The Life of Pablo*. Much like Ye needed to experiment with *Graduation* and *808s & Heartbreak* to elevate his production, the aforementioned were necessary to do the same on this project.

Lyrically, it's Push's greatest hits on steroids. The coke raps are there of course and they're home runs but the album offers a lot more nuance and poignant moments than Pusha T gets credit for. "Santeria" for example, Pusha raps with enraged sadness on the murder of his road manager De'Von Picket:

Darken my doorstep, they told me the day's gone
You listening, De'von?
As I'm talking to your spirit, for God's sake
I'm dealing with heartbreak

DAYTONA maintains daunting consistency with quality rhymes that cover a range of topics, themes, and beliefs in organized fashion. What makes Pusha's rhymes rather remarkable is his ability to hit with gut punches and feverish imagery such as on "Baby Come Back" when he remarks on climbing the ladder to success high enough to see "complexions fade".

Lastly, the cover art. Upon its unveiling it unsurprisingly garnered a lot of attention and controversy. It wasn't because Kanye paid $85,000 cash for the licensing fee, it was the fact that it was a photograph of Whitney Houston's drug riddled bathroom in her Atlanta home at the peak of her crack addiction. A lot can be taken from the imagery and according to Push, Kanye stated that "this [the photo] is what people need to see to go along with this music."[80] And after several listens it makes sense.

Crack has terrifying staying power once it infiltrates someone's life and it doesn't discriminate despite its urban prejudices. When taking a step back and examining everything that surrounds the

169

photo, it's quite an awakening. On the outside is an affluent Atlanta mansion but on the inside is a catastrophe of pain. At its soul is a Diva beloved by many. The cover art is all encompassing of what *DAYTONA* embodies—brutal and beautiful. This is what people need to look at when listening to this album.

Rap Analysis:
Eve & Dr. Dre, "Let Me Blow Ya Mind"

by Martin E. Connor

Every once in a while, I get a request from a reader that I absolutely love, because it's a request for me to analyze a song that is criminally under-appreciated. Amy's recent ask for me to take a look at Eve's "Let Me Blow Ya Mind" is one such case. It's not because it's one of Dre's best beats (although it is,) or because it's got a killer hook (although it does.) It's because of the mesmerizing contrast between the simplicity of Eve's rhythms on the one hand, and the head-banging groove she still somehow manages to jam the track full of. Her rhythms on paper would be pretty easy to write down, but—because of how she delivers them—they end up being nearly hypnotizing. This has led to Eve being underrated more generally, because the one thing that she's really good at (riding the beat) is one of the things that musicians and audiences understand the least.

I recently made a rap song where I took dozens and dozens of bars from 100 different songs by 50 different artists, and freestyled through all of them by means of categories that grouped their flows together based on rhythmic similarities. Some rhythms were syncopated, some were on-beat, some were really complicated, etc. Obviously Kendrick was in there, as was André 3000, Notorious B.I.G., Lauryn Hill, Talib Kweli, Nas, and Lil Wayne…no surprises so far. But at the end of the list, who did I find but—Eve! I expected those other rappers with technical reputations to show up, but not her. What did her inclusion among such a legendary group teach me about her rap?

It showed me that Eve's rap taps into some really fundamental facts about rap that many people gloss over, or ignore completely,

171

when discussing the rhythmic elements of rap. The undeniable reality is that most of rap's rhythms will always sound extremely similar to each other (in theory, at least). This is because there just aren't that many different rhythms that rappers can pull off while still meeting all of rap's innate requirements. These requirements include the fact that the song's tempo must be quick/slow enough to talk over, and that the rapper must take breaths every so often. Even within a single beat with four 16th notes, there are only 12 possibilities for separate rhythms. When we expand this to a full bar and its own 4 beats, we are still left with only 240 possibilities. This might sound like a lot—and, certainly, there are more than 240 rhythms in rap's history—but this quick-and-dirty estimation is still very small when compared to the number of different possible rhythms in instrumental musics like jazz. Trumpets, basses, drums, and saxophones obviously aren't constricted by rap's strict requirements around both communication and breathing.

So if there aren't really that many possible rhythms in rap, then how come we never get bored of it?

The answer is found in the amazingly diverse world of rappers' vocal timbres, as well as rappers' varying amount of rhythmic swing. And, unsurprisingly, Eve brings both of those things in abundance on "Let Me Blow Ya Mind."

First, let's identify her lines where the rhythms are fairly standard, and which I was able to find in tons of other songs. These include what I call the 8th note rhythm (which has 2 evenly spaced syllables on every beat), the waltz rhythm (which has a 16th note right before, right on, and right after the beat), and the offbeat rhythm (which is two 16th notes followed by an 8th note.)

First, Eve's 8th note rhythm on "Let Me Blow Ya Mind:"

"WHICH one, PICK one,

THIS one, CLASsic"

I found this in tons of other songs, including Puff Daddy's verse on "Welcome To Atlanta," Lil Wayne's verse on "I'ma Dope Boy," Big Sean's song "A$$," Game's song "Westside Story," Lil Wayne's song "Who Wanna," and a second Game song, "How We Do."

Now, Eve's waltz rhythm:

"a LOT more, than YOU, to GET rid, of ME"

I also found this rhythm on Nas' "N.Y. State of Mind," A Tribe Called Quest's "Vibes and Stuff", "and Kanye West's "'Niggas In Paris."

Lastly, here's Eve's offbeat rhythm:

"EAsy come,

EAsy go,

EVie gon' be

LAS-tin'"

I found this rhythm in a Mos Def freestyle, on Big Sean's verse on "Mercy," Pharoahe Monch's "Body Baby," and André 3000's verse on "Aquemini."

So, for three of Eve's bars from "Let Me Blow Ya Mind," I found 10 other rappers who had 13 of their own songs that used the exact. same. rhythms.

The reason this doesn't sound like rhyme-biting, or plagiarism, is because each of these rappers delivered these same rhythms in their own unique way. They made these rhythms unique—not by changing where the syllables fall and where they don't—but by changing a.) how far behind the beat they are, and b.) how their voices rise and fall as they say them.

For example, let's look at Eve's waltz rhythm again:

"a LOT more, than YOU, to GET rid, of ME"

She pronounces these lyrics in a sharp and staccato manner; she doesn't linger on each syllable, but instead cuts it off sharply... takes a brief pause...and then moves quickly onto the next one. She also says them in a way that is both dismissive and disbelieving, a feeling that she reinforces by mockingly raising her voice to a higher pitch about halfway through. When she pronounces this part, she is also pretty far behind where the drums are falling.

But now take a look at how A Tribe Called Quest raps this same waltz rhythm on "Vibes & Stuff:"

"FROM fat, to SKINny

from FREEda, to WINNy"

Here, Q-Tip's rhythms are a lot more laidback than Eve's. He drawls from one syllable to the next in a smoother, more legato way, connecting them all closely together. He doesn't pronounce each word sharply, but instead maintains an evenhanded voice that remains in a conversational tone. This is how two rappers can have the same exact rhythms, but have completely different sounds and feels to them.

As a second example, take Eve's offbeat flow:

"EAsy come,

EAsy go,

EVie gon' be

LAS-tin'"

Here, Eve positively explodes off the beat on the syllables "ea-", "ev-", and "last," as she says them more loudly, and says them right on top of the beat. This is her hard-hitting Philly flow coming through full force.

In a freestyle on YouTube though, Mos Def finesses these same exact rhythms into something much smoother and mellower:

"STANdin' five

TEN i be

ROCKin it

WHEN i be"

Mos' pronunciation of the words are much less edgy, and much more rounded. He's feeling the full weight of the entire rhythmic phrase, and not just focusing on this 3-note rhythm's first syllable.

We've now gotten to the heart of the matter. Eve's style is so catchy because she takes rhythms that we've been hearing all our lives, and then restyles them into something completely new and super sticky with her swing and with her delivery. I've tried to use this big comparison in order to draw close attention to those defining features of her style. Such features aren't complicated rhythms, like Talib Kweli's signature style, or a super unique voice, like Aesop Rock. Instead, her legendary status rests on her ability to take really simple rhythms, and make them stick in your ear like glue…and pulling off a trick like that just goes to show that Eve really has blown our minds with this song.

Invasion of Privacy
Is Cardi B's Victory Lap

by Lindsay Zoladz

Cardi B did not bite Beyoncé, not literally, but behold the way she sinks her teeth into the pronunciation of Queen Bey's name on "Best Life," the sixth song off her debut album, *Invasion of Privacy*. Like a lot of great rappers, there is an immediate, surface-level joy in hearing Cardi B say things, a culinary zest she can draw out of certain consonants and vowels. "I took pictures with Beyoncé," she growls, "I met Mama Knowles / I'm the rose that came from the concrete in the Rolls." It's a memorable moment on an album overflowing with them, and it is endearing, how awestruck she sounds at the details of her own life. Making Chance the Rapper sound like the least animated person on a track is no easy feat, but Cardi bodies him on "Best Life": A word, out of her mouth, is worth a thousand words. And so somehow it's all there—the struggle, the triumph, the pitbull tenacity with which she is going to hold onto her moment—in the way she enunciates "Beyoncé." She savors it the way Biggie did "Sega Genesissssss." It's the evidence of an arrival.

Instagram star turned rapper to be reckoned with Cardi B came up in such an unconventional, thoroughly modern way[81] that I was not sure we needed something as old-fashioned as a major-label debut album from her—I was not sure this was a format in which someone so quintessentially of-the-moment would still need to thrive. What a delight, to be proved so wrong. Confident and bountiful, *Invasion of Privacy* makes a strong case for its own necessity. It is a victory lap for the things Cardi has already proved she can do ("Bodak Yellow" is here, as is its spiritual sequel, the exuberant "Bickenhead"). But just as thrillingly, it is also

177

a first glimpse of muscles we didn't even know Cardi could flex: She makes a convincing case that Migos need a fourth member on "Drip"; she recruits J Balvin and Bad Bunny for the irresistible "I Like It" (quite possibly a "Despacito" in the making, or at the very least the year's first serious Song of the Summer contender); on songs like "Ring" and "Thru Your Phone," she reinvents the rap ballad as something too forceful to be dismissed as fluff. Though it features a few too many guest stars, *Invasion of Privacy* squanders remarkably little of its runtime. It's not a vibe or a mood so much as a relentless collection of bangers.

Cardi was able to translate her Instagram confessions into bars so seamlessly because the principle of her delivery is the same: She makes a convincing case that whatever she is saying is the most important thing that anyone is saying in the world at that moment. "Bodak Yellow" turned pettiness into something operatic, and her rhymes on *Invasion of Privacy* have that same urgency. The nudes found in a cheating man's text history becomes a matter of life and death on "Thru Your Phone" ("I'ma make a bowl of cereal, with a teaspoon of BLEACH!"), while "Money Bag" becomes a frenzied fairy tale about the glory of being Cardi B. "He can tell from the front I got ass behind me," she brags, emphatically, "and I park my Bentley truck on my Versace driveway."

Much has been made of the scatological shamelessness with which Cardi talks about her own body. "I wanna fart [but] I'm around soo many people in a small room," she tweeted to her 2.7 million followers a few weeks ago; I am not sure how many people were in that room, but I'm guessing the number was fewer than 2.7 million. An early *Fader* profile[82] led with Cardi telling the journalist, in vivid terms, how much she needed to "take a shit"; the first line of her *Rolling Stone* cover story[83] was "Cardi B is butt-naked in the doorway of her hotel room, yelling about her vagina." When Cardi raps about her body, it is sometimes a profession of sexual prowess and desirability ("They remind me of my pussy, bitches mad tight," she says on *Invasion of Privacy*'s opening track, "Get Up 10"). But what feels new and even radical about her perspective is the sense of humor she has about her own body—the kind, frankly, usually reserved for only male rappers talking about their dicks. I have not heard a funnier rap verse this year than the one in the middle of "Bickenhead," which is basically an X-rated Green Eggs and Ham:

> Pop that pussy while you work
> Pop that pussy up at church ...
> Put your tongue out in the mirror
> Pop that pussy while you drive
> Spread them asscheeks open, make that pussy crack a smile

Especially within the pop universe, the (sexual) female body is still almost exclusively described by men, so there's an immense power to the way Cardi boasts and jokes about her own existence within a female body that I don't think we've quite heard since Missy Elliot. Even when she's rapping about looking like a snack (or, more accurately, a whole entrée) it's impossible to objectify Cardi because she is such a complex subject within her own rhymes, because she is so gloriously alive within her own skin.

"Ain't no more beefin', I'm just keepin' to myself," Cardi raps on "Best Life," "I'm my own competition, I'm competin' with myself." Some might hear it as a swing at Nicki Minaj (who makes a similar claim on her 2012 single "Come on a Cone"), but if you're not quite as quick to read everything one successful female rapper says as a shot at another successful rapper, it just as easily reads as an homage. Too many people have tried to manufacture beef between the two of them, but it's impossible to deny that Nicki Minaj's previous success has macheted a path for Cardi—and Cardi, to her credit, seems aware of that.

Still, *Invasion of Privacy* pulls off a few feats that none of

179

Minaj's three albums have been able to: It is able to fuse the soft and hard sides of Cardi into a coherent whole. On songs like, say, The Pinkprint's "Grand Piano," Minaj has a tendency to indulge in a mawkish sentimentality that gives fuel to her more sexist haters who believe, as Peter Rosenberg infamously said, that her softer, poppier songs mean she can't also create "real hip-hop."[84] Given this, one of the most impressive things about *Invasion of Privacy* is how Cardi has found a way to make her ballads (the songs about heartbreak that would traditionally be interpreted, simplistically, as "softer" and more "feminine") hit with a force that make them difficult to trivialize. "Thru Your Phone" crackles with visceral anger, while the Kehlani collaboration "Ring" wields its defiant vulnerability like a Louboutin heel to the neck.

It is a failure of imagination to assume that Cardi B's triumph is necessarily a loss for Nicki Minaj, who is rumored to have new music coming out later this year. "Ain't a bitch in my zone," Minaj rapped six years ago, on her second record, "In the middle of nowhere, I just feel so alone." Now, at last, she's not. Cardi's rise has forced us to recognize new trajectories of success, new stories—and so it feels unsuitably old-fashioned to assume that there can still be only one successful female rapper at a time. I am curious to hear the kind of music Minaj will make when she's not the only female rapper in her zone; the challenge just might make her sharper than ever. And anyway, neither she nor Cardi should get too used to being the only female rapper in the pop world for very long. *Invasion of Privacy* is likely to inspire many more.

At the end of a whirlwind weekend during which everyone—from Oprah to Erykah Badu—seemed to be paying their respects to Cardi B, she appeared as the musical guest on Saturday Night Live. During her second song, the bouncy, melancholy single "Be Careful," the camera pulled out to reveal that, as it has been rumored for months, Cardi was indeed pregnant. It was an elegant, calculated reveal, reminiscent of Beyoncé herself, who famously announced her own pregnancy during her 2011 MTV Video Music Award performance. Cardi, as ever, has proved to be an astute student of televised spectacle.

On SNL, Cardi worked within her limitations. She is still a bit hesitant as a live performer (although it's understandable why she would have been especially nervous that night, given what she was disclosing) and on stage her flow can sometimes feel over-practiced rather than instinctual. And yet, as she finally revealed her secret in her own time, it was hard not to be moved.

Back when the pregnancy was still just a rumor, plenty of armchair skeptics criticized Cardi's decision to have a baby at such a "pivotal" moment in her career: Was she squandering her success? And yet there's something quintessentially Cardi about it all, the blunt reminder of the facts of the female body, the yearning for traditional milestones ("I wanna get married, like the Currys, Steph and Ayesha shit," she raps on "Be Careful") even as she carves out her own unique path. It was a complicated image: There she stood alone in bridal white, as though marrying herself and her own ambition, glowing with the promise of a family even as she rapped a bitter song about a partner's infidelity. Cardi B became famous by presenting herself as an open book, and yet her power in that moment came from how much control she had over it all, how carefully she'd orchestrated the timing and the staging of this reveal. Perhaps the best way to protect against invasions of privacy, Cardi B has taught us over the past year, is to become the writer, director, and star of one's own life.

Notes & References

54 Maas, Emily, "Mac Miller Turned to Drugs After 'Blue Slide Park' Criticism," Billboard (January 29, 2013) https://www.billboard.com/articles/columns/the-juice/1535980/mac-miller-turned-to-drugs-after-blue-slide-park-criticism

55 Chesman, Claire-Donna, "Mac Miller, Brain Surgery & Learning to Slow Down," DJ Booth (August 10, 2017) https://djbooth.net/features/2017-08-10-mac-miller-brain-surgery

56 Phillips, Yoh, "Mac Miller, 'Faces' & Why We're Attracted to Artists Killing Themselves," DJ Booth (August 2, 2018) https://djbooth.net/features/2018-08-02-mac-miller-swimming-album-review

57 Chesman, Claire-Donna, "Mac Miller Scores a Heavenly Battle for Peace on 'Swimming'," DJ Booth (February 3, 2015) https://djbooth.net/features/2018-08-02-mac-miller-swimming-album-review

58 Reichard, Raquel, "Bad Bunny is the trap en español rapper collabing with all your faves," The Fader (March 21, 2018) https://www.thefader.com/2018/03/21/bad-bunny-latin-trap-interview

59 Lopez, Julyssa, "Reggaeton Pioneers The Noise Are Coming Together for a Rare Reunion Show at New York's Red Bull Music Festival," Remezcla (2018) http://remezcla.com/music/rbma-festival-new-york-the-noise-reggaeton/

60 Ortiz, Muñiz, J, Jorge "'Boricua Guerrero' marca historia del reguetón," El Diaro de San Juan (July 28, 2008) https://www.pressreader.com/usa/el-diario/20080728/281908768921610

61 Cepeda, Eduardo, "Tu Pum Pum: As Reggaeton Goes Pop, Never Forget the Genre's Black Roots," Remezcla (2018) http://remezcla.com/features/music/tu-pum-pum-1/

62 Ortiz, Muñiz, J, Jorge "'Boricua Guerrero' marca historia del reguetón," El Diaro de San Juan (July 28, 2008) https://www.pressreader.com/usa/el-diario/20080728/281908768921610

63 Dominguez, Tony, "15 Reggaeton & Hip-Hop Collaborations You Probably Forgot About," Remezcla (2018) http://remezcla.com/lists/music/hip-hop-reggaeton-collabs/

64 Khal, "Everything You Need to Know About the Girl Behind the 'Cash Me Ousside' Meme," Complex (February 7, 2017) https://www.complex.com/life/2017/02/cash-me-ousside-how-bow-dah-meme

65 Smith, Dianna, "'Cash me outside' teen from Boynton nursed her mother through chemo," Palm Beach Post (February 9, 2017) https://www.palmbeachpost.com/entertainment/cash-outside-teen-from-boynton-nursed-her-mother-through-chemo/ihuBqx1BFi56bWXyO9sboL/

66 Weiss, Jeff, "Searching for Tomorrow: The Story of Madlib and DOOM's Madvillainy," Pitchfork (August 12, 2014) https://pitchfork.com/features/article/9478-searching-for-tomorrow-the-story-of-madlib-and-dooms-madvillainy/

67 Mason, Andrew, "MAD SKILLS: MADLIB IN SCRATCH MAGAZINE," Scratch Magazine/Stone Throws (May 8, 2005) https://www.stonesthrow.com/news/2005/05/mad-skills

68 "PHOTOS: MAKING MADVILLAINY," Scratch Magazine/Stone Throws (March 1, 2004) https://www.stonesthrow.com/news/2004/03/making-madvillainy-photos

69 Alapatt, Egon, Eothen, DiGenti, Brian "BLUNTED ON BEATS: MADVILLAIN INTERVIEW IN WAX POETICS," Scratch Magazine/Stone Throws (February 8, 2004) https://www.stonesthrow.com/news/2004/02/blunted-on-beats

70 Murphy, Bill, "PHANTOM MENACE: REMIX MAG INTERVIEW WITH MADLIB AND ENGINEER DAVE COOLEY," Remix Magazine/Stones Throw (May 5, 2005) https://www.stonesthrow.com/news/2005/05/phantom-menace-remix-mag-interview-with-madlib-and-engineer-dave-cooley

71 Mao, Chairman, Jeff "Madlib (2016)," Red Bull Music Academy (2016) http://www.redbullmusicacademy.com/lectures/madlib-2016

72 Mao, Chairman, Jeff "DOOM," Red Bull Music Academy (2011) http://www.redbullmusicacademy.com/lectures/doom-lecture

73 Horowitz, Matt, "Interview: Dave Cooley," Grown Up Rap (September 12, 2017) https://grownuprap.com/2017/09/12/interview-dave-cooley/

74 Pemberton, Rollie, Sylvester, Nick, "Madvillain: Madvillainy," Pitchfork (March 25, 2004) https://pitchfork.com/reviews/albums/5579-madvillainy/

75 "MADVILLAINY by Madvillain," Metacritic (March 23, 2004) https://www.metacritic.com/music/madvillainy/madvillain/critic-reviews

76 Henderson, Eric, "Review: Madvillain, Madvillainy," Slant Magazine (December 17, 2004) https://www.slantmagazine.com/music/madvillain-madvillainy/

77 Nostro, Lauren, "Danny Brown's 25 Favorite Albums," Complex (October 1, 2013) https://www.complex.com/music/2013/10/danny-brown-favorite-albums/

78 Nagshineh, Alex, "Cover Story: Madlib (ft.DOOM)," Bonafide Mag (October 26, 2016) http://www.bonafidemag.com/cover-story-madlib-interview/

79 Hahn, Bryan, "Pusha T Breaks Down "DAYTONA" On New "KingPush Radio" Beats 1 Show," HipHopDX (May 25, 2018) https://hiphopdx.com/news/id.47001/title.pusha-t-breaks-down-daytona-on-new-kingpush-radio-beats-1-show

80 Snapes, Laura, "Kanye West paid $85,000 to use Whitney Houston bathroom photo on Pusha T album," The Guardian (May 25, 2018) https://www.theguardian.com/music/2018/may/25/kanye-west-paid-85000-to-use-whitney-houston-bathroom-photo-on-pusha-t-album

81 Zoladz, Lindsay, "Bloody Slippers: The Fairy-Tale Come-up of Cardi B," The Ringer (September 21, 2017) https://www.theringer.com/2017/9/21/16345124/cardi-b-bodak-yellow-career-rap-rise-nicki-minaj

82 Kameir, Rawiya, "Cardi B Did It Her Way," The Fader (June, 2016) https://www.thefader.com/2017/06/22/cardi-b-cover-story-interview

83 Spanos, Brittany, "The Year of Cardi B," Rolling Stone (October 30, 2017) https://www.rollingstone.com/music/music-features/the-year-of-cardi-b-200589/

84 Frank, Alex, "Peter Rosenberg on Nicki Minaj's New Music: "She's Potentially the Greatest Female MC of All Time"," The Fader (April 22, 2014) https://www.thefader.com/2014/04/22/peter-rosenberg-on-nicki-minajs-new-music-shes-potentially-the-greatest-female-mc-of-all-time

Part 3
FRESH PERSPECTIVES

Hip Hop Writing in 2018

by Gary Suarez

In the U.S. and abroad, no genre matters more today than hip-hop. While still centered around American cities and urban centers, its listeners reside everywhere a streaming platform can reach. The Billboard charts depend on rap, as do Spotify's global charts. Short of the Country Music Awards, no televised awards show could stay relevant in 2018 without it.

Despite this music's international appeal and adoption, far too often the hip-hop conversation seems confined to its country of origin, with special dispensation given to Toronto as if some Major League Baseball expansion team. Such myopic discourse leaves burgeoning scenes around the world, as well as nations with long-running rap traditions, in states of artificial self-containment even in our digitally democratic age. While Twitter bozos ranked Jay-Z albums every other week in an exponentially mundane and fruitless pursuit, Latin trap poured out of the Caribbean, Korean rappers conjured massive fanbases, and UK drill shook London to its core, to cite but a few examples. Journalists representing those regions and or otherwise connected to those communities helped to raise awareness online, with some publications more or less devoting themself to the sounds booming through their streets.

Nonetheless, hip-hop writers felt compelled to talk about Drake, and Nicki, and Kanye, and Travis. In a year characterized by its steadily downsizing media climate, during which we saw gutting layoffs and more than a few shutdowns, few could truly blame the remaining desperate outlets for mining the superstars and their respective myriad dramas for every last click. Decades from now, academics will at least have extensive documentation and corresponding commentary of what Cardi B did on Instagram in a given week.

Still, writers did the damn work, and some did it exceedingly well. Shrewd critics at outlets like *DJ Booth* and *Vibe* thrived within the margins of commercially acceptable content, elevating listicles and hot take essays from the perfunctory doldrums of the formats. Even *Pitchfork*, a publication regularly and, at times, unfairly derided by many for its critical takes on rap releases, acknowledged the need for more dedicated attention by creating a whole new vertical devoted to this music and its artists, helmed by an African-American editor and predominantly populated by writers of color.

As hip-hop singles topped the Billboard Hot 100 chart more weeks than any other song, media outlets, including many traditionally perceived as white, appeared to focus more of their attention on this music and the surrounding culture. Those mainstream moves put rappers on magazine covers and in year-end list roundups, presenting these artists to wide readerships and a potentially greater overall listenership. While rap music assuredly benefited from the broadness of the coverage, it led to more than a few raised eyebrows and, in a number of cases, censure from those arguably closer to it.

Cringeworthy opinion pieces, social media gaffes, and less objectively offensive works elicited the now all too familiar bouts of fleeting outrage. Yet it also prompted some editors and writers in hip-hop journalism to ask existential questions of the field and the craft. Speaking for outlets that had long catered to the music and to African-American artistry, several lamented that the acts they covered devotionally or otherwise faithfully had abandoned them for *New York Times* interviews, *Vanity Fair* profiles, and Forbes exclusives. The migration of rap music criticism away from progressively vanishing reviews sections towards the platforms of mostly white YouTube personalities leaves grizzled veterans and eager new jacks with deep concern over the industry's future.

While it would be naive and ignorant to dismiss these issues outright, they inadvertently cloud our appreciation for the abundant musical bounty of 2018. Whatever your preferred flavor of hip-hop, from lyrical boom bap to shouty SoundCloud bangers and everywhere in between, there was no shortage of material to enjoy. Every week, streaming platforms added scores of new releases--singles, EPs, albums, mixtapes--from major label signees and aspiring newcomers alike. All that music provided continuous infusions of ideas that fueled rap journalism and criticism, and the clamor for greater diversity by both readers and writers yielded some truly great results.

Donald Glover's "This Is America" Is a Nightmare We Can't Afford to Look Away From

by Tre Johnson

Donald Glover may be done making things for you to enjoy. His newest single as Childish Gambino, "This is America," joins the second season of his FX series, *Atlanta* ("Robbin' Season"), in showcasing a darker, more sinister vision than anything he's done before. Both works take his audience on a macabre journey through a nation where entertainment is more important than justice. People are dying in "This Is America," but all they want us to do is sing and dance. It's an upsettingly vivid illustration of the Faustian bargain that black America makes on a regular basis, trading our bodies for our expression and freedom.

Directed by Glover's longtime collaborator Hiro Murai, the video for "This Is America" opens with an act of horror: Glover shoots a hooded, handcuffed black guitarist execution-style, and a couple of schoolchildren rush in to drag his body offscreen. More children join Glover to dance around the massive warehouse where the video takes place as more and more chaos unfolds. The setting evokes Michael Jackson's 30-year-old landmark "Bad" video, which made use of a similarly abandoned city space to grapple with internal conflicts about a black artist's placement in society. In "This Is America," cars are set ablaze, a man drops to his apparent death from a balcony, and Glover mercilessly guns down a joyful church choir. The children dance unfazed all the while, each time bearing a different type of witness to what's happening. A child is the one to handle Glover's weapon after each shooting, and it's children who sit in the rafters above, recording the bedlam with their phones. Our normalization of racist violence has come at the cost of not only black lives, but black innocence.

Like several other notable works of black American art in recent years, "This Is America" is about absorption. Onscreen and in real life, the black body gets exposed to so much terror and injustice and keeps going. How does the black body endure, and in what ways or spaces is it allowed to live out its emotions? Beyoncé's *Lemonade* used the body as a diary of past pains and potentially redemptive experiences. *Get Out* showed us the price of a body that is literally inhabited by the constant white gaze. Lena Waithe's *The Chi* on Showtime has reminded us of how often black people – particularly children – are asked to absorb the dangers of America and still required to be happy. *Black Panther* is about a hero who has the ability to absorb the violent energy thrown at him and reflect it back.

But this is America, and while there are no superheroes here, Glover's video calls back to the long history of black folks coming up with ways to barter our physical existence for a slice of the pie. It's meant trafficking in our pain to get paid even a little, a dynamic steeped into our conjoined history with America. Throughout the video, he acts out a familiar tightrope walk for many hip-hop artists who have found success through revisiting painful experiences. "Get your money, black man" is sage advice that has been passed on through generations. Glover keeps dancing as he talks about the relationship between materialism, blackness, consumption and exploitation.

"This Is America" reflects the desire to use every one of our available platforms to punch at America's conscience. So we keep recycling our trauma into art, which mainstream America then consumes and judges on the same scale as black entertainers' less burdened white peers. That tension has been at the heart of countless pop-culture flashpoints: Kendrick Lamar losing the 2014 Best Rap Album Grammy to Macklemore; *Lemonade* losing

189

2017's Album of the Year Grammy to Adele's *25*; the dramatic Oscars finish between *Moonlight* and *La La Land* in 2017. It bears repeating that blackness rarely gets the liberty of being free from its circumstances, while the rest of America gets to sit back and be entertained by us. Glover forces us to look at exactly who we are as a result.

With *Get Out*'s Sunken Place, Jordan Peele gave a name to the desperate, gasping, hellish depths that surround Black America – a place that so many of us are trying to escape while others seem to dive and wallow in it. There's an echo of this image in "This Is America," which closes with Glover running frantically in the dark with indistinct people in close pursuit. After a breathtaking four minutes of violence, somehow this moment is the most terrifying of all. Why are they trying to capture him: for causing so much destruction, or for revealing the truth about our country? As the mob closes in on him, the thought occurs that his captors plan to return Glover to his scripted role in a culture where the black entertainer isn't a mirror, but a toy. This is America. Shut up and dance.

To Be Seen Is to Be Heard:
Visibility Is No Longer an Option

by Yoh Phillips

Beyoncé was one of the first high-profile rule-breakers to break free from album release tradition.[85] In an age of oversharing and leaked intel, she operated with the secrecy of a vigilante cleaning up crime in Gotham City. December 13, 2013 will be remembered as a redefining hour for an industry that's historically slow to embrace change.

The unannounced approach of her self-titled, fifth studio album is often what Houston's queen is championed for, but what I will remember about that day is going into my job at Olive Garden and seeing my co-workers crowd around iPads and iPhones to watch her new music. They weren't playing the album as a work of audio, but viewing the visuals for each song. To be seen and to be heard were equally a part of the *Beyoncé* experience.

In contrast to this innovative method that was moving the needle, 106 & Park had little over a year left before their final cancellation. The days of hosts Free and AJ, Julissa and Big Tigger, and Terrence J and Rocsi were receding memories of ancient afternoons. As the final countdown-format series standing in a post-YouTube world, BET's 14-year staple was like the last Blockbuster left after the arrival of Redbox. What was once a celebrated shortcut to unseen premieres, hip-hop titans, and exciting newcomers was now a dated detour.

When the environment shifts, the creative climate adjusts to complement the transition. Look no further than 1981, when music as a visual medium was strongly affected by the launch of MTV, a gift to a generation entering the '80s. Initially, the cable network promised a service airing music videos for 24 hours, which

191

was an enticing offer during a period where such a possibility was unheard of.

In a 1982 promotional advertisement filmed to attract potential investors, J.J. Jackson—the late MTV VJ—stated, "This is an age group, a generation, that has expressed itself through its music. It's grown up with television and if you want to reach these young adults talk to them through music. Reach them on the channel they were born to watch."

Jackson, who was one of five famed VJs that helped introduce the network in its infancy, made music television sound like a birthright for Generation X. The motto "I want my MTV" allowed what was made for them to be *claimed* by them. It was their intersection of music and media, no one else's. The platform proved capable of being more than just a voice, unlike radio. MTV could be the face of progression, showing the faces of those ushering in a new age of music and entertainment.

An opportunity to be seen is what vehicles of visibility like *American Bandstand* (1952), *Soul Train* (1971), and MTV offered. The platforms to spawn from their bridge between artist and audience were instrumental in television becoming a medium for music introduction. Hip-hop doesn't grow into a global wildflower without *The Arsenio Hall Show* (1989), *Yo! MTV Raps* (1988), and *The Fresh Prince of Bel-Air* (1990) turning the small screen into a stage for representation. They broke barriers between art, culture, and consumerism that accelerated rap's unique voice, visual swagger, and striking attitude within the mainstream market.

Michael Jackson doesn't become the King of Pop without moonwalking during *Motown 25* while performing "Billie Jean." Hype Williams doesn't capture the magic of hip-hop's Jiggy Era without music videos increasing the stock of artists. Countless other moments of cultural significance go unseen, unnoticed, or are simply nonexistent without a vision for visual outlets. MTV cultivated the demand that got the gears turning for video series, but the power of its influence was dated by the generation just acquiring Walkmans, VCRs, and cable television.

That's why MTV's 2017 attempt to reboot TRL was a nostalgic trainwreck. It was an old show for a new audience who wasn't born during the boom that brought their dominance. MTV was not the channel they were born to watch.

Ironically, the combination of social media's celebrity access and the mobile model of smartphones has lead to a modern version of MTV's 24-hour station. What television platforms used to provide isn't necessary now that Instagram, Twitter, Snapchat, and YouTube function as modern alternatives. The artists of today have adapted to a dawn where disconnecting is a form of invisibility. Before, being seen increased the probability of being heard by a wider audience. In 2018, the vehicles of visibility play an imperative part in building and maintaining an audience.

The value of music videos changed forever after MTV's launch, and it's no coincidence the visual art form suffered as albums sales plummeted, budgets dried up, and their function as televised billboards failed to increase attention around a release. Recently, as of the last few years, there's been a resurgence in the power and lasting impact of music visuals as a form of creating mass attention. Drake's ability to pick singles has always been a strength, but with the release of *Scorpion*, the Toronto juggernaut displayed an understanding of music video spectacle that boosted the album's omnipresence.

Karena Evans, the 22-year-old director who has been behind the best videos of Drake's career, deserves credit for the album's record-breaking success. The videos alone brought a sea of attention toward the popular pop star that has had an impact on his 2018 commercial dominance. Visibility has long been Drake's superpower, and in 2018, he's had his strongest visual presence ever.

JAY-Z followed in his wife's footsteps and created a contrasting visual companion[86] for his latest and best post-retirement album,

4:44. The Brooklyn-born rap genius and his pop goddess partner have mastered creating a visual language that communicates the excellence of their music.

Weaved throughout *4:44*'s footnotes, *Lemonade*'s poetic cinema, and the superb "APESHIT" is an understanding of how, in a time where visibility can be curated into an unforgettable experience, they have perfectly entered the post-MTV age ahead of many of their contemporaries. It's not simply about shooting grandiose videos but finding the middle ground between two mediums able to converse as one.

Twenty-two year old Tierra Whack understands social media and what it means to hit the pulse of being seen in order to be heard. The madness of releasing a 15-minute visual project through Instagram is a method that only a child of the internet would consider. Whack's 2018 debut album, *Whack World*, is fit for the microwaved attention spans of the Instagram-era of artist discovery. If Vine was still around, she would already be a star.

Fifty-year-old Will Smith is more than twice the age of Tierra Whack, but he is also adjusting to this phase of clip-based content with ingenious vision and present-day awareness. Smith is a rare elder of the old school who has managed to complete a full social media resurgence through consistent and thoughtful videos that succeed with substance for what they lack in length. Instagram has been Smith's medium of choice since December of 2017. The account functions as an ongoing, day-to-day diary, providing his 22 million followers with sage wisdom, fatherly humor, and refreshing entertainment.

Elders often face scrutiny for being out of touch, but the successful rapper turned pop culture icon is a leading example of how to gracefully live in the now with acceptance instead of resentment.

Joy is what Will Smith deposits in the culture's bank of content, a stark contrast to how Kanye West has utilized his social currency. West, much like Smith, is a master of visibility. Outbursts, antics, exceptional work—any and all forms of publicity have been used by the Chicago-born controversialist. Over the last 21 months, under the Trump administration, West has become an ugly caricature of the man hip-hop believed they knew. Yet, in the midst of destroying his legacy and the dwindling whatever goodwill he has left with the public, he's still seen success.

Kanye's latest single, "I Love It" with Lil Pump, debuted at No. 6 on Billboard's Hot 100 and reached No. 1 in Canada, Finland, New Zealand, and Sweden. The music video—executive produced by Spike Jonze, Kanye West, and Amanda Adelson—was premiered during the 2018 Pornhub Awards, and has already amassed over 190 million views. He is no longer the trainwreck that's hard to look away from, but the heavy smog that you can't help but inhale. By leaning into the absurd and ridiculous, and doing it visually, West has scored his biggest hit in years.

With an influx of content the visual saturation is no different than the audio saturation, and so going shorter, creative, and concise is now the name of the game. Visibility is about communicating with the present in the spaces where the conversations are already being had. Frank Ocean building a staircase throughout the duration of his 2016 visual album *Endless* didn't receive much, if any, fanfare. It wasn't the kind of video that goes viral, especially considering its Apple Music exclusivity. The lone video release from his critically acclaimed album *Blonde*, "Nikes," is a similar case. Selectivity to where and how you want to be seen is a creative decision, but one that severely limits reach and the prospect of going viral.

Emmanuel Maduakolam recently wrote an excellent editorial for Hypebeast[87] on how TV has become the new radio for rising artists looking to expand their reach. Shows like FX's *Atlanta* and Issa Rae's *Insecure* are programs that turn music from emerging acts into the soundtracks of their series. Essentially, MTV wanted to make a channel that merged radio and television, and now that ethos has entered the pop culture.

Dreamville's EARTHGANG recently had their new, Arin Ray-assisted single "Stuck" featured in a recent episode of *Insecure*. Prior to its release, the Atlanta duo took their talents to *COLORS* and premiered a previously unreleased record, entitled "Up." With over a million subscribers, the German YouTube live performance series is one of the best visible platforms for emerging artists. In just the last week, esteemed names like 6LACK and Jay Rock appeared on the blossoming forum for artist discovery.

Soon, *COLORS* will be required during an album rollout like joining the cast of Everyday Struggle or being interviewed on The Breakfast Club. If you consider the popularity of *Bless The Booth*, reaction videos, viral challenges, NPR's Tiny Desk, and late night hip-hop favorites like Desus and Mero, the options to be seen are broad and crucial when considering how navigating these spaces are building bridges between artists and audiences.

In his excellent op-ed on Kanye West and white freedom, Ta-Nehisi Coates poetically takes readers back to his upbringing in 1980s Baltimore. He described discovering the myth of Michael Jackson through classmates due to the lack of cable in his household and parents whose radio selection wasn't fixated on stations playing the latest and greatest in pop music. It reads like a fable, almost impossible to believe there was a time where the royal highness of our world was only witnessed through imitation dances and stories of red jackets and werewolves. But that speaks to the limitations that still existed, separating people from pop culture.

Coates crystallized a time much different than the now. Before, it was possible to be big and still invisible to many. In 2018, there's no excuse to not be visible. Even The Weeknd, who built his brand on mystery, has ditched the mysterious persona. The music industry has long been headed toward pivoting to a visual-dominated medium. Today, it takes more than just great songs to be heard. It takes imagination, collaboration, and great presentation.

It takes being seen.

Visibility isn't an option, but a requirement in the days where WiFi is free at McDonald's and the camera is always facing you. Everyone is watching.

Why Can There Only Be One Dominant Woman in Rap?

by Kiana Fitzgerald

**"I heard these labels are trying to make another me /
Everything you're getting, little hoe, is because of me."**

Nicki Minaj delivered this pointed jab on London On Da Track's "No Flag," which dropped last August. Her whole verse is a thinly veiled Uzi aimed at an up-and-coming female rapper, and not just any new girl—one who bears a striking similarity to her. Everybody with a working brain did the math: light-skinned, physically enhanced, beautiful, theatrical bars, from around the way in NYC. It's gotta be Cardi B, right? Doesn't matter either way, because that's what the internet ran with.

As this assumption spread far and wide, Nicki took to Twitter and insisted no, it was not about Cardi, that she had written the verse well before Cardi really started taking off. But it was enough to convince people that something was brewing. Weeks later, G-Eazy dropped his Billboard Top 10 single "No Limit" featuring ASAP Rocky and Cardi. "My career takin' off, these hoes jogging in place," she rhymed. "Swear these hoes run they mouth, how these hoes out of shape?" She then drops an indisputable bomb: "Can you stop with all the subs? Bitch, I ain't Jared."

It wasn't long before she was visiting the Breakfast Club for the inevitable interrogation all contributing members of the culture must face. The conversation took a turn for the obvious and Cardi was barraged with a series of questions about the "No Limit" verse and its intended target. "You and Nicki don't have a beef do you?" asked Charlamagne. "No," Cardi replied flatly. Charlamagne pressed further: "Got you. She's just not your cup of tea?" Cardi was visibly flummoxed but kept cool, stating the two had talked and that was that.

The next month, October, Migos dropped "MotorSport" with both Nicki and Cardi, and promptly had everybody thinking the two had subbed each other on the same damn song. The song in which Cardi literally says: "Why would I hop in some beef when I could just hop in a Porsche? / You heard she gon' do what from who? That's not a reliable source." The words themselves apparently weren't enough, as speculation of a bubbling beef continued. For the record, before the song dropped, the two had both been spotted jamming to one another's music, Cardi tweeted lyrics to Nicki's "Win Again," and Nicki tweeted a seemingly heartfelt congratulations when Cardi's "Bodak Yellow" hit No. 1 on the Billboard Hot 100.

"I feel like people wouldn't even be satisfied if me and her was making out on a freaking photo," Cardi told *Complex* that October. "I feel like people just want that drama because it's entertaining." Meanwhile, Nicki addressed the beef rumors in a now-deleted string of tweets, saying that men in the hip-hop community are pushing animosity on female rappers. "These are men in our culture who simply refuse to let it go," she tweeted. "They don't do this to male M.C.'s."

She's right.

Dreezy, a female rapper out of Chicago, says she's constantly dealing with outsiders reaching to stack her against someone else, purely because of gender. "I always feel like I'm getting compared to other females," she told *Complex*. "It's kind of stupid because they don't do that to the male counterparts. They all coexist, you feel me?" Elaborating, she pointed to how men have been moving together in the past year. "I think last year might have been one of the years that we had the most collab tapes from artists," she said. "But when it comes to females, it's like the pit of death, like crabs in a barrel. We gotta fight for the top type of stuff."

Oakland's Kamaiyah feels like beef between women is manufactured by men, as Nicki stated. "You see all the men are widespread in every lane, in every sector," she began. "They don't do that. What it is, is that the men are messy and they make the females go against each other. Men be like 'Ahh, that bitch ain't fucking with you.' So now you're high, you're like, 'Fuck that. These hoes ain't fucking with me. I'm that bitch.' Now nobody wanna get along because everybody wanna be 'that bitch.'"

The relationship between men and women in hip-hop reflects the relationships found inside and outside of the general workplace. According to research[88] conducted by the Harvard Kennedy School in 2015, "men behave in a sexist manner towards women in order to remove them from male-dominated spaces, regardless of social status"—an approach called social constructionist theory. The study continues by bringing evolutionary theory into the picture, which explains how sexist behavior is "in response to a threat to a male's position in a social hierarchy." As the gender that largely built hip-hop, men have free reign in the genre and—consciously or subconsciously—want to keep it that way. One way this plays out is, when women are pitted against each other, they're occupied and out of the way, ensuring they take up as little space as possible.

Elizabeth Mendez-Berry, a hip-hop critic during the '90s, says the belief that there could only be one dominant woman started way back when. "There was a strong sense that there was only room for one woman in the game at any given time," she wrote me via email. "Or at least one type of woman, so it was Kim or Foxy. There was definitely a moment with Missy and Lauryn and Kim and Foxy and Eve, but I'd say that was the exception rather than the rule."

Whether it was an anomaly or not, the '90s era gave us "Ladies Night," the 1997 feminist anthem disguised as a Lil' Kim album cut remix and *Nothing to Lose* soundtrack feature. In addition to Kim, Missy Elliott, Da Brat, Angie Martinez, and the late

Left Eye were featured on the track. When *Complex* spoke with Missy in January,[89] she reminisced about the collaboration coming together. "To see so many strong, powerful women come together: No egos, and everybody just having fun," she said. "It seemed like every woman out there came out and supported that record and that moment. I would hope to see that again at some point before we leave this Earth."

After "Ladies Night," there wouldn't be another chart-topping, mainstream rap collab between multiple women in the '90s and early 2000s. Missy would duet, so to speak, with another female MC, but the numbers seldom ventured past two. Later, post-2010, songs like Ludacris' "My Chick Bad" remix with Trina, Diamond and Eve would bring the female-led posse cut back to mainstream. But it took some time to get there again.

Looking back, you can pinpoint the moment when female rap took a hit and things shifted: Missy Elliott got sick. Lil Kim went to jail. Left Eye died. And according to Frannie Kelley, co-host of the Microphone Check podcast and producer of the women-focused music podcast Good As Hell, it got more complicated from there. "Trina was sort of moving between labels," Kelley said. "She was still around, playing shows, but she wasn't in the album release cycle conversation. Latifah gets into movies, Da Brat starts doing radio. All of this shit happened in a five year period."

Kamaiyah remembers things the same way, and figures that the dwindling number of female rappers might be why things have ended up so restrictive today. "The numbers of female rappers went away, so it made it easier for it to make it look like it was only room for one," she said. "Because if you are the only one, then you have this mentality that there can only be one." Kamaiyah's thoughts mirror a 2012 George Mason University study[90] on gender issues and their impact on organizational culture and performance. Research revealed that women are less supportive of other women in conditions where they are both underrepresented in a workplace and feel there are only a few opportunities for advancement. In other words: The smaller the space for women to succeed, the more likely they are to turn on one another for success.

Let's apply that to hip-hop. Once the leading cast of female rappers dwindled, the space for women in rap restricted by default—if there are fewer women rapping at a prominent level, there's less room needed for them. That tightened space in the rap landscape was the perfect breeding ground for competition.

Kelley recalls who was there when the dust settled after the pool of female rappers shrunk. "Into that gap comes Nicki [Minaj]," she explained. Nicki, who crossed over from Young Money's resident female MC to international pop star. Nicki, who passed up Aretha Franklin just last year for most Billboard Hot 100 hits of any female artist, ever. She's been in the game now for a decade and—despite her current, highly observed absence—she's working just as hard as she was when she first popped up, pumping out quotable, chart-dominating features while she readies her upcoming album. If she hasn't reached it yet, she's on her way to legit icon status in pop culture, through her style, personality, and of course, bars. She redefined what it means to be a female rapper, and did so in such a major way that it affected every woman entering the game after her. "Everybody that kind of comes up and around her, gets compared to her," Kelley said.

Kid Fury, host of the wildly popular culture commentary podcast The Read, says the Nicki comparisons new female MCs are faced with are unnecessary and unfair. "Women are completely treated differently when it comes to rap," he said. "They're not even allowed to like, stick a thigh through the door before somebody is like, 'Who is this bitch trying to come in here and rap that isn't Nicki Minaj?'"

Nicki's presence in rap is so commanding that any woman who tries to follow her is immediately questioned by her army of online fans, the Barbz. Bbymutha is someone who has been dragged into the pit of Nicki comparisons. The Chattanooga rapper released a song called "Rules" last year that generated buzz on social media and YouTube. In addition to praise, it brought about confusing feedback. "People were trying to tell me that I should've sold it to Nicki," she said. "And I'm just like, why would I have done that? Why? People take what I say the wrong way. I was just like, 'Nicki couldn't have made a song like this.' And I said that because it came from a personal place."

Kid Fury recognizes that women are pushed to compete in ways that men aren't. "As competitive as rap is, men aren't given the space to feel threatened by one another like that," he said. "As many of them can rap over the same beats, have the same colorful dreads, have the same jewelry and piercings and tattoos, and talk about literally the same thing—all this music sounds the same right now."

According to Frannie Kelley, the mechanics of the rap industry allow this kind of duplication to happen and still lead to viable success for artists who are not so original. "The industry throws resources at middling, mediocre, pointless men, and refuses to throw money at women unless they have proven themselves on a level well past reason," she said. "And yet they've built this entire fanbase and brand for themselves, and a body of work."

The crux of what is wrong with this game can be explained by, of all people, Chris Rock. To paraphrase him: true equality is the ability to be equally as bad as white people, or in this situation, men in general. Men are afforded the ability to be morally flawed, but they'll still get a deal, chart high on Billboard, and maintain an undying fanbase. Women can be pristine, spit the hardest bars in the room, be funny AF and/or ooze sex appeal, and will just get a toenail in the door. Men are consistently gallivanting about on tour together, and dropping joint albums left and right; women, meanwhile, are encouraged to stay in their separate lanes, when they're not being asked to specifically go after each other on wax.[91] Women like Nicki and Cardi, who are both so badass and dominant that they have the world confused about how to handle them at the same time.

If art imitates life, life imitates art. The patriarchal inequities we're currently debating as a society (primarily via the #MeToo movement) are displayed front and center in our female hip-hop stars' jockeying for pole position. The patterns that have taken ahold of society as a whole represent what we're seeing in hip-hop. Men want their territory, and they're both surreptitiously and overtly encouraging women to take each other out of the equation so they can keep it. They do this in order to remain confident in their place, and of their own abilities. Women end up aiming to best each other because they know space alongside men is limited. Competition equals survival, and nowhere is that more true than hip-hop. If the way women are positioned in society at large is any indication, a new era of female rappers will still be duking it out long after Nicki and Cardi lay down their mics.

Nothing Lasts Forever:
The Rise and Fall of Kanye and Drake

by Bijan Stephen

Nothing lasts forever, and the salient feature of dynasties is that they come to an end. Kanye West and Drake have been figuratively warring over the airwaves for about a decade now, with neither party—nor their affiliated hip-hop constellations—quite ready to give up the battle for control of the summer. Winning that war means winning the year: Nothing goes quite so well with hot weather as a hot beat, and these two have them in spades. The rivalry came to a head this year with the G.O.O.D. Music release of Pusha T's sublime *Daytona*, almost entirely produced by West, and Drake's messier *Scorpion*.

On "Infrared," Daytona's last track, Pusha makes the rivalry explicit: He follows up on a relatively old beef,[92] accusing Drake of relying on a ghostwriter for some of his lyrics. (It's important to note that the beef—between Lil Wayne's Cash Money label, which hosts Drake, and the Clipse, which granted Pusha T his entrée into rap stardom—began, in 2006, over who wore the A Bathing Ape brand first.[93] It's that old, and that petty.) Drake responded with a couple of anemic diss tracks, "Duppy Freestyle" and "I'm Upset," in which the pop star variously announces he's in shock at Pusha's audacity and is thinking about buying a semiautomatic pistol and a bulletproof vest. As many have noted, "Infrared" was a feint: Pusha fired back with "The Story of Adidon," which featured a picture of Drake in blackface on the single's cover, made digs at Drake's father and mother, and revealed that the rapper was hiding a child. The beef was ultimately quashed by J Prince, the legendary CEO of the equally legendary Rap-A-Lot Records, but it seems that Pusha and Kanye have won the summer again.

205

The theatrics, which took place in May, may have generated some excitement, but Kanye and Drake share a larger problem: Their time in the spotlight as the kings of rap and pop, respectively, appears to be coming to an end. Even as Kanye attempts to solidify his position as rap's preeminent auteur with a spate of G.O.O.D. Music albums, and Drake moves to secure his legacy with *Scorpion*, both seem to have missed their slide into irrelevance. Hip-hop is a young person's game; so is pop. A new class of unaffiliated artists, working in the shadow of these two giants, have been awaiting their turn in the spotlight; this summer, they might be the real winners.

In an aesthetically savvy move, Kanye announced earlier this year that he'd be releasing five albums by well-known artists in the G.O.O.D. Music stable, all produced by him. They included Nas's first album in six years, a collaboration with Kid Cudi, a solo outing from Teyana Taylor, and the albums by Pusha T and West himself, though aside from *Daytona*, the efforts have been mostly unremarkable. Add to this his embrace of Trump and his outrageous tweeting, and it seems that Kanye is grasping at straws. On all of the albums, the production is characteristically his: The samples are heavy and well-chosen, and even where the rapping is weak, they shine. The problem, however, remains: Nearly all of the albums are retreads of ideas that West ran through in the early '00s. It seems his originality has gone missing.

Scorpion, Drake's fifth solo effort, suffers from the same affliction. Yet where the G.O.O.D. Music artists keep it short, Drake goes long: At 25 tracks, *Scorpion* is a tedious and repetitive listen that reprises all of Drizzy's hobbyhorses—anxiety, money, naked need, problems with women, and his perpetual hope for transformation.

A large part of the album has Drake addressing the rumors about his son. "Single father, I hate it when I hear it," he confesses on "March 14." "I used to challenge my parents on every album /

Now I'm embarrassed to tell'em I ended up as a co-parent / Always promised the family unit / I wanted it to be different because I've been through it / But this is the harsh truth now." The album also finds Drake resting on his formidable laurels—animals that lose a fight but don't die limp back home to lick their wounds. "Who's givin' out this much return on investment? / After my run, man, how is that even a question?" he raps on "Survival," *Scorpion's* first track. But a general sense of exhaustion wends its way throughout the album. Drake sounds tired, uninspired, and uninterested in his usual subject—himself.

Meanwhile, younger artists like Cardi B and Rico Nasty have released albums that are quiet masterpieces, innovative and, above all, fresh. There's none of the ennui or ambivalence about success that now feels characteristic of Kanye and Drake, two dudes who have been on top for so long that it's gotten boring; there's a flame in these younger women and their cohort that's been missing since *Views* and *The Life of Pablo*.

Rico Nasty's latest album, *Nasty*, dropped in mid-June, and it is nothing short of a declaration that it's time for the existing order to be upended. "Bitch I'm charged up!" Nasty yells in "Bitch I'm Nasty":

> **Bitches wanna beef, get you burnt up, I am the best, bar none**
> **And I'm screamin', "Fuck Trump! Black girls, stand up!"**
> **Bitch I'm nasty, and I don't give a fuck like, what is classy?**
> **Smokin' on cat pee and my voice is raspy**
> **I know these hoes can't stand me**
> **I'm a black queen in a black coupe**
> **With some black niggas in some black suits**
> **If you run up on us, then they gon' shoot**

It's a thrilling performance that makes *Nasty* one of the best rap albums of the year; even that glancing reference to Trump feels contemporary in a way that renders Kanye's latest efforts to address his presidential fandom so much empty bunk. In "Ye vs. the People," Kanye attempts to explain: "I feel an obligation to show people new ideas / And if you wanna hear 'em, there go two right here / Make America Great Again had a negative perception / I took it, wore it, rocked it, gave it a new direction / Added empathy, care, and love and affection / And y'all simply questionin' my methods"—which only proves he doesn't get it. Nasty's distaste for Trump is rooted in her love of black people, which is itself a political act; Kanye's love of Trump grows out of his inability to process Trumpism as an ideology of real consequence, as something more than aesthetics.

While not explicitly political, Cardi B's studio debut, *Invasion of Privacy*, also boasts a liveliness that Kanye and Drake seem to lack. Released to rave reviews in early April, it's almost explicitly made for the summer. "I Like It," which features the Latino pop star J Balvin, sounds like it was scientifically engineered in a lab somewhere to be blasted at the neighborhood block parties that seem to spontaneously generate when the temperature rises above 80°F. Cardi's having fun. Consider her verse on "I Like It":

Hotter than a Somali, fur coat, Ferrari
Hop out the stu', jump in the coupe (coupe)
Big Dipper on top of the roof
Flexing on bitches as hard as I can
Eating halal, driving the Lam'
Told that bitch I'm sorry though (sorry)
'Bout my coins like Mario (Mario)
Yeah, they call me Cardi B
I run this shit like cardio

Compared to the old heads, the kids are alright.

What's frustrating about Kanye's and Drake's mutual decline are the occasional flashes of brilliance that the two still display. The Kanye-produced *Daytona* is pure old-school magic: It sounds like a classic, and will undoubtedly go down as Pusha T's best album since he and Malice (now No Malice) made *Hell Hath No Fury* in 2006. "This ain't for the conscious, this is for the mud-made monsters / Who grew up on legends from outer Yonkers / Influenced by niggas straight outta Compton, the scale never lies / I'm two-point-two incentivized," Pusha raps on "The Games We Play." Part of the appeal is that Pusha returned to his cocaine-dealing roots and found the ground there fallow and fertile. As a result, the bars on *Daytona* are some of the best of the year, and Kanye's sample-heavy production elevates them to the sublime.

As for Drake, his recent songs "God's Plan" and "Nice for What," both from *Scorpion*, are bops in the classic Drake mold, written explicitly for women ("Workin' hard, girl, everything paid for / First-last, phone bill, car note, cable / With your phone out, gotta hit them angles," he raps on "Nice for What") or for his homies ("And you know me / Turn the O2 into the O3, dog / Without 40, Oli, there'd be no me / Imagine if I never met the broskies," he says on "God's Plan," about his frequent collaborators). The old brilliance is there, the same ease that suffused 2011's *Take Care* and 2013's *Nothing Was the Same* and vaulted Drake onto the top of the charts and the world.

But the world has changed. Both of the genres that Kanye and Drake defined have now moved on as a new generation—people like Cardi B and Rico Nasty and Tierra Whack—comes onto the scene. Over the last two years, a certain self-confidence has been punctured, and music has started to capture the rising sense of alarm, the realization that things might not turn out the way we thought they would. That takes ferocious sounds. If the rappers at the top of the game can't provide them, others will.

How Desus & Mero Redefined Hip-Hop in Late Night

by Dylan "Cinemasai" Green

On February 14, 1981, Blondie's Debbie Harry introduced Funky 4 + 1 to the Saturday Night Live stage. The Bronx group became the first rap act to ever perform on television, their lead MC Sha Rock shepherding a then-unknown culture into the late-night sphere.

In 1989, Arsenio Hall introduced De La Soul as "the hippies of hip-hop" on his eponymous late-night show before the group performed "Me Myself & I," the very song they crafted to tell fans and critics alike to stop calling them hippies. The show's final episode on May 27, 1994, was capped with a huge freestyle session featuring MC Lyte, A Tribe Called Quest, a handful of Wu-Tang Clan members and Guru from Gang Starr, among others.

Fast forward 20 years to March 2009, The Roots become the house band for Late Night with Jimmy Fallon before they all upgraded to The Tonight Show following Jay Leno's departure in 2014.

As hip-hop has grown more and more popular since the Boogie Down Bronx days, it has continued to creep further and further into late-night television. So far, in fact, that premiere artists like Kendrick Lamar and Chance The Rapper have taken to premiering songs via talk shows. Rap performances on late-night TV bring in millions of viewers to shows that a younger generation probably wouldn't care about otherwise; Colbert's given stage time to plenty a rapper, but you won't catch him waiting in line for a papaya juice.

Yet, few things feel as hip-hop within the late-night sphere as Desus and Mero turning the internet into their own personal bodega stand.

Both Desus Nice (born Daniel Baker) and The Kid Mero (born Joel Martinez) are Bronx natives. Desus had a literature degree from College of Mount Saint Vincent and a shitty social media job for an accounting firm. Mero worked as an aide at a junior high school and would spend off hours playing Call of Duty and hanging outside the bodega "[hoping] someone would buy me a beer," as he told *Rolling Stone*[94] in 2015. To vent their frustrations and get some jokes off, they both took to Twitter, a social media clout-building decision that eventually led them to television.

The comedy duo has been tearing up the airwaves at Viceland since October 2016, turning the two-man Uptown act they perfected on shows like Uncommon Sense and the Complex web series Desus vs. Mero and their Bodega Boys podcast into the self-dubbed "Number one show in late night." The pair work within the confines of many other late-night shows: they riff on current events and gossip on and off of the internet before they interview an "illustrious guest"—who, of course, receives a rainbow over their head with a message of their choice. (The earliest guests got rocks, which have apparently appreciated in sentimental value). There's no live performance element, but it's their approach to—and reverence for—hip-hop as a whole that makes the show resonate with the entirety of the culture.

Beyond interviewing rap and rap-adjacent stars from Rae Sremmurd and Jean Grae and Quelle Chris to Fat Joe and Method Man, Desus & Mero's entire approach is rooted in the bare-knuckle joking and jumped turnstiles culture that birthed hip-hop in the first place. No matter the guest type—rapper, entertainer or politician—every question comes from a place of honesty and passion; fandom that can't be faked. Mero's boisterous personality is the live version of the all-caps mixtape reviews he used to write for *Noisey*. (This is still the best Danny Brown review[95] I've ever read in my life.)

211

Stylistically, neither of them dons a suit; they stunt in streetwear and the freshest sneakers and Timbs and regularly sport merch from underground rappers like Your Old Droog and Conway The Machine, among others. Every guest signs their big wooden table, which is adorned with graffiti. They may be on my TV and computer screen thanks to Vice Media, but hearing them jump between flaming Trump, hot basketball takes and cracking on DJs Envy and Akademiks brings me back to the days when I'd listen to my barber take on the world while trimming my fade.

In April, I took my first trip to the Apollo Theater to see their 5 Borough Tour. Their opening DJ had the entire upper deck swag surfing before the duo even stepped onto the stage. When they arrived, both men were flying their respective Jamaican and Dominican flags, with Desus turning his back to the crowd to reveal a red silk Diplomats jacket. The Harlem applause was deafening. Mero commented that he'd never watched Showtime at the Apollo as a kid because he didn't always have cable. "You gotta rub the stump, it's tradition," Desus replied. In his fresh white Timberlands, Mero walked over to his co-host and humped the stump. Endless laughter. The Bronx-bred Bodega Boys had conquered Harlem and delivered an Apollo experience I won't soon forget.

Making it on TV and retaining an edge is no easy task, especially as a representative of hip-hop. For every Atlanta or The Chi that does hip-hop culture proud, there are a dozen shows like The Mayor or The Get Down that don't make the cut. Desus & Mero are the physical manifestations of The Roots playing Fishbone's "Lyin' Ass Bitch" as Michele Bachmann walked across the Tonight Show stage, and the overt diss to Arsenio that De La Soul slipped onto De La Soul Is Dead. They're the synthesis of Cipha Sounds and Russell Peters by way of a corner store cypher. This shit is in their blood.

They're not the first hip-hop presence on late-night TV, but they're definitely the most potent and relevant, and they did it by being themselves.

Get the Bodega Boys their Emmy already.

The Rise of the Rap-tor: Inside Hip-Hop's Complicated Relationship With Hollywood

by Shawn Setaro

In the summer of 2000, Dr. Dre and Snoop Dogg headlined the Up in Smoke Tour. The packed bill was bookended by Eminem (in what may have been one of the last times in his life that he opened up for anybody, anywhere), and a mini-reunion of the surviving members of NWA.

Right before Ice Cube's solo set during the tour's Boston-area show, the host of the night decided to hype up the crowd. "Do we have any Ice Cube fans in the house?" he asked. "How many people saw *Boyz n the Hood?*"

While introducing a rapper by mentioning a movie may seem odd at first, it's a good bet that many of the people in that crowd knew Cube not as the firebrand MC on "Fuck tha Police," "AmeriKKKa's Most Wanted," or "Check Yo Self," but rather as Doughboy or *Friday's* Craig Jones. Even 18 years ago, Ice Cube had already largely transitioned from being just a rapper into an actor.

And he was far from the only one. Many of Cube's rap peers like Queen Latifah, LL Cool J, and Will Smith were at that point more recognizable for their onscreen roles than their rhymes.

As time went on, the trend only increased. A 2017 study[96] by Dr. Tia Tyree of Howard University showed that the number of rappers starring in movies went from a total of five throughout the entire back half of the 1980s to 36 in 2002 alone.

This is not unprecedented. Comparable rises have happened before with related professions. Singers, after all, historically have not been shy about being on camera in other situations. Whether it was Frank Sinatra's golden arm, Diana Ross singing the blues, or Dolly Parton working 9 to 5, there's a long list of vocalists on the silver screen.

"If you look back at the history of things, singers have made good transitions to acting," *The Hard Way* director John Batham told *Jet* back in 1991. "There are emotional ties between singing and acting."

For Ludacris, the answer is a lot simpler—he was comfortable around cameras.

Luda's acting career began when John Singleton, impressed by the rapper's music videos and personality, asked him to audition for 2003's 2 Fast 2 Furious after fellow rapper Ja Rulex backed out of the film.[97] When I reach Ludacris on the phone, the radio DJ-turned-rapper-turned-actor is very clear about how important his video experience was in his new career.

"Half of the battle is being comfortable in front of the cameras, in my opinion," he says. "That can do a lot for someone when they're just starting to act. You have to get used to that before you can really focus on your crap in the first place. It makes it a little easier transitioning just because [musicians] are already very used to cameras being in our faces and being able to fully dive into our art."

Fredro Starr of Onyx has been acting since before his group's 1993 debut album came out. His career includes parts in everything from *Save the Last Dance* to *Moesha* to *The Wire*. To Fredro, the same qualities that made him a successful rapper helped as a thespian—timing, a knack for performing in front of live audiences, and, most importantly, being outgoing.

"To be a good rapper, you definitely don't wanna be a shy person. That's the first rule," he explains. "You have to be ready for the spotlight."

"HALF OF THE BATTLE IS BEING COMFORTABLE IN FRONT OF THE CAMERAS. YOU HAVE TO GET USED TO THAT BEFORE YOU CAN REALLY FOCUS." - LUDACRIS

But all of this doesn't explain how rappers got to appear in so many films in the first place. The practice really took off in the early 1990s, with the rise in popularity of the "hood film." As a way for projects like *Menace II Society, Juice,* and *New Jack City* to give the viewer a sense of veracity, moviemakers turned to casting rappers, either in bit parts or sometimes even as leads. This was, Dr. Tyree points out, similar to the way films of the Blaxploitation era used pro football players like Jim Brown and Fred Williamson to "authentically reflect the Black urban experience." Tyree, whose interest in the intersection of rappers and film dates back to a middle school viewing of *Krush Groove*, says that both football players and rappers act as a kind of shorthand to the viewing audience.

"At that time, football players had a lot of credibility in the black community," she explains. "They were looked up to in the black community. They're powerful forces, not only in physical presence but in what they were doing outside of the football field. So it's easy to say, 'I want to utilize you as a tool. I have a movie role, and you can help me create a shortcut.' Because movies are only a certain finite period of time. The quicker I can get my audience to understand my character, the faster I can get them engrossed into my story. When I see Ice-T on screen, from his lyrics I know that he is a bad, street guy, and that's exactly who I'm trying to convince the moviegoer that this character is. So by putting Ice-T in that place, I create a shortcut for the moviegoers."

The scholar says that you can see that kind of shortcut almost everywhere. With the exception of a handful of what she calls "elite rappers" like Ice Cube, Queen Latifah, and Will Smith, most MCs end up playing a version of their rap persona. The most commonly cast artists were what Tyree describes as either "hardcore" or "party" rappers—which she found corresponds to playing, respectively, bad guys and good guys in film.

"Unfortunately, black men who were rappers in this Hollywood system were stereotyped, really playing to these extremes," she says. "Either they were good guys—the party rappers, the fun rappers; or they were the bad guys—the gangster rappers and the hardcore rappers. This dynamic is what made the rappers work in the Hollywood system."

Xzibit, who has gone from rapping to hosting the successful TV show *Pimp My Ride* to acting in projects like *Empire* and an *X-Files* movie, says he was offered a bunch of "stereotypical shit" when he first started appearing in films, and turned it all down. "You could always be thug No. 1, thug No. 2. But give me something with some bones and some meat to it," he says.

When Common decided to give acting a go ("I started trying to play piano and do other things and nothing felt natural, so I went to an acting class and it changed my life," he remembers), he had a different experience. He says that he almost didn't land his first role—one that remains a favorite of his to this day—as Sir Ivy in the 2006 film *Smokin' Aces* specifically *because* he was a rapper. Writer/director Joe Carnahan didn't want the MC's rap personality to come through onscreen.

"He definitely was not looking for me to be the persona of Common that he already knows," the Chicago rapper recalls. "I didn't want to work with directors that thought, 'I want to work with this dude because he's a rap artist.'"

According to Common, honing his skill as a storyteller in songs like "Testify" is what got him ready to appear in front of the camera. And in turn, acting has made him a better writer.

"With what we do with storytelling as writers, it allows us to be able to dig into characters and what the story of a person's life may be," he reveals. "I think acting took me deeper into the empathy and understanding of humanity. It was another angle to tackle it from as an actor. When you write, you use your imagination and your experiences, whether it be things you experienced or things around you. But in acting, you take a story that's already there and a character that already has certain elements and pull from experience that you may or may not have had. The beauty of it is you do research, so it takes you even deeper in some instances in understanding empathy and what a person is."

Krondon, a veteran MC who recently got his first major acting role as the villain in The CW's Black Lightning, found that even more than writing his own material, it was penning songs for rappers like Snoop Dogg that prepared him for being onscreen.

"I've been able to write for some of the best and biggest names in music," he says. "And in order to do that, I had to put myself in those shoes, empathize and sympathize completely, and role play, in order for them to actually take the songs and use them and stand behind them—and, in some cases, like Snoop Dogg, go publicly and say, 'Yeah, this guy did that.' It prepared me [for acting], and I didn't even know how much it would prepare me."

And Krondon's longtime friend Xzibit sees a very direct connection between writing rhymes and acting.

"It's just an extension of what I was already doing in music," Xzibit explains. "You're telling stories. Some people take their environment, some people take other people's experiences, and put them into rhyme. The same thing with acting. You have to pull from a place that's not necessarily your everyday life, and that's how you have to build your characters. [That's] what every performer should do."

Phonte Coleman, a rapper and singer best known for his time with the Durham, North Carolina rap group Little Brother, agrees. The rhymer, who lately has made the transition into voiceover and acting work, sees a huge overlap between the two art forms.

"The reason why I think so many rappers are able to make that transition into acting is because rapping pretty much is acting," he says. "Every time you get behind a mic, you record a verse, you're capturing a performance. It may not be, 'To be or not to be,' but it definitely does involve getting into a character of some sort. You're playing some version of yourself, and that is acting. So I think that's why so many rappers are able to make that jump. The transition is seamless."

"EVERY TIME YOU GET BEHIND A MIC, YOU RECORD A VERSE, YOU'RE CAPTURING A PERFORMANCE. IT MAY NOT BE 'TO BE OR NOT TO BE,' BUT IT DEFINITELY DOES INVOLVE GETTING INTO A CHARACTER." - PHONTE

It is not automatic, however, that being a good rapper (or ghostwriter) means you will be a good actor onscreen. Dan Charnas was the co-creator of VH1's *The Breaks*, which chronicled a group of young people striving to succeed in the burgeoning hip-hop industry of 1990. Casting the central character, an aspiring rapper named Ahm (ultimately played by actor Antoine Harris), led to a disagreement with the show's co-creator Seith Mann.

"When we first went into this, I was very sure of myself in the conviction that rappers tend to be very good actors because there was something endemic to the experience of being a hip-hop MC and doing videos," he says of the show's casting process. "Seith was of the conviction as a director that he'd rather have an actor first and a rapper second. And this was a point of contention between us at first because I'm like, it's so much easier to teach a rapper to act than an actor to rap. What I discovered is that Seith was absolutely right, and I was wrong."

Despite that, the show used a number of rappers in roles both central (Method Man, Afro) and peripheral (Phonte Coleman,

219

Torae). The program's auditioning experience, though, left Charnas with a tempered view of rappers' potential to move into the acting world.

"MCing is a skill, and to do it well you have to be gifted or practiced. Acting is very much the same," he sums up. "There's very few people who are gifted. Most people get to it via practice. Thinking that you can only go to rappers and get a good pool of actors is like trying to catch lightning in a bottle, to use a horrible cliche."

Once Xzibit started acting, he quickly realized that, as long as he was popular, the people making the films he appeared in didn't care whether he was a good actor or not. He learned the hard way by watching one of his early roles, alongside Ice Cube in the 2005 film *XXX: State of the Union.*

"I looked at that movie and I was like, Wow, that fucking sucks really bad—my performance, anyway," he remembers. "So I was like, I gotta take this shit seriously. Because of the popularity I had at the time, I knew they were putting me in the movie because it was putting asses in the seats. They don't care if I do well or not. They just fucking wanna get their bottom line."

In her study, Tyree points out that in recent years, it is mostly those who already have plenty of practice onscreen who have been taking most of the movie roles. It's in marked contrast to the early 2000s, where dozens of rappers per year were ending up in films.

"The elite rappers have become staples in Hollywood," she explains. "They are trusted now that they can be a little bit more versatile. When we need someone to be in this space between hip-hop culture and Hollywood, we know that these few rappers can do it well. So there's no need to search for that one rapper that's doing something great because we've achieved the few we need."

But the trend of rappers acting will continue, she believes, for the same reason most things in America happen: the almighty dollar.

"This is about movie making and money making," she closes. "Blackness and hip-hop culture have always been commodified in U.S. culture. When you can take blackness and hip-hop culture and translate into the big screen, you're going to see and find success. Hollywood has proved that by consistently casting rappers in film over a 25-year period. It's voyeurism and it's a desire to see and understand blackness that allows rappers to find their place in Hollywood."

Today's Fun Hip Hop Is Good, But It Needs A Deeper Message (Sometimes)

by Amir Ali Said

Trap music, modern-day "R&B", and drill music are cool. I listen to it. Whether I'm at a party, out with friends, or at home alone, it gets regular spins. I enjoy the music just like most of my generation. The music sounds good, it makes us dance, and we have a good time. But that's the thing, that's all it does. When the song is over, and we're waiting for the next song, what did we actually hear? What new thing did we learn? What did we get? Most of the time we didn't get anything besides a good beat and a few clever lines. In other words, we haven't learned anything new and there was no real message besides partying and debauchery. But hey, we're just having fun, right?

For me, that distinction isn't mutually exclusive. We can have fun and learn at the same time. I've grown up playing sports, running through park sprinklers, and attending parties while still learning. Life itself is a constant learning process, and music has always been a big part of that. And lest we forget, embedding a powerful message in the music is one of the most important features of African-American (Black) music. In the '60s, '70s, and '80s, fun music was played at parties and most of it still had a message. The same could be said about a lot of hip hop music of the '90s. Each generation in these eras were by and large committed to making music that was both entertaining and informative. But I don't think that a similar parallel can be drawn with my generation, as the bulk of artists in my generation are not focused on making music with a strong message.

When you consider the previous generations that came before mine, it appears that my generation is the first group to make fun music (music with very little substance or staying power) almost exclusively the primary goal. In the '60s and '70s, musicians like James Brown, Stevie Wonder, and Nina Simone all made music that was enjoyable. People danced and had a good time to it, and when the song was over, they also learned something. In this way, they got a better return from the music of their generations. Songs like James Browns's "Say It Loud – I'm Black and I'm Proud," Stevie Wonder's "Superstitions," and Nina Simone's "Mississippi Goddam," were mainstays in the African-American (Black) community. "Say It Loud – I'm Black and I'm Proud," a dope funk song about being proud of your black heritage at a time when black lives mattered little in America, was a crowd pleaser and a commercial success. "Superstition" was another commercial success that had a message. The song largely served as a warning, discussing popular superstitions and their negative effects. "Mississippi Goddam" was a jazz tune Simone wrote in response to the Alabama church bombing in 1963. All of these songs that I mentioned here spoke to the issues of their time and still remained entertaining.

In the '80s, when hip hop began to hit a new stride, the trend of delivering a powerful message with fun music continued. In the early '80s, Grandmaster Flash and The Furious Five released "The Message." While commercially successful, "The Message" served as an authentic take of the struggles in the inner-city. In the mid-'80s, Run-D.M.C. sent a strong message to the world. With their debut album *King of Rock*, they furthered their rap-rock-fusion style, demanded respect for hip hop, and crowned themselves as the kings of rock. In the late '80s, Eric B. & Rakim released their debut album, *Paid In Full*. Featuring Rakim's dense lyricism and Eric B's soulful production, *Paid In Full* not only had a message, it raised the bar of lyricism in hip hop forever.

In the '90s, fun music still had a message. In the early '90s, A Tribe Called Quest released two classic albums. In '91, they released *Low End Theory*, featuring Q Tip's notorious "record company people are shady" line on "Check The Rhime." And in '93, they released *Midnight Marauders*, featuring "Award Tour," "Electric Relaxation," and "Steve Biko (Stir It Up)." Around the same time, Public Enemy was making waves with their infamous "Fight The Power" track. By the mid/late '90s, there was no shortage of music with a message. Nas released his debut album, *Illmatic* in '94, Tupac put out *All Eyez On Me* in '96, and Gangstarr dropped *Moment Of Truth* in '98. Each album was as fun as it was educational.

While I understand every generation will have its own take on music, I believe certain core features should always be preserved. Everyone isn't going to be a revolutionary, and I don't think it's reasonable to expect that. But the vast majority of music makers within a given generation should at least try to make music (sometimes) with messages other than unchecked fun. And using youth as an excuse for not making music with substance is the worst kind of deflection of cultural responsibility. Stevie Wonder was just 22 years old when he released "Superstition." Run and DMC were 21 and 22 (respectively) when *King of Rock* was released. Rakim was 19 when he rhymed on *Paid In Full*. A Tribe Called Quest were a group of 21 year olds when they released *Low End Theory*. And Nas was 20 when he released *Illmatic*. These were young men, just one or two years older than me, revolutionizing music.

There will always be rappers who primarily make so called lyrical music and there will always be rappers who make fun music. But keep this in mind: In the '80s and '90s, lyrical rappers were the dominant group that shaped the overall scope of hip hop. Today, lyrical rappers are the outliers, and the fun rappers dominate the market. So what will be the long-term effects of xan-poppin, lean-sipping, gun-bar ladened music? Every day, teenagers listen to contemporary hip hop and draw inspiration from it. But today's popular hip hop is largely disposable.

At this rate, the future seems grim. If this cycle continues, what kind of music will the next generations create? What will happen to those from my generation who don't learn anything from our music other than fun? Will they be productive, critical thinkers? Or will they be non-productive and ignorant? And what about other forms of art? What effects will today's hip hop have on artists (and their work) who primarily listen to and draw inspiration from hip hop? If hip hop, long a source of information and inspiration, becomes a watered down fun city, what will happen to those people living in at risk communities? And what will happen to pop culture as we know it?

So how do we rectify this situation? Well, there isn't just one answer to that question. But I believe it starts with acknowledging where we've erred as a generation. Then we should try to discover, study, understand and appreciate the history of powerful music that came before us. This does not mean that my generation should look to copy what came before. It means, we should aim to build upon what came before. And this includes incorporating substance just as much as it includes making fun music.

Black Skinhead:
Vic Mensa and The Distortion
of The Skinhead Subculture

by Elijah C. Watson

Black skinhead. Aside from being the name of a 2013 Kanye West song, the phrase has been perceived as oxymoronic. A pairing of words that arguably don't belong together, considering the latter's association with white supremacists and neo-Nazis.

This association wasn't always like this. The skinhead subculture was born out of racial unity, a term used to describe a group of people brought together by fashion and music in London, England in the 1960s. But the subculture transformed into something entirely different following its inception, so much so that the skinhead aesthetic — short hair, boots, a white t-shirt, jeans, and suspenders — became synonymous with white nationalist values.

Recently, a picture of Vic Mensa performing live at New York City's Bowery Ballroom began to circulate on Twitter, with a number of fans comparing his appearance to American History X's Derek Vinyard (famously portrayed by Edward Norton). In the film, Norton is a neo-Nazi skinhead whose violent acts against black people land him in prison and contribute to his younger brother's death.

The black skinhead aesthetic isn't new for Mensa. Last year, he practically wore the same wardrobe seen in the photo for his "OMG" video. There's also an old Instagram post from the video shoot captioned with "Black Skinhead." However, the comparisons to Norton came with this picture, most likely because of Mensa's newfound build and bald head.

But it's fascinating to note just how synonymous the aesthetic and the term skinhead has become with white supremacy, considering both have its origins in black culture.

The skinhead subculture was originally tied to working-class youths in London, England in the 1960s. Considered the first wave, this iteration of the movement was an offshoot of another youth subculture called mod. Skinheads were categorized as such because of their close-cropped or bald heads, but their fashion was inspired by mod as well as the Jamaican rude boy subculture.

Jamaica has a storied history with the United Kingdom, the island country serving as a British colony between 1655 and 1962. Following World War II, a mass migration of Jamaicans to the UK occurred, with many of them filling up vacant jobs throughout the country. Along with sharing the same jobs with British people, Jamaican immigrants also inhabited the same working-class and poor neighborhoods as them. Being in such close proximity to each other the rude boy and skinhead youth subcultures were bound to converge.

Black Jamaicans brought with them music such as dub, ska, rocksteady, and reggae, as well as fashion items such as striped suits, thin ties, and pork pie or Trilby hats — both of which were a part of the rude boy subculture that rose to prominence in Kingston, Jamaica, in the early 1960s. A name used to describe rebellious and violent youth frustrated with poverty and inequality throughout Jamaican shantytowns, rude boys became an integral part of the skinhead subculture.

The look of the skinhead was as cool as it was intimidating. The work boots, straight-leg jeans, trousers, suspenders, and button-down shirts a practical clothing style that reflected their economic circumstance.

"The clean-cut, neatly pressed delinquent look owed at least as much to the rude boys as it did to the formalized and very hard stereotypes of the white lumpen males," Dick Hebdige wrote[98]

227

in his 1979 book *Subculture: The Meaning of Style*. "… through consorting with the West Indians at the local youth clubs and on the street corners, by copying their mannerisms, adopting their curses, dancing to their music…"

In his 2016 BBC Documentary *The Story of Skinhead*, Don Letts — a black Jamaican — explored the relationship between the two, with skinheads acknowledging how influential the rude boys subculture was.

"It was unique and it was a bond we had with our black friends," Tony Haddow said. "It was something we could all share in. I mean even what we were wearing — the trousers up high and things like that — that all came from Jamaica I would say rather than the state."

As the skinhead subculture rose to prominence, Jamaican artists created a new genre dedicated solely to the group — skinhead reggae. Desmond Dekker, the Skatalites, Symarip — these artists and bands catered to the British and Jamaican skinhead alliance. However, with skinhead's rise came its commodification. The subculture was mutating into a trend as well as a tactic to enlist white youth into far-right political groups.

Throughout the 1970s, groups such as the National Front and the British Movement took advantage of disaffected youth, using them to promote their fascist ideology.

"We were trying to think about race wars," Joseph Pearce, a former National Front member, said in *The Story of Skinhead*. "Our job was to basically disrupt the multicultural society, the multi-racial society, and make it unworkable."

"[Our goal was to] make the various different groups hate each other to such a degree that they couldn't live together," Pearce added. "And when they couldn't live together you end up with that ghettoized, radicalized society from which we hoped to rise like the proverbial phoenix from the ashes."

The politicization of the skinhead subculture as well as its adoption in the burgeoning punk scene distorted it from its roots even further. By the late 1970s, the general public had come to view the skinhead subculture as how it's perceived today across the world — a group that promotes racism and neo-Nazism.

Although this doesn't seem to be Mensa's intent to shed light on the origins of the skinhead subculture, it's a way to highlight how this group's multicultural roots were appropriated into something entirely different. Aside from the viral wardrobe, the artist wore another outfit reminiscent of the subculture's early beginnings.

The striped outfit, the tie — the button on his right is even a direct nod to the rude boy subculture's influence on the skinhead aesthetic, with the item reading "Rude Boy" in all caps.

Mensa has always utilized punk signifiers throughout his career. However, it's this most recent iteration that has gained the most attention because of its association with skinhead subculture. But it's important to note that what Mensa might be doing — whether intentional or not — is a form of reclaiming. A reminder — and introduction — to an aesthetic that didn't originally belong to violent white nationalists, but working-class British and Jamaican people celebrating each other's culture.

The Real Story of South Florida Rapper XXXTentacion

by Tarpley Hitt

The corner house on a rich but unremarkable street in Parkland, about four miles from Marjory Stoneman Douglas High School, belongs to a scrawny 20-year-old with a tree tattoo in the middle of his forehead. He stands about five feet six inches tall and weighs 125 pounds with shoes on. The kid bought the house in November, moved in shortly after, and made the place his own, decorating in the sparse, halfhearted way you'd expect from a teen homeowner but with occasional high-end touches, like an industry-grade recording studio on the first floor.

Today two cars — a black BMW and a colossal van — are parked out front in one of those circular driveways that are popular in the suburbs. A team of landscapers dots the edges of the property, ensuring the shrubs stay pruned. There are a half-dozen Wi-Fi networks to choose from, all named variants of "Theworldwithin."

The $1.4 million Tuscan-style home has no doorbell, but a rotating cast of kids routinely answers knocks on the door. Around noon on a recent Thursday, it's a blond boy with a peach-fuzz mustache and a cursive face tattoo. When the owner is requested, Peach Fuzz grumbles something inaudible and disappears behind the wooden door. He returns trailing his five-foot-six friend, who is shirtless, barefoot, and a little angry.

In real life, the homeowner is strikingly pretty, with huge irises and a jolt of blue hair pulled into two french braids. He's covered in tattoos: Most prominent are an elephant head on his throat, "17" on his temple, and "Cleopatra," his mother's name, scrawled on his chest. He is charismatic, quick to laugh, and slightly condescending. When a visitor, who found the place from a stray speeding ticket, says she's surprised he came outside, he says, "The word would be 'dumbfounded.'"

In the past six months, this guy has rarely left his house. That's partly because he was working on an album that, when it dropped this past March 16, debuted at number one on the **Billboard 200**. But it's mostly due to the fact he's on what his lawyer calls "modified house arrest" while awaiting trial for a disturbing list of criminal charges, including domestic battery by strangulation, false imprisonment, and aggravated battery of a pregnant woman.

"I'm going to domestically abuse y'all little sisters' p** from the back."**

He denies the charges, saying in a September 2017 Instagram video: "Everybody that called me a domestic abuser, I'm going to domestically abuse y'all little sisters' pussy from the back."

But today, after some back-and-forth, the homeowner — whose real name is Jahseh Dwayne Onfroy but whom the world knows as the polarizing SoundCloud artist XXXTentacion — lets the door swing open and leads the way to his blue-lit studio. "Take off your shoes," he says.

For the next two hours, Onfroy sits cross-legged on a comfy chair and talks openly about astral projection (he's for it), feminism (he's against it), and systemic oppression (it's over, apparently) while declining to address or reflect upon the criminal reasons he's unable to leave his house. "Would I change anything about my journey?" he says at one point. "Fuck, no."

The controversial rapper emerged onto the public stage in early 2017, when a single he uploaded to SoundCloud burst out of underground music circles and into the mainstream. The track was short, distorted like most of his songs, and named an imperative "Look at Me!" But as listeners and media took his instruction to

231

heart, they uncovered details about Onfroy's past, including the brutal allegations of domestic abuse.

When the claims surfaced, the singer joined a lineup of controversial male figures, from Chris Brown to Harvey Weinstein, whose accusations of abuse have spurred a national conversation about an age-old question: Can great art be separated from problematic artists? But unlike Brown, Weinstein, or many of their peers, whose work was well known before it became controversial, Onfroy's celebrity and extreme criminal charges are closely tied. As the singer's friend and fellow rapper Denzel Curry once said in an interview with *Hot New Hip Hop*[99]: "The thing with X is, when he got into trouble, that's what blew him up."

In many ways, Onfroy's continued commercial viability is a testament to what accused assailants can still get away with in the court of public opinion, especially when their victims — like Onfroy's — are low-income and women of color.

But after a review of hundreds of pages of court documents, a two-hour talk with the singer, and interviews with his alleged victim, old friends, collaborators, fans, and foes, what emerges is not a portrait of a supervillain. Instead, it's a grim picture of a banal, unglamorous, half-likable kind of figure whom women around the world encounter every day — someone who isn't profoundly addled as much as pathetically insecure, obsessed with power, and incapable of following one essential directive of human conduct: "It's so simple," his accuser says. "Just don't hit anybody."

Once, when Onfroy attended the beige strip of concrete buildings called Margate Middle School, a classmate had a crush on him. In the idiom of preteen infatuation, she showed it by hitting him. The boy asked his mother if he could hit back. Her answer: Give the girl three warnings; if she keeps hitting, you have to handle it.

Onfroy took those words to heart. When the girl next bothered him, he says, he "slapped the shit out of her and kneed her."

His mom was surprised. "[She] realized how serious I took her," Onfroy says. "Her word was my bond."

Onfroy's tumultuous but intensely close relationship with his mother, Cleopatra Bernard, was one of the defining aspects of his early life and tied to the pattern of fighting that characterized his adolescence. He didn't live with her while growing up; she was 17 or 18 when she had him and in a hard spot financially. "Raising a kid was, honestly, one of her last priorities," the singer says. He spent the first decade of his life cycling through the homes of friends, family, and babysitters.

"From what I can remember, I've never seen Jahseh living with [his mom]," his half-sister Ariana Onfroy, a recent Howard University graduate with a burgeoning YouTube presence, says in a video she posted in April. "He was always living with other people."

Separation from his mother, whom Onfroy describes as "exactly like me, but probably more pretty," affected him as a kid. When she was around, she'd buy him gifts: clothes from the prep staple Abercrombie & Fitch and the phones of the moment: first the Kyocera slide-up and then the Motorola Razr. When Bernard was gone, the void rattled Onfroy's self-esteem. "My mom was the one who dressed me," he told an interviewer in 2016. "My mom was the one who told me that I looked nice this morning or that I needed to go take a shower."

"I used to beat kids at school just to get her to talk to me, yell at me."

Onfroy picked fights with other students to get his mother's attention. "I chased her," he says. "I used to beat kids at school just to get her to talk to me, yell at me." After he was expelled from middle school for fighting, Bernard moved him to a residential program for troubled youth, Sheridan House Family Ministries, where he happily stayed for a few months. ("I've heard Jahseh is

233

something of a rap star now," says one administrator, who declined to give his name.) But after he turned 12, Onfroy most consistently lived with his grandmother, Collette Jones, in a Lauderhill gated community. "My grandma really feels like my mom," he says. "My mom almost feels like more of a sister."

Soon after starting school at Piper High in 2012, Onfroy graduated to more serious offenses, including armed robbery, burglary, possession of a firearm, resisting arrest, and possession of oxycodone, according to a 2016 interview with the underground hip-hop podcast *No Jumper*. He made it to his sophomore year at Piper before leaving for a stint in juvenile hall. Though short, still tatt-less, and with an "Iamsu! Afro" and a Wiz Khalifa-style patch of dyed hair, he established himself as one of the most volatile personalities in juvie, where he previewed an explosive, over-the-top machismo that would later become his brand.

In the *No Jumper* interview, he describes rooming with a gay inmate whom he repeatedly calls "a faggot." He says he told a guard: "If he does anything I disapprove of, I'm gonna kill him." After a week or two, when his cell mate "started staring," Onfroy responded by placing the boy's head on a concrete slab in the cell and stomping. "I was gonna kill him," he says, "because of what he did, because I was naked. He was staring at me. I started strangling him."

The boy screamed. "The guard hears him, and I've got his blood all over my hands, all of my chest, literally... I was going crazy. I smear his blood on my face, on my hands. I got it, like, in my nails. I got it all over me. I was going fucking crazy."

The guards opened the cell and pulled Onfroy off. "I told you I would kill him," the rapper reports saying. He contends the guards didn't charge him. Instead, they told him to clean up. His mother was visiting, and when she spotted blood under his fingernails, she asked what had happened. When he responded, "This n**** did some gay shit, so I had to crack his head open," she began crying.

Onfroy first told this story two years ago, but there are no records of the incident, and he declines to discuss it now. He says he's moving away from that version of himself ("I'm like, really, really nice").

After juvie, Onfroy ordered a snowball microphone on eBay and — along with a goofy, slow-moving kid named Stokeley Clevon Goulbourne, who would later become known by the stage name Ski Mask the Slump God — began making music. The pair started a collective called Members Only and began working on the beginnings of two mixtapes — *Members Only Vol. 1 and Vol. 2* — which would come out the following year.

Onfroy's early efforts exhibited two traits that would become his signatures: a wide-ranging taste in genre and a forceful determination to have things his way.

In August 2014, for example, South Florida videographer Daniel Calle was booking a show of local acts at a venue in Hollywood, Florida. Calle, who has a hip-hop-Seth Rogan vibe, recalls Onfroy reached out to him and said he would perform.

"It was like, 'My bad, dude, I can't get you on this show,'" Calle recalls. "But he shows up anyway. He's like, 'I'm performing.'" Calle tried to stop him. Despite his size, Onfroy had a way of making things happen. "You have to understand," Calle says, "he's very sure. He's very absolute."

In late May 2016, Onfroy was preparing to perform at an impromptu venue next to a thrift store in Oakland Park. As concertgoers crowded in, Onfroy spotted a girl from across the room. She had a model's frame, dark eyeliner, inch-long acrylic nails, and a head of short, loose curls. Onfroy beelined for her. "He locked eyes with me," the girl says. Then he grabbed her by the throat. "He made it seem sexy."

The girl, Geneva Ayala, knew Onfroy a little and was about two years older. (She has rarely spoken to the media but agreed to talk on the record with *New Times* in part because #MeToo has changed the atmosphere for abuse survivors.) Although she hadn't seen him in ages, they had been loosely flirting over social media for more than a year. "Me and you are going to be together before I'm famous," he had once messaged her.

He was right. Two years later, after the pair had been dating for five months, Ayala would come forward and accuse Onfroy of the unrelenting, torturous domestic abuse that would send him to jail, to house arrest, and to jail again, then launch him meteorically into the spotlight.

Like Onfroy, Ayala had a chaotic home life. Her mother wasn't interested in kids, she says; her father was busy with 13 others. At the age of 4, Ayala moved in with her grandmother in Miami, where she cycled through grade schools to escape bullying. At the age of 12, she returned to her mom. Though their relationship was rocky, Ayala didn't want to leave: "You can almost be in love with your mother. That's how I was."

But when Ayala was 16 years old, her mother stopped paying for the electricity, then the water. At the end of the month, she ordered Ayala to move out. Her mother was pregnant, moving in with her boyfriend, and leaving her daughter behind. "She told her that they had a shelter in Homestead that she could go to," one witness later recalled to state prosecutors, who would spend months investigating Ayala's abuse claims.

Then he grabbed her by the throat. "He made it seem sexy."

After that, Ayala home-hopped. She stayed with neighbors for a while, occasionally at a motel her uncle owns in Hollywood, with her grandmother, and in parks when necessary. She worked overtime at a Pizza Hut to pay for food and incidentals.

When Ayala met Onfroy in November 2014, she had been living with her high-school boyfriend. Their relationship was strained. They fought often, and after a particularly bad argument,

236

the boyfriend took to Twitter and posted an illicit picture of Ayala, exposing her without consent.

Onfroy, who saw the photo, messaged her and insisted on fighting the boyfriend. Ayala didn't know Onfroy at all, but he was emphatic. "He was like, 'Your boyfriend's not supposed to be doing shit like this,'" she says. He set a date and time. The day of the fight, she met Onfroy with two friends at a Coral Springs movie theater, but her boyfriend never showed. The group hung out instead. Onfroy intimated that he liked Ayala and at one point pulled her onto his lap in a surprising but not off-putting way. "I liked him too," she says. "I thought, *He's cute. He seems intelligent.*"

When he dropped her off later that night, she forgot her phone in the car. She and Onfroy made arrangements to meet at a McDonald's the next day, but the exchange soon slid into a hangout. "There's a Vine from that day," she says. "I've got the short, curly hair and he's making weird noises, like Doodlebop noises."

They spent the next three days hanging out constantly, walking around neighborhoods, taking the bus to far-flung stops, smoking cigarettes. One day it rained, so they stopped at the motel Ayala's uncle owns and spent hours spilling their life stories. Onfroy bought her gifts — thoughtful ones, not the standard bracelet or teddy bear. "He got me a pillow," Ayala says. A pillow? "Well, I didn't have one."

On the fourth day, the two separated and fell out of touch. They didn't see each other for 18 months, until he grabbed her by the throat at his Oakland Park show. After that gesture, he held her for a moment and then disappeared. They saw each other briefly during the performance and hugged, Ayala remembers. He was sweaty.

Later, Onfroy invited her and a friend to an afterparty at the North Miami home of a hard-core porn star, Bruno Dickemz, who happened to moonlight as the singer's manager. The girls agreed.

At the party, Onfroy and Ayala found themselves in a corner, catching up. Ayala was still living with her boyfriend, but their relationship had soured. On the spot, Onfroy offered to let her live with him. He said he liked her and had always pictured them together. She agreed to think about it. The next morning, she started packing.

Ayala moved into Dickemz' house with Onfroy that day and almost immediately noticed something was off. According to her deposition and an interview, two weeks after moving in, Ayala admired a childhood friend's new grills in a Snapchat video she posted. It prompted Onfroy to grab her iPhone 6S, smash it on the floor, and strike her hard in the face. He later fixed the phone, but Ayala was stunned. "I got slapped for no reason," she says, "and he kept acting like everything was cool."

Later that day, Ayala says, Onfroy hit her again. "I was really lightheaded, because the slap was so hard," she recalls. "It was one of those slaps where you hear ringing." She sat for a second in a daze. Onfroy told her to wait and then left the room. He returned holding a long-handled barbecue fork and a wire barbecue brush. "He was like, 'Which one do you want me to use?'"

Ayala was confused. "Like, use for what?" In a deposition given seven months later, she recounts to a prosecutor: "He told me to pick between the two, because he was going to put one of them up my vagina." She chose the fork. Then, Onfroy began pulling up her black-and-white striped dress. He lightly dragged the fork against the skin of her thigh. Ayala passed out.

"When I came to, I remember just thinking, I *cannot let this happen to me*," she says. "*This, right here, cannot happen to me.*"

"I got slapped for no reason," she says. "And he kept acting like everything was cool."

Ayala wanted to leave. But it was clear Onfroy wouldn't "be comfortable" with that, she says in the deposition. She hadn't broached the subject of leaving either because, according to the deposition, she "felt scared to be open with him." When she did talk, he'd say she sounded stupid. "I barely spoke," Ayala says.

So when Onfroy moved to Orlando in late June 2016, Ayala went with him. The depositions detail a pattern of regular, torturous abuse that summer, with daily verbal attacks and physical incidents every three or four days. According to Ayala's statement, he beat her at times, choked her, broke clothes hangers on her legs, threatened to chop off her hair or cut out her tongue, pressed knives or scissors to her face, and held her head under water in their bathroom while promising to drown her.

"His favorite thing was to just backhand my mouth," Ayala says. "That always left welts inside my lips." Onfroy would also try to guilt her with near-attempts at suicide, she says. He would fill a bathtub, dangle a microwave over the water, and threaten to let go.

Onfroy's triggers were, in some ways, predictable — usually jealousy — but also erratic. Small things could set him off: like her humming another rapper's verse or asking a friend what music he was playing.

"Once, we were all in the car, and my ex made a joke," says Talyssa Lee, who was dating one of Onfroy's producers in 2016. "[Ayala] just laughed as a reaction... When we got in the house, [Onfroy] walked into the other room and started beating on her."

Lee, who didn't know Ayala or Onfroy before the week of the car ride, noticed marks on Ayala's body within hours of meeting her. "It was very clear that [Onfroy] was avoiding her face," she says. "He was hitting her under the chin, on her back — her ribs were all bruised up."

Almost as disturbing as the overt abuse, Lee says, was the lack of response from anyone around the pair. "All the boys around him, they witnessed that shit," she says. "I can't just sit here and hear a girl screaming in the next room... her voice gurgling because she's being held underwater."

On July 14, 2016, Onfroy was arrested in Orlando for allegedly stabbing his new manager, a guy nicknamed "Table," who the singer claimed had been stealing from him. He bonded out only days later, but returned to jail in Broward County shortly after for earlier charges of armed home invasion and aggravated battery.

While Onfroy was in custody, Lee and a few other friends helped Ayala escape. Shortly thereafter, she moved to Texas, safely far from Onfroy.

But by August, the two were talking again. In September, when Onfroy was released on $50,000 bond and placed under house arrest, they decided to move in together. They found a place in Sweetwater: an apartment complex near Florida International University where three friends were living.

Soon, Onfroy learned she had been with someone else. Though they made up, the perceived transgression left Onfroy with a hysterical paranoia that she was hiding something, Ayala says.

On one occasion, he woke her in the middle of the night, took her outside where two of his friends were waiting, smashed a glass bottle, told her to tell him about the other man or he would "fuck [her] up," and beat her while the others watched, according to her deposition. On another, he threatened suicide by dangling himself from a 12th-story balcony, holding onto the railing with only his legs.

These episodes could erupt out of nothing. When Onfroy wasn't angry, Ayala says, they got along. They were trying to have a baby, and when a pregnancy test returned positive, Onfroy was happy, she says.

But the morning of October 6, 2016, while their roommates were out and Ayala was lying on Onfroy's chest, he snapped. "He's like, 'You need to tell me the truth right now or I'll kill you and this jit,'" Ayala says in her deposition, "the jit meaning child."

For the next 15 minutes, she claims, Onfroy punched, slapped, elbowed, strangled, and head-butted her with unprecedented force.

When Ayala saw herself in the mirror, she says, her temples were swollen, her eyes were leaking, and she felt as if her head were "going to pop." Around that time, she began to lose vision. She vomited. According to the deposition, Onfroy was still hitting her when their roommates walked in.

Ayala says she begged the onlookers to take her to the hospital. But Onfroy forbade it. The roommates placed tea bags on her eyes and antibiotic ointment on her cuts. Onfroy dressed her in a pink hoodie and sunglasses and drove her to North Miami, where he confiscated her phone and left her in Dickemz' back room for two days.

According to the deposition, at 2 a.m. October 8, after 30 straight hours of sleeping off her aches, Ayala left the back room for the first time, went to the kitchen, and pretended to make Onfroy something to eat. She opened the refrigerator door as far as it could go, blocking his view of the kitchen, kicked open a nearby side door, and ran out into the street.

The next morning, Sweetwater Police arrested Onfroy and later charged him with aggravated battery on a pregnant victim, domestic battery by strangulation, false imprisonment, and witness tampering. He pleaded not guilty and bonded out for $10,000 but was soon detained by Broward County officials for violating his house arrest.

Weeks later, Onfroy's single "Look at Me!" which had been online for nearly a year, began to climb the charts.

It's relatively rare that a song becomes popular years after its release. But when it happens, the track is usually buoyed by something else — maybe a movie or a commercial — that thrusts it into the public consciousness. For Louis Armstrong's once-overlooked single "What a Wonderful World," it was a feature in *Good Morning Vietnam*. For the Proclaimers' "500 Miles," it was the cult classic Benny & Joon. For Onfroy, it was likely his arrest.

The rapper had originally recorded "Look at Me!" in December 2015 with two South Florida producers, Jimmy Duval and a guy named Rojas who calls himself "The Underground DJ Khaled." The song was posted to Rojas' SoundCloud account, but received little reaction. The track was grainy and gleefully crude (*I'm like, bitch who is your mans/Can't keep my dick in my pants*"), with an earworm of a hook. It attracted a few diehard fans.

Then, more than a year later, in January 2017, the heavily distorted single — a far cry from the polished production of most mainstream hits — exploded onto the charts, attracting an endorsement from rapper A$AP Rocky and prompting Adam Grandmaison, a tattooed former BMX biker and hip-hop tastemaker, to sign on as Onfroy's manager. There was so much hype that when Drake previewed a similar-sounding song January 28, fans accused him of plagiarism, which compounded Onfroy's fame.

Throughout all of this, the rapper maintained his innocence to the domestic abuse charges. His attorney David Bogenschutz declined *New Times*' request for comment on the defense, and his management has made no official public statement rebutting the allegations. But in a recorded call from jail that was widely shared on social media, Onfroy claimed Ayala had cheated on him and then blackmailed him. She had been hit by someone else, he said. "Geneva fucked my homeboy… She tried to bribe me and my mother and my people for $3,000," he says, laughing. "Stop believing the motherfucking rumors. I did not beat that bitch; she got jumped. Bye."

In another call that also was passed around social media, he claimed Ayala had never been pregnant: "For all you dumb fuck ass n****s that thought this stupid bitch was pregnant, I've got the paperwork signifying that she wasn't pregnant. So when I get out, I'll fuck all your little sisters in the fucking throat hole."

As Onfroy sat behind bars, media began to question whether

the controversy had fueled his fame. In February 2017, *Pitchfork* published the 2,200-word piece "XXXTentacion Is Blowing Up Behind Bars, but Should He Be?"[100] and a March *Washington Post* article about "Look at Me!" wondered whether Onfroy's rise had "more to do with the public's ghoulish interest in the repugnant crimes he may have committed."

"Stop believing the rumors. I did not beat that bitch; she got jumped."

Nearly six months after his arrest, Onfroy left Broward County Jail after pleading no contest to his 2015 charges of armed home invasion, robbery, and aggravated battery with a firearm. He got out March 26 and, just days later, announced a surprise show in downtown Miami. The rapper barely promoted the event, but by 9:30 p.m. April 7, a massive line had formed outside the venue.

One attendee, Sebastian Alsina, estimated in a blog post that more than 350 people crowded into the small warehouse. But before Onfroy could perform, a squadron of cops in full tactical gear crashed the party and pushed their way to the front. They called for the venue's managers and insisted everyone leave. Instead, the crowd rioted. "The streets were flooded," Alsina wrote. "Cars were being jumped on, people were being trampled, bottles being shattered just to get a sight of X."

The surprise show foreshadowed the next year of extreme commercial success and sinister developments in the rapper's criminal case. Onfroy would soon drop two mixtapes and embark upon a nearly sold-out tour. He joined the ranks of hip-hop magazine *XXL*'s 2017 "Freshman Class," a major list of up-and-coming artists. ("He really won by a landslide as far as the #1 pick," *XXL* editor in chief Vanessa Satten told the morning talk show *The Breakfast Club*.) In August, "Look at Me!" went certified platinum, and Onfroy released his first album, *17*, which debuted at number two on the *Billboard* albums chart. Weeks later, Onfroy signed a reported $6 million record deal with Caroline, a subsidiary of Capitol Records.

Though his fame grew, Onfroy's reputation soured. After he appeared in the *XXL* list, many publications criticized the magazine. "XXXTentacion should not be on this cover," Tom Breihan wrote in a June article on *Stereogum*[101], a music website. "We should not continue to make him famous." The same month, *The Outline*, another website, published the article "Do Not Co-Sign XXXTentacion." In September 2017, *Pitchfork* published new details of Ayala's alleged abuse[102], prompting more publications to pull back from covering him.

The rapper tried to repair the damage. In October, he announced plans to donate more than $100,000 to a domestic abuse charity. Then, in December, he planned an "anti-rape" event during Art Basel Miami Beach. But neither effort bore fruit: The anti-rape event was canceled after one of his fans vandalized the venue, and Onfroy says he never donated to any abuse charities, electing instead to contribute to several children's causes.

On November 27, 2017, Onfroy's attorneys submitted a document signed by Ayala, stating she would not testify against him in court. Ayala now says she signed it at the rapper's request, knowing that prosecutors, not victims, decide whether to pursue domestic abuse charges. "And I was scared," she says. "He always invited all his fans to go to every court appearance... When I walk out of the courtroom and onto the street, what are people going to do?"

Suspecting coercion, prosecutors over the next few weeks charged Onfroy with 15 counts of witness tampering and harassment relating to both the domestic abuse charges and earlier alleged crimes. As evidence, they submitted recordings of 213 phone calls the singer made from jail to friends and witnesses including Ayala. When *New Times* requested to hear the calls under Florida's Sunshine Law, Onfroy's lawyers objected, claiming among other things that the audio was exempt because it amounted to a "confession." A judge granted an emergency hearing in private and then sealed the records until this September.

Talyssa Lee, who says she witnessed Ayala's abuse, contends she received one of those phone calls. "Jahseh called me from jail and threatened me... He was telling me to stop speaking with Geneva, to stop [talking about the abuse] online, because he knew I was telling the truth."

The new charges affirmed the media's distaste for Onfroy but didn't deter fans. When his second album, *?*, dropped in March 2018, it quickly garnered enough sales and streams to hit the top of the *Billboard* charts. Its success placed Onfroy in the league of top chart staples such as Drake, J. Cole, and Kendrick Lamar.

The 18-track, 37-minute album is an exercise is breaking down genre barriers, jumping between trap, alt-rock, metal, and reggaeton — an explicit effort to please everyone. "I was trying to appeal to every market," Onfroy said in an April interview. "Even if there's someone who doesn't like the entire album, you have to like at least one song."

The question of how to treat Onfroy's music remains tricky. Just last month, the streaming platform Spotify announced a new "hateful conduct" policy that prohibited the music of Onfroy and accused sexual predator R. Kelly on its playlists. Many applauded the gesture. But, as a spokesperson for Onfroy pointed out on Twitter, the new policy excluded many other alleged — largely white — abusers, including David Bowie and Gene Simmons of Kiss. Just two weeks later, Spotify reversed its policy, reportedly because several artists, including Kendrick Lamar, threatened to pull their music from the platform. The question of ethical listening will likely come up again soon, however, because Onfroy has intimated a new album might drop in June.

Back in Parkland, in the dim recording studio of his $1.4 million home, Onfroy explains why he's not a feminist. Feminists aren't looking for equality, he says. They want empowerment. "Women may see or feel that they're belittled," he says, "but you're only belittled if you want to be belittled." Take, for instance, Hillary Clinton, he says. "She ran [for president] and she wasn't killed for it. That says everything."

In this post-#MeToo moment, when abuse allegations "can go off hearsay," Onfroy argues, "women are almost more powerful than men."

After coming forward with her allegations, Ayala was abandoned by many of her friends. Only Talyssa Lee, the stranger she'd met in Orlando, stood by her story publicly. Ayala received phone calls from Onfroy's family and friends telling her to drop the charges.

Much of the harassment often came online. Ayala's Twitter account was hacked and taken over by an impersonator, who tweets often about Onfroy. Her Instagram account was deleted after too many fans "reported" her posts.

But people tracked her in real life too. She took a job at a Dunkin' Donuts but had been working there only a week before Onfroy's fans found her. They began showing up every day, harassing her, taking photos of her, and trying to follow her home. Ayala quit after three weeks. "I can't even go to the mall or Walmart without being noticed and eyed down," she says.

Perhaps most disturbing, after he allegedly beat her in the apartment near FIU, Ayala found herself in need of surgery to repair nerve damage and a fracture near her eye. The procedure would cost around $20,000, so Ayala, who has no health insurance, set up a GoFundMe campaign to crowdsource the money. The page quickly raised several thousand dollars, including $5,000 from Onfroy himself.

But within a week, GoFundMe received reports from Onfroy's fans claiming Ayala had misrepresented the cause of her injuries. So the website deleted her page, freezing the funds that had been raised. When *New Times* reached out to GoFundMe for comment, the company investigated the suspension. A spokesperson wrote back the following:

"If a campaign is reported, our team looks into it to request sufficient information regarding the use of funds. In this case, the campaign was reported to us, and we reached out to the campaign organizer to collect additional information. Sufficient information was provided, and the campaign has been reactivated."

(Update: Since this story's publication, thousands in new donations have poured into Ayala's GoFundMe account.)

Nearly two years after they first met, Ayala now rents a room in a house 20 minutes south of Onfroy's place. It's the first room she's had to herself. "I'm saving up to move somewhere else," she says, "somewhere in the country, where there aren't any people."

When It All Falls Down:
The Twisted Nightmare
of Kanye West and Trump

by David Dennis, Jr.

Imagine one of the biggest rappers in the world standing in front of the president of the United States on live television with free rein to say whatever is on his mind. Imagine that rapper advocating for more mental health institutions to curb black incarceration rates. Imagine he or she arguing for the freeing of prisoners such as Larry Hoover[103], and for the creation of more jobs in the deeply troubled urban areas of Chicago. Imagine this musical artist advocating for an end to oppressive stop-and-frisk laws.

That sounds like the culmination of decades of rap music being a way to amplify the voices of those marginalized in the United States. And if anyone had told you a decade or so ago that Kanye West would be that rap ambassador to the White House, you would not have been surprised. After all, West built a big part of his career on being the most successful semiconscious rapper ever to stand up for black people. However, the reality of West's meeting with Donald Trump last week was more twisted nightmare than utopian rap dream.

Last week, we didn't get the Kanye West who spoke up for us. We got something unfamiliar, terrifying and ignorant. We got a West with Make America Great Again hats (he said the red cap "made him feel like Superman"). He's been calling Trump a genius for a while (and Trump returned the favor). We got an unending vomitlike array of misinformation. But maybe that's the Kanye West we should have seen coming for a long time.

We can't spend years celebrating West for his free thought then wonder why the women in his life aren't able to rein him in.

West's new alt-right image emerged seemingly out of nowhere this spring with a tweet of a MAGA hat and sudden praise for Trump, rants about slavery being a choice and a desire to do away with the 13th Amendment that abolished slavery. And it's fueled by the same superficial ideas of activism that West has coasted on for his whole career.

In the past month, West has shut down his Twitter and Instagram feeds again. After a one-week hiatus, he returned, live from Uganda, with a Periscope rant about "mind control." He also streamed a recording session from Uganda, where he's apparently working on a new album called *Yandhi* (due Nov. 23). It went for 11 minutes and was called "Spaceship calling earth| 3 Domes Uganda."

The Kanye who called out a president for racism has been replaced by a Kanye who buddies up to a president who calls African countries "s—tholes" and defends the military acumen of Robert E. Lee. But while this "new" Yeezy is a tragedy for fans who mourn the loss of someone they've believed in for years, the real tragedy is that New Kanye and Old Kanye are one and the same. New Kanye is a persona that has been hiding in plain sight all along — a Kanye West who never went beyond the surface on issues but was given the benefit of the doubt because of his otherworldly genius.

West has won 21 Grammys on 68 nominations. The indomitable Quincy Jones has 79 nominations, and the others just above West include Paul McCartney, Stevie Wonder, Jay-Z and Henry Mancini. West's first three studio albums were all nominated for the most prestigious Grammy, album of the year.

It was as if the absence of street subjects automatically meant the presence of political awareness. No.

There have been Billboard Music Awards, Soul Train Music Awards, World Music Awards, MTV Video Music Awards, Webby Awards, NAACP Image Awards. And the list of accolades goes on and on. And in just a matter of months, he made all of that irrelevant. The more he becomes a lackey for Trump and spouts ill-informed rhetoric, the more that long list of awards gets pushed to the footnotes of his legacy.

West cut his teeth as a producer first, helping Jay-Z refine his sound by infusing sped-up soul samples on the MC's classic 2001 *The Blueprint*. West's dreams of being a superstar rapper were mostly met with skepticism back then, despite his enthusiasm and self-confidence. "He interrupted our studio session," Jay-Z said in 2017, "and stood on the table and started rapping. ... We were like, 'Could you please get down?' And he was like, 'No, I am the savior of Chicago.' He ain't even have a record."

West, who signed to Jay-Z and Dame Dash's Roc-A-Fella Records, was an anomaly for a brand built on authentic 'hood tales from artists such as Philadelphia-based Beanie Sigel and Freeway, Harlem's Cam'ron and, of course, Brooklyn's own Jay-Z himself. West was something different. He wore collared Ralph Lauren shirts and made songs about girls picking majors at college.

The prospects of West having a successful career were bleak in the early 2000s, as rap was dominated by the likes of 50 Cent, Jay-Z, DMX, Nelly and Cash Money Records, all of whom talked about either their lives in the streets or how many women they had sex with in the clubs. Musings about religion and the ills of spending money on Jordans didn't translate to chart-topping hits. Jay-Z said it himself in 2003's "Moment of Clarity": *If skills sold, truth be told / I'd probably be lyrically Talib Kweli / Truthfully I wanna rhyme like Common Sense / But I did 5 mill' / I ain't been rhyming like Common since.*

But something unexpected happened. West spoke to (and stop me if this sounds familiar) an underrepresented middle-class sector of rap fans who wanted someone to speak to their everyday lives. People who neither grew up ducking gunshots nor got rich enough to wear million-dollar watches. His debut 2004 album, *The College Dropout*, hit that population to massive success. His first single, "Through The Wire," about a car accident, was on the Billboard Hot 100 pop charts for 24 weeks.

His second single, "Slow Jamz" featuring Jamie Foxx and Chicago's Twista, was about playing oldies with a lover, and it topped the charts. "All Falls Down" is about the downfalls of materialism and was a huge hit as well. The miracle, though, was "Jesus Walks" (co-written by Che Smith). It's a song about wanting to create a song about Jesus — that would play in nightclubs.

Not only was it big all over radio and at the desired nightclubs, it won best rap song at the Grammys and appeared on lists of best songs of the year, of the decade and of the 2000s. *Rolling Stone* has "Jesus" as No. 273 on its list of the 500 Best Songs of All Time. *The College Dropout* is a classic album, a touchstone for the millennial generation and also in music overall.

West was the missing link between perennial underground "conscious" acts such as Common, Talib Kweli and Mos Def and conscious superstar artists such as Kendrick Lamar, J. Cole and Chance the Rapper of the 21st century. But not being "gangsta" doesn't make one automatically "conscious." West was gifted with a conflation of characteristics that he didn't quite earn: Dude was grouped in with the conscious and politically aware even though, compared with that community's music, West didn't quite measure up.

He never rapped with an understanding of American politics with the kind of depth of, say, Public Enemy's Chuck D. He never grappled with American foreign policy like Mos Def. He didn't articulate Pan-Africanism like Black Thought. Yet West was given the mantle of being rap's political leader: "Kanye was going to be the new leader, and I was fine with that," Questlove (who has since changed his mind) wrote in his 2013 *Mo' Meta Blues*. It was as if the absence of street subjects automatically meant the presence of political awareness. No.

West is allowing himself to be party to endangering the most vulnerable members of society.

West's role as leader of rap consciousness would only be elevated in the fall of 2005 when, during a live benefit telethon for Hurricane Katrina, West looked directly at a camera and proclaimed, "George W. Bush doesn't care about black people." The impact of this moment cannot be overstated. The comment took West from being one of the most popular rappers in America to one of the most recognizable celebrities in the world. And one of the most political — despite the fact he never really articulated what he meant.

Sure. We can deduce that West was referring to the endless images of black suffering on television in Katrina's aftermath. And/ or the ensuing disorganized Federal Emergency Management Agency assistance and botched humanitarian efforts. Or Bush's inaction being about the race of the people he was supposed to aid. There was a need for West's remarks. There's a place for unfiltered anger in certain situations, and West captured the feelings of many in his telethon comments. It was also important to break the post-9/11 moratorium on criticizing the president.

But West never followed up with any depth with regard to his thoughts on Bush and Katrina. The closest he came was an onstage rant at MTV's $2 Bill Concert days later. There was little conviction. There was a lack of substance:

"People are like, 'Yo, aren't you scared that something's going to happen to you?' I was like, 'I can think of a lot worse things that could happen to me, like how about not eating for five days? Or how about not knowing where my f—ing family is?' Everybody's always concerned about theyself. … I just feel like America's always been pushing the [impoverished] under the counter, trying to act like it's not really there. … And what happens if you're cleaning the kitchen and you're always dusting something under the counter? If you spill something, it's going come up and be in your f—ing face."

But the toothpaste was out of the tube: Kanye West was a bona fide activist. A symbol of black resistance and of political rap even if he didn't have the depth, desire or understanding needed to live up to that distinction.

Then, in 2007, West's mother died. Donda C. West was a professor and a single mother from the time Kanye was 3. She instilled in him a confidence that would make him so outspoken and sure of himself as an adult. Donda West was featured in his early videos and was the inspiration behind *Late Registration*'s "Hey Mama." Nothing was the same.

In 2009, Taylor Swift walked onstage at the MTV Video Music Awards to accept an award for best female video only to have her acceptance speech interrupted by a leather-clad West, who had spent most of the night on the red carpet with a bottle of ever-emptying Hennessy in his grip.

"Yo, Taylor, I'm really happy for you, Imma let you finish, but Beyoncé has one of the best videos of all time. One of the best videos of all time!"

It was another off-the-cuff live TV moment that galvanized the country. But this one felt different. It felt mean-spirited and

253

was treated as such — Swift's innocent white girl persona and its historical implications only added fuel to the fire. The immediate logical leap came from the idea that the absence of his mother was somehow the cause of Kanye's outburst.

When West went on The Jay Leno Show days later, Leno brought up his mother, asking what she would think of his actions.

"So many celebrities, they never take the time off. I've never taken the time off to really — you know, just music after music and tour after tour. I'm just ashamed that my hurt caused someone else's hurt. My dream of what awards shows are supposed to be, 'cause, and I don't try to justify it because I was just in the wrong. That's period. But I need to, after this, take some time off and just analyze how I'm going to make it through the rest of this life, how I'm going to improve."

And now, more than 10 years later, armchair therapists on social media and beyond use Donda West's death to justify her son's behavior. The idea being that if she were still alive, she'd have stopped West from jumping onstage that night. That she'd even have stopped him from marrying Kim Kardashian. That Donda West would use her scholarly intellect to teach her son about the ills of his political marriage to Trump. This notion is, of course, placing the burden of a grown man's actions onto a black woman. And, to a similar point, blaming West's political shift on his marriage to Kardashian further infantilizes a grown 41-year-old man.

But that's the Kanye West story: a man who has been crowned a prince of conscious rap without having to do the actual work of deep engagement with the issues — while having the blame for his harmful tactics placed on those around him. We can't spend years celebrating West for his independence and free thought then wonder why the women in his life aren't able to rein him in.

West is in the middle of one of the worst career meltdowns we have ever seen and only has himself to blame. His endorsements of Trump are not mere publicity stunts. They are not Andy Kaufman-esque trolling or subversive genius. His pro-Trump rants are not a phase, or a harmless form of album promotion. And West is not harmlessly ignorant — because there is no such thing.

Not as long as his words are used to raise campaign funds, and to further endear some to a political force pushing through legislation that is putting toddlers in cages. The stakes are higher than that of simply upsetting a president who doesn't like black people, or embarrassing a pop star at the VMAs. West is allowing himself to be party to endangering the most vulnerable members of society.

So don't feel sad that West's career has reached a point of no return. Don't mourn. Mourn those affected by his latest White House stunt. Because, compared with them, Yeezy's career is immaterial. *Come on, come on I'm tellin' you all / It all falls down.* If only Kanye West himself could understand that concept.

From 40 to Dilla:
The Beauty of Raging Against
the Dying Light
by Yoh Phillips

I. The Cancer of Time Is Eating Us Away

"I know that, one day, I will have to face the situation where I'll stop drawing for good, and I am working at learning how to live with such a concept. But if, or when I do it, it won't be because my hand will be too shaky to hold a pen." —Jean "Moebius" Giraud.

Learning of an illness without a cure often comes without preparation. The revelation is spontaneous and painful, like the sudden collapse of a lung. First comes the panic, then fear and anxiety, all falling upon the flesh like frigid raindrops downpouring on a cloudless June afternoon. No umbrella for comfort; no raincoat for convenience. To be baptized in bad news.

The two main themes of Pusha-T's "The Story of Adidon" are dissection and disclosure. He is Dr. Peter Benton rather than Terrence Thornton, the surgeon operating instead of a rapper battling. Unveiling the existence of Drake's son and the now-defunct Adidas rollout was more impressive than any rabbit pulled from a magician's hat, but the lyrics poking fun at Noah "40" Shebib's multiple sclerosis hit the hardest. "*OVO 40, hunched over like he 80—Tick, tick, tick,*" he rapped, "*How much time he got? That man is sick, sick, sick.*"

The luxury of time has been Pusha's biggest boast throughout the rollout of his latest album, *DAYTONA*. Taunting 40 with the idea that his time may soon be up is cruel irony, topped only by the release of "The Story of Adidon" just 24 hours prior to World MS Day.

Without the knowledge that 40 is battling a disease, hearing Pusha's lyrics is like being told a distant relative has been ailing in silence. The imagery of him sick and hunched over is jarring, but adds new light upon what Drake rapped four years prior on "0 to 100 / The Catch Up":

"I got 40 in the studio, every night, late night / Gotta watch that shit, don't want to make him sicker / That's my nigga"

Noah "40" Shebib is a man of the shadows. Which is why it may be surprising to learn the Toronto native was a child actor before becoming the architect, producer, engineer, and best friend of the biggest rapper in the world. For someone who operates in the background, it's hard to imagine him existing in the spotlight. When Drake and Shebib entered the industry together, before the 2009 release of *So Far Gone*, the 35-year-old producer was four years removed from being diagnosed with multiple sclerosis. In 2005, on his 22nd birthday, Shebib had his first bout with the nervous system-destroying chronic illness. 30 days later, he was unable to walk.

Soon thereafter, sensory complications began to sprout; 40 could no longer process hot and cold temperatures. In a rare, 2011 profile on *The FADER*, the mastermind producer briefly touched[104] on the three-plus years he spent working his way back to his feet: "I was walking slower than grandma for six months, then like grandma for six months," he explained to writer Nick Sylvester. Multiple sclerosis affects each person differently and currently has no cure. With disease-modifying drugs, exacerbations can be managed, but there's no promise in feeling well tomorrow.

"The most difficult things about living with MS, he says, are 'explaining to people how MS works, justifying the effects of MS, and the "but you look so good" syndrome. I wish people knew how unpredictable the disease is. One day I can walk five miles and the following day only 500 feet. It is very difficult for people to grasp that concept.'"—Noah "40" Shebib

When the dots begin to connect, it makes sense why Shebib doesn't go on tour; why only a door separates 40's condo from the multi-million dollar OVO studio and office space. You begin to wonder whether Drake's perpetual release schedule is tied to a team racing against an unpredictable clock. 40 hasn't kept his condition a secret—he's an ambassador for the National Multiple Sclerosis Society—but the status of his day-to-day is unknown.

40 has only conducted a handful of interviews, and they mainly focus on the creative process behind the music, not the health of the creator during it. He is the OVO owl who stays away from unwanted eyes and unnecessary cameras. He is a man of the shadows, private as a vigilante and mysterious as a house filled with balloons.

Pusha's nod toward time could simply be malicious, the petty remark of a villain going for the kill. Or, just like Adonis, maybe Pusha knows something we don't. Tick, tick, tick.

II. Time: The Donut of the Heart

"I know why this has happened," Ali said. "God is showing me, and showing you"—he pointed his shaking index finger at me and widened his eyes—"that I'm just a man, just like everybody else." —Muhammad Ali, "My Dinner With Ali"

During his first, initial stint in the hospital, 40 worked off a laptop and portable keyboard. He decided nothing would hinder his ability to create. "...I said, 'I've got this disease, I'm going to live with it. I'm going to win it and my story is going to be that much better when I get there.' I made that decision very early on in my diagnosis," he told *CNN*[105] in a 2012 interview. These are the words of a fighter; a man who will challenge whatever odds he must to be an artist. They're bold, beautiful, and inspiring words, but they aren't delivered without fear.

Multiple sclerosis could strip away the fine motor control of his fingers, hindering the hands that have played the piano since he was three years old; hands that have produced on and engineered every Drake album since *So Far Gone*. The mind may conjure the vision, but God is in the hands.

The potential pitfalls of MS remind me of what Jordan Ferguson wrote in his 33 1/3 book about James Dewitt Yancey, better known as J. Dilla, and his classic album, *Donuts*:

"Lupus is a monstrous disease, causing the body to essentially become allergic to itself. Coupled with TTP, the pair formed a brutal tag-team of ailments that damaged Dilla's kidney and left the joints in his hands swollen and stiff, particularly cruel punishment for a man who spent his life flipping through stacks of records and tapping out beats on the pads of a sampler."

J. Dilla, much like 40, was private about his personal health. Dilla was diagnosed with thrombotic thrombocytopenic pura, or TTP, an incurable, rare blood disease, sometime after returning from a 2002 European tour. Kelly Carter of the *Detroit Free Press* noted[106] how TTP is a disease that causes kidney failure, severe blood-sugar swings, and immune system issues. Jay Dee's body was fighting an internal war, but this wasn't the knowledge of the public.

We weren't supposed to know about the extended months spent between the walls at Cedars-Sinai hospital or the countless treatments of dialysis. Dilla's hematologist, Dr. Aron Bick, would say the incurable medical condition didn't become a handicap. "He didn't want to be a professional patient," Dr. Bick notes in Ferguson's 33 1/3 dedication to *Donuts*.

On *Nobody's Smiling* deep cut "Rewind That," Common, over the No I.D.-produced soul loop of "Telegram" by Eleanore Mills, touches on his time spent living with Jay Dee, from meeting the acclaimed producer in Q-Tip's basement to watching his fallen friend waste away in their California apartment. "*The beats got iller, but the sickness was still there,*" he raps, illustrating how Dilla's illness didn't hinder the potency of his creations, but that as his health progressively got worse it only hurt more to witness.

Hearing Common open up about Dilla's final days makes me wonder how Drake must feel if, in fact, his best friend's health is truly in decline. Throughout the A Side of *Scorpion*, Drake touches on various lines from "The Story of Adidon," but he doesn't make a single reference about 40's health. On the album where Drake is his most paranoid, betrayed, and alone, he's also at his most rich and famous, but no amount of money in the world can help cure an incurable disease.

On "Is There More," the outro that concludes *Scorpion*'s Side A, Drake raps, "*I got fear of havin' things on my mind when I die,*" a rare mortality reference from the man who promotes more life. The fear of dying with words unsaid is true for any man, but for creatives, the fear of dying with ideas unmade is equally as frightening. Dilla was, without question, a vessel of limitless potential. His mind still had ideas left to create; there was plenty of music unborn. The tragedy of life is how fragile bodies are, and the likelihood of flesh expiring before genius.

Nothing stops the clock toward our final hour. Nothing on this Earth slows down the haunting tick, tick, tick.

III. Rage, Rage, Against the Dying of the Light

"To whom much is given, much is expected. To whom much is given, much can be taken away. A reminder that life is fragile and we should cherish and fear that sobering fact. Heroes eventually die" —John Noire

Jean "Moebius" Giraud wrote the opening quote that begins this article in 1989. It's from the opening pages of the prolific French artist, cartoonist, and writer's art book, *Chaos*. Moebius wasn't naïve about his future, nor the inevitability that old age affects an artist's ability to create. He decided that drawing was an expression of joy, and even if his work would suffer due to the shaky hand of an elder, he would continue until there was no more joy in creating.

By the time of his death at the age of 73, it wasn't the shake of his hand, but the decline of his vision that caused doing what he enjoyed to become more strenuous. Life has a way of being a Shakespearean comedian when it comes to the things we lose. It's always the invaluable, never the replaceable.

At the time, Moebius was earning more money than ever for his work, but it wasn't capitalism that drove him to draw; it was the sense of purity the craft brought to his soul. Joy is the driving force when creating is the purest euphoria. During my recent interview[107] with DJ Premier, 52, the veteran producer acknowledged that joy and love, not celebrity and money, are the driving forces behind his advanced career.

Preemo recently brought his drum machine to his ailing father's home during their final days together. He has found in his craft more than an outlet for creativity, but a companion for comfort and distraction. I sense the same for Dilla, who looked toward music to express his awareness and acceptance of time running out.

Donuts is a testimony of how the presence of death and decay did not defeat James Dewitt Yancey. When you read of his mother

261

massaging his fingers after they swelled to a size impossible to program his drum machine,[108] that's the persistence of a warrior and determined craftsmen. When you hear of Dilla touring in Europe during December 2005, performing from a wheelchair, it's the resistance of an inevitable faith.

Being able to spend his 32nd birthday at home, and not in the hospital, on the day of *Donuts'* release, was a brief, but beautiful victory in a long war that Dilla was determined to fight until the bitter end. That unwavering spirit takes me back to the aforementioned Muhammad Ali, and how the champ resisted being overcome by Parkinson's disease. Ali's long-term degenerative disorder took the floating from his feet and the poetry from his tongue; the celebrity athlete was robbed of the very tools that defined him, but he didn't stop as if he were signed to Bad Boy.

In 2016, Gay Talese wrote[109] an excellent Ali story for *Esquire* detailing a trip to Cuba to meet Fidel Castro in 1996. There's one quote that has continued to stick with me:

"But the mind behind his Parkinson's mask is functioning normally, and he is characteristically committed to what he is doing: He is spelling out his full name on whatever cards or scraps of paper his admirers are handing him. "Muhammad Ali." He does not settle for a time-saving "Ali" or his mere initials. He has never short changed his audience."

Even after his boxing career ended, and throughout his battle with Parkinson's, Ali never lost the desire to be a symbol of strength and a provider of joy for people. Ali wasn't bested by the thing he could not control. Dilla wasn't bested by the illness he could not cure. 40 said that nothing will ever stop him from making music, and he has made good on that promise 13 years straight. In the *CNN* interview where he talked about his MS, 40 displayed the fortitude of a man who will not be bested.

Time is the one resource we never get more of, the one thing we can't barter or trade for in life. All we get is a lifetime, no matter how long or short that may be. Health will not always be in our control, even when we consciously treat our bodies as holy temples. What will never change, in sickness or in health, is the desire to do what brings us joy. It is the best thing—the only thing—we can do with our time.

I wish Noah "40" Shebib a long life, and the strength to do what he loves until there's no love left. I commend him for being the most recent example of a man raging against the dying light. And I hope, when my time comes, that I find the will that he has to rage against the final tick, tick tick.

Notes & References

85 Watercutter, Angela, "BEYONCÉ'S SURPRISE ALBUM WAS THE YEAR'S MOST BRILLIANT RELEASE," Wired (December 13, 2013) https://www.wired.com/2013/12/beyonce-album-social-media/

86 Taylor, Ben, "'4:44' One Year Later: Reframing a Legacy Through JAY-Z's Short Films," DJ Booth (June 29, 2018) https://djbooth.net/features/2018-06-29-jay-z-444-short-film-reviewing

87 Maduakolam, Emmanuel, "How TV Became the New Radio for Emerging Artists," Hypebeast (September 5, 2018) https://hypebeast.com/2018/9/tv-new-radio-music-atlanta-insecure

88 Kuznekoff, H., Jeffrey, Kasumovic, M., Michael "Insights into Sexism: Male Status and Performance Moderates Female-Directed Hostile and Amicable Behavior," Harvard Kennedy School (2015) http://gap.hks.harvard.edu/insights-sexism-male-status-and-performance-moderates-female-directed-hostile-and-amicable-behavior

89 Fitzgerald, Kiana, "Exclusive: Missy Elliott on Her New Mountain Dew Collab and What It's Like to Work With Morgan Freeman," Complex (Jan 30, 2018) https://www.complex.com/pop-culture/2018/01/missy-elliott-talks-mountain-dew-collab-morgan-freeman

90 Tucker, Dorothy, "Women vs. Women: When Female Competition Is a Destructive Force," CBS Chicago (October 24, 2016) https://chicago.cbslocal.com/2014/10/06/women-cant-always-count-on-women-in-the-workplace/

91 Petridis, Alex, "Lady Leshurr: 'They wanted to pit me against Nicki Minaj – I wasn't feeling that'," The Guardian (September 1, 2016) https://www.theguardian.com/music/2016/sep/01/lady-leshurr-they-wanted-to-pit-me-against-nicki-minaj-i-wasnt-feeling-that

92 Ramirez, Erika, "Meek Mill vs. Drake: A Full Timeline of the Rap Beef & Who Weighed In'," Billboard (July 31, 2015) https://www.billboard.com/articles/columns/the-juice/6641784/meek-mill-drake-timeline

93 Jenkins, Craig, "Drake Fails to Grow on Scorpion," Vulture (July 2, 2018) https://www.vulture.com/2018/07/drake-scorpion-album-review.html

94 Weiner, Jonah, "How Desus and Kid Mero Went From Twitter Cranks to Comedy's Hottest Duo," Rolling Stone (March 31, 2015) https://www.rollingstone.com/culture/culture-features/how-desus-and-kid-mero-went-from-twitter-cranks-to-comedys-hottest-duo-76473/

95 Mero, Kid, The, "Danny Brown's 'Old' - The Kid Mero Review," Noisey (October 18, 2013) https://noisey.vice.com/en_au/article/6emne6/danny-browns-old-the-kid-mero-review

96 Tyree, Tia, "Making Movie Money: A 25-Year Analysis of Rappers' Acting Roles in Hollywood Movies," Journal of Hip Hop Studies (2017) http://jhhsonline.org/wp-content/uploads/2017/10/Making-Movie.pdf

97 "John Singleton Reveals how Ja Rule Blew His Chance to be in 2 Fast 2 Furious," Grantland (2015) http://grantland.com/hollywood-prospectus/john-singleton-reveals-how-ja-rule-blew-his-chance-to-be-in-2-fast-2-furious/

98 "Skinhead: the Evolution of a Subculture and Society's View Thereof," The Undisciplined (2014) https://theundisciplined.com/2014/07/04/skinhead-the-evolution-of-a-subculture-and-societys-view-thereof/

99 Findlay, Mitch, "Denzel Curry Talks Living With XXXTentacion, Love Of Goku & More," HotNewHipHop (January 24, 2018) https://www.hotnewhiphop.com/denzel-curry-talks-living-with-xxxtentacion-love-of-goku-and-more-news.42776.html

100 Hogan, Marc, "XXXTentacion Is Blowing Up Behind Bars. Should He Be?," Pitchfork (Febuary 7, 2017) https://pitchfork.com/thepitch/1437-xxxtentacion-is-blowing-up-behind-bars-should-he-be/

101 Breihan, Tom, "Let's Talk About This Year's XXL Freshmen," Stereogum (June 14, 2017) https://www.stereogum.com/1946638/lets-talk-about-this-years-xxl-freshmen/franchises/status-aint-hood/

102 Hogan, Marc, "XXXTentacion's Reported Victim Details Grim Pattern of Abuse in

Testimony," Pitchfork (September 8, 2017) https://pitchfork.com/thepitch/xxxtentacions-reported-victim-details-grim-pattern-of-abuse-in-testimony/

103 Main, Frank, "If Larry Hoover were freed, he'd bring 'fear of God' to streets, advocate says," Chicago Sun Times (October 11, 2018) https://chicago.suntimes.com/news/if-larry-hoover-were-freed-hed-bring-fear-god-streets-advocate-says-donald-trump-kanye-west/

104 Sylvester, Nick, "Noah "40" Shebib: Best He Ever Had," The Fader (October 13, 2011) https://www.thefader.com/2011/10/13/noah-40-shebib-best-he-ever-had

105 Tinker, Ben, "The beat goes on for music producer diagnosed with multiple sclerosis," CNN (April 17, 2012) http://thechart.blogs.cnn.com/2012/04/17/the-beat-goes-on-for-music-producer-diagnosed-with-multiple-sclerosis/

106 Carter, Kelly, "JAY DEE'S LAST DAYS," Detroit Free Press/Stones Throw (February 25, 2006) https://www.stonesthrow.com/news/2006/02/jay-dee-s-last-days

107 Phillips, Yoh, "DJ Premier Wanted to Produce for Drake & Kendrick Lamar for Years—Finally, He Got One," DJ Booth (Jun 29, 2018) https://djbooth.net/features/2018-06-29-dj-premier-interview-drake-scorpion

108 Fitzpatrick, Rob, "J Dilla: the Mozart of hip-hop," The Guardian (January 27, 2011) https://www.theguardian.com/music/2011/jan/27/j-dilla-suite-ma-dukes

109 Talese, Gay, "Boxing Fidel," Esquire (Jun 6, 2016) https://www.esquire.com/sports/a45516/muhammad-ali-boxing-fidel/

Credits

Acknowledgments

Amir Said and Amir Ali Said:

We would like to thank the guest editors who helped us select the clips for *Best Damn Hip Hop Writing: 2018* — Thank you, Gary, Kiana, Dart, Martin, and Yoh. We would also like to thank and acknowledge all of the writer's whose work appears in *Best Damn Hip Hop Writing: 2018* — Thank you: Erin Ashley, Josie Duffy Rice, Donna-Claire Chesman, Cherie Hu, Yemi Abiade, Gary Suarez Kathy Iandoli, Martin E. Connor, John Vilanova, Dart Adams, Rich Juzwiak, Sharine Taylor, Christopher Pierznik, Craig Jenkins, Donna-Claire Chesman, Julianne Escobedo Shepherd, Eduardo Cepeda, Meaghan Garvey, Gino Sorcinelli, Alec Stern, Eric Diep, Zach Quiñones, Martin E. Connor, Lindsay Zoladz, Tre Johnson, Yoh Phillips, Kiana Fitzgerald, Bijan, Dylan "CineMasai" Green, Shawn Setaro, Elijah C. Watson, Tarpley Hitt, David Dennis, Jr.

Amir Ali Said acknowledges:

Thank you to my father, Amir Said, for presenting me with this challenge and for offering his guidance and continued advice.
—Amir Ali Said

Amir Said (Said) acknowledges:

Amir Ali Said, my son, best friend, and Superchamp co-founder, As always, thank you for your friendship, knowledge, courage, and curiosity. Your leadership in this endeavor was impressive and invaluable. It was a privilege to watch you learn and grow as you assumed the challenge in taking the lead with this book. Thank you for coming to Paris and making sure that we did nothing (aside from going to the movies for reliev) until we completed this book. More importantly, thank you for bringing your energy (I really needed it) and giving me back a piece of Brooklyn. And thank you for spending my birthday with me. Aslo, an extra thanks for facilitating so many different tasks in the final hour, I love you, Son, Alhumdulillah!

This book took a lot of careful planning and required the support in various forms from a number of different people (I thank you all!), but there are some people I am compelled to single out here: Anna, thank you for your tireless commitment to Superchamp and your timely copyediting. Fergusson, what can I say, you always come through; Marine, Thank you for helping to keep me steady; Isabelle, Thank you very much for believing in what Amir and I are building with Superchamp, and thank you for your kindness and generosity and doing reads with me when you know that I would rather be doing something else — Ça fait 6 mois après *La robe jaune dans le parc* et ce poème chante encore, et depuis que tu as pris les Teddy Smith's rien n'est plus pareil; Christophe, thank you for your advice; Géraldine, Thank you for doubling up, c'est pas *Memento* hein mais c'est une grand chose et je te remercie ton assurance; Sibel, thank you for staying on top of things and making sure that I had what I needed, getting to this point would not have been possible without your support; Nicolas, merci pour ton patience et comprhénsion, c'est sur que mon agenda est fou mais on trouve toujours un moyen — *On n'est pas bien là!*; Danny, thank you for the kind words and the reenforcement for what it means to be black and living in France; Marcelle, thank you for all of your support and for considering all the things that I've already considered but still telling me anyway; Céline, thank you for making sure that this book went through, on time, et je te remercie pour la bulle dans le resto sushi, Pizza is ready ! Abdulai, thank you for making everything add up and for always reminding me what must be done next.

—Said

About the Editor

Amir Ali Said is the co-founder of Superchamp Books and the editor of the *Best Damn Hip Hop Writing* series a writer, publisher, actor, and filmmaker from Brooklyn, New York. His first book, *Performance Day*, was published in 2013. His latest book, *Everyday Routine*, was published in 2017.

About the Series Editor & Creator

Amir Said is the co-founder of Superchamp Books and the creator and series editor of the *Best Damn Hip Hop Writing* series. He is a writer, musician, and publisher from Brooklyn, New York, now living in Paris, France. He's written a number of books including *The BeatTips Manual*, *Ghetto Brother* (co-written with Benjy Melendez), *Medium Speed in the City Called Paris (Poetry)*, and *The Truth About New York*. His new books, *The Art of Sampling, 3rd Edition* and *Camouflage*, will be published in the fall of 2019.

CPSIA information can be obtained
at www.ICGtesting.com
Printed in the USA
FFHW012352110419
51693368-57113FF